THE APOCALYPSE OF YAJNAVALKYA

REVELATIONS CONCERNING
THE NATURE OF HUMANITY
AND THE GODS

LIBRARY
OF
CERNÊ

LIBRARY
OF
CERNÊ

Paperback ISBN
979-8-9879087-0-9

e-Book ISBN
979-8-9879087-1-6

Library of Cernê

An imprint of
Atlas Global Enterprises LLC
530-B Harkle Road, Suite 100
Santa Fe, New Mexico 87505
USA

libraryofcerne.com
curator@libraryofcerne.com

AND NOW FEAR NOT,
YE RIGHTEOUS,

WHEN YE SEE THE SINNERS
GROWING STRONG AND
PROSPERING IN THEIR WAYS:

BE NOT COMPANIONS WITH
THEM, BUT KEEP AFAR FROM
THEIR VIOLENCE;

FOR YE SHALL BECOME
COMPANIONS OF THE HOSTS
OF HEAVEN.

~ Enoch ~

CONTENTS

INTRODUCTION   1

BOOK I   THE AGES OF MAN
Chapter 1   The Dawn of Humanity   7
Chapter 2   The Golden Age   13
Chapter 3   The Silver Age   27
Chapter 4   The Bronze Age   57
Chapter 5   The Iron Age   71
Chapter 6   The New Age   99

BOOK II   THE DIVINE QUATERNITY
Chapter 7   Infinity   125
Chapter 8   Eternity   133
Chapter 9   Mind   141
Chapter 10   Matter   151
Chapter 11   Maya   155
Chapter 12   The Eightfold Way   167

BOOK III   THE SHADOW OF DEATH
Chapter 13   The Ivory Tower   177
Chapter 14   Making a New Man   207
Chapter 15   Defiling the Innocent   231

BOOK IV   THE PATH OF RIGHTEOUSNESS
Chapter 16   Feast and Fast   265
Chapter 17   The Power of Breath   281
Chapter 18   Awaken the Sleeper   291
Chapter 19   Personal Apotheosis   305

CONCLUSION   319

INTRODUCTION

These are the words of Yajnavalkya. May they be a blessing for the righteous and a curse upon the sinners of the earth.

The time has come, oh Seeker of Truth, for you to awaken to the reality of your existence, a reality that has been hidden from you for many millennia. For you find yourself at the end of an age. The final judgment is at hand, wherein all the works of evil shall be destroyed, and the world shall be made new again. I have returned to open your eyes and to deliver a message to those with the courage and faith to see it for themselves.

Perhaps my name is a stranger to you. Know that, in the last age, Yajnavalkya wrote books to aid in the spiritual elevation of earthly humans such as yourself. By way of those books, you were introduced to your divine self, the *ātman*, and were charged with discovering it through practices that I shall briefly discuss again in this text. In making this discovery, you shall be transformed, elevated, and freed from the attachments, sufferings, and anxieties that plague the minds of many who dwell upon the earth today. The great and divine *Matsya Purāna* foretold the return of Yajnavalkya as the harbinger of the hosts of heaven, who are coming with irresistible might to destroy the armies of evil.

What follows are four distinct but interrelated stories that together reveal the true nature of the reality in which you find yourself. As you look out upon the chaos and insanity of your world, you, no doubt, feel a certain trepidation, anxiety, and confusion. With each passing day, events are becoming more and more extreme. Tyranny and war are consuming the nations of the earth, and billions cry out for the blood of billions more. How, then, to make sense of it all?

First, you must recover the past you have lost. The impoverished history you know is far removed from the true story of humanity. Your ancestors trace a path not of thousands of years, but hundreds of thousands, and the record of this history has been written in stone, ice, clay, papyrus, and parchment for all to see. The voices of your forebears cry out and you must hear them now, for in hearing and understanding lies the foundation for what is to come next.

Second, you must discover the true nature of God, the cosmos, and yourself. Know that religion has blinded you to God by separating you from Him. You must realize that no intercessor is required, for God is within you and all around you. The limitless power of Infinity and Eternity generate and sustain all Creation, even your body and mind, and you must understand their paradoxical workings if you are to realize your highest potential.

Third, you must see your enemy, the one who seeks to turn you away from the true nature of God, the cosmos, and yourself. These insidious, cunning beings have spent millennia developing their science of ruling you, a science you shall learn for yourself. Their power grows by way of lies and fear, and the refusal of the masses to see those beings for what they are allows them to continue, unimpeded, with their destructive plans. But fear not, for they are possessed by cowardice and hubris, both of which increasingly expose their presence and their evil ways with each passing day. Damned by God during a bygone age, they plot to ruin the earth and humanity, making it impossible for you to join His kingdom. They will fail, for the righteous shall learn how to find salvation and grow beyond the reach of the evil ones.

Fourth, you must find and walk the Path of Righteousness. You will learn how to purify your body and mind, freeing yourself of a host of afflictions. Then, you shall turn this recovered vitality towards awakening and elevating your spirit, which is the course of evolution that has been set before you, and precisely that from which your enemy seeks to keep you. For herein lies true liberation, wisdom, light, and love beyond anything you have yet experienced. Know ye not, ye are a god? You are His child, after all, and beyond the veil of your material body lie wonders and an existence free from the grasp of those who seek to bind you in servitude for all time.

The goal of this work is to prepare you for the great battle that draws nigh. For events are upon you that bewilder the ignorant, driving terror into their hearts and turning them against their brothers and sisters in humanity. Know this, that long ago your ancestors in the remotest antiquity took to the heavens, escaping obliteration by a celestial event far beyond their control. The human forces of all the cosmos have now turned their gaze back towards Planet Earth, for they know the evil that is consuming it, and the time of their return is at hand. You must be ready to join them in the spiritual and technological bounty they bring with them, or be annihilated for choosing the evils of ignorance and materialistic greed.

There will, doubtlessly, be moments where your deepest-held, most cherished beliefs will be challenged, even shattered. Such is the way of truth, for against its light no shadows or ignorance can stand. Your task is to persevere and have faith that you will not be led into darkness and sin. As you read, listen to your heart, for it shall provide you with the courage required to cast out your demons and embrace the truth. Though you may, at times, feel completely untethered, know that a new foundation rises to meet your feet, one that will support you for all eternity in truth and righteousness.

Let us proceed now, for time is a precious resource you can no longer afford to waste.

BOOK I
THE AGES OF MAN

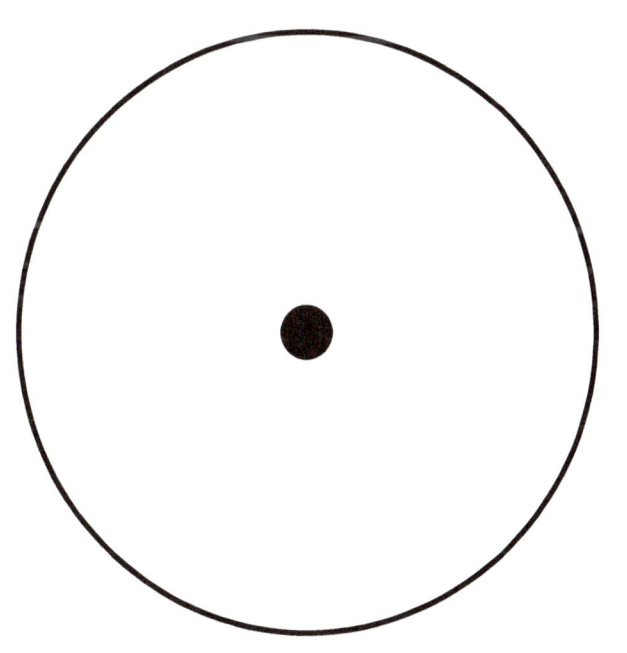

CHAPTER I
THE DAWN OF HUMANITY

To be fully human, mankind must know their history, yet this history is precisely what mankind has forgotten. The mind of humanity is afflicted with amnesia, eyes blinded, and memories darkened. For reasons that shall become clear, this story has been deliberately hidden from you, a problem that shall now be rectified.

THE FIRST HUMANS

First, you must understand where your species originally appeared on earth and how long *Homo sapiens* have truly inhabited this planet. Until recently, your scientists believed East Africa was the birthplace of the species, based on 200,000-year-old human remains discovered in Ethiopia.

They were wrong. In the first decade of the new millennium, in a cave thousands of kilometers away in Morocco, archeologists unearthed more than twenty human bones from at least five individuals. These remains proved to be 100,000 years older than those found in Ethiopia and suggest that *Homo sapiens* originated in Northwest Africa and then dispersed eastward across the continent.[1]

[1] **Ewen Callaway,** "Oldest Homo Sapiens Fossil Claim Rewrites Our Species' History," Nature, June 7, 2017, https://www.nature.com/articles/nature.2017.22114

What significance does this discovery hold for you, oh Seeker of Truth? This cave, Jebel Irhoud, sits in the shadow of the highest peak in the Atlas Mountains, a peak once known as Mount Atlas and now called Toubkal. This great mountain is the highest peak for over 2,000 kilometers in any direction. Though the cave is easy to miss, the mountain, located a mere 130 kilometers away, is not. Your ancestors used it as a landmark, and it appeared frequently in their stories and legends. More importantly, this mountain, and the lands surrounding it, figure prominently in human history, in the establishment of humanity's oldest civilization, and in the people who came to be known as the Atlanteans, of whom you shall read much in the forthcoming pages.

This birthplace of humanity sets the stage for the rest of this revelation.

THE SUPERNOVA THAT CHANGED HISTORY

The earliest-known humans who inhabited North Africa 300,000 years ago were called the Achuleans. Their numbers consisted of not just *Homo sapiens*, but also *Homo erectus*. Their descendants, the Aterians, emerged 150,000 years ago and spread across North Africa, from Mauritania to Egypt, becoming great travelers as well as observers of the heavens.

Approximately 41,500 years ago, these Aterians witnessed a great unleashing of unfathomable cosmic power when a star at the end of its life exploded in earth's proximity. Today, scientists know it was the star Geminga that went supernova and forever changed this planet and its inhabitants.

For thousands of years, humans have periodically seen such events in the night sky and have written records dating back over 2,000 years. The Geminga supernova changed human history well before the time of that writing, but the effects are still visible today, captured in the geologic and biologic records of the planet. Debris from the supernova did not crash to earth until tens of thousands of years later, but catastrophic events immediately befell all living beings.

A mass extinction happened throughout Oceania, which you know as Australia, and which faced the supernova when it exploded and thus endured an intense, unobstructed gamma ray burst. The blast lasted only a few seconds, but it irradiated and killed nearly all life, human and megafauna alike, in the region of earth that faced it. The rest of the planet not directly facing the cataclysm was gravely affected, as you shall learn, but was spared annihilation.

The Scientific Record

When Geminga exploded, the bombardment of radiation caused earth's magnetic field to temporarily reverse, in what is known today as the Laschamp event. The geologic record marks this history, as do tree rings in New Zealand. An ancient lava flow that spewed out molten stone and then solidified, over and over, froze in time a record of magnetic particles. Layer after layer, they all point in the same direction, aligned with the magnetic North and South Poles—until they suddenly switch directions at the time of the supernova.

The explosion of Geminga was visible for months, and radiation continued to rain down, though in a less deadly form. It was at this time your ancestors found a new use for ochre: as a sunscreen that protected them from the deadly rays.

Furthermore, the great force of the explosion swept clean vast swaths of space, leaving an unusually low density of atoms. This empty expanse, known as the Local Bubble, continues to grow to this day and has reached a present breadth of 350 lightyears. [2]

[2] Richard Firestone, Allen West, and Simon Warwick-Smith, *The Cycle of Cosmic Catastrophes* (Rochester, VT: Bear & Company, 2006), 176.

The Genetics of Modern Humans

Radiation of this magnitude has the power to change the basis of life, the very genetic makeup of the human species. Genetic mutations can be neutral or detrimental, and some give rise to new forms of life.

Following the supernova, a new Y-chromosomal haplogroup—one of the major patrilineages of all present-day humans—emerged in Ethiopia, which, like the whole world, received the radioactive fallout. Your scientists call this new haplogroup E1b1b, or E-M215. It does not produce visible traits but serves as a historical marker in the very fiber of your being, recounting the story of this cosmic event.

One male Aterian living in Ethiopia was exposed to radiation, experienced this genetic mutation, and passed it on to his sons who, in turn, continued passing it on. From that single human being, a unique Y chromosome group formed, and from that group, the rest of human history unfolds. Over the next 20,000 years, this haplogroup split, with some heading north to Mesopotamia to become the present-day Israelites, and some heading west to the Maghreb. As shall be revealed, this is the birth of two great patrilineages: the Sons of Adam and the Sons of God.

The Atayal Legend

While any inhabitants of Oceania were likely wiped out in the supernova's aftermath, tribes living farther north survived to tell tales about what they experienced. One tribe called the Atayal arrived on the island of Taiwan 45,000 years ago, before the supernova appeared, and they passed down stories about the evil sun that suddenly appeared in the sky.

One legend tells a tale of two suns—one, the normal yellow sun; the other, smaller and blue. For months on end, the bright yellow sun burned during the day, as it always had, and the blue sun rose at night, after the yellow sun had set. The blue sun shone brightly, nearly as brightly as the yellow sun, causing the Atayal to endure perpetual day.

The legend also describes periods in which both suns sat in the daytime sky at the same time, and the Atayal called the blue sun evil because it burned the grass, caused the plants to shrivel up, and made their island stiflingly hot. As you are aware, the changing position of the blue sun in the sky can be explained by the orbit of your planet around the yellow sun.

The Atayal people decided they needed to do something about this evil blue sun wreaking havoc on the land, so two people, a father and his son, decided to slay it. They went on a long journey and eventually stood close enough for the son to draw his bow and loose an arrow into the blue ball of fire. With one shot, the boy pierced the evil sun, causing it to disappear from the sky, so that days and nights returned to their normal pattern.

The legend also describes blood oozing out of the pierced evil sun, scalding the earth beneath. In truth, when radiation from the Geminga supernova hit the atmosphere, it generated a surge of unnatural, nuclearly unstable elements, including carbon-14, beryllium-10, chlorine-36, aluminum-26, and immense amounts of nitrate. While some stayed in the atmosphere, most infused the clouds and fell to the earth as a reddish-brown rain. [3]

[3] **A. Cooper** et al., "A Global Environmental Crisis 42,000 Years Ago," Science 371 (February 19, 2021): 811–818; **K. Hughen** et al.,"14C Activity and Global Carbon Cycle Changes over the Past 50,000 Years," Science 303 (January 9, 2004): 202–207; **Paul A. Mayewski** et al., "Major Features and Forcing of High-Latitude Northern Hemisphere Atmospheric Circulation Using a 110,000-Year-Long Glaciochemical Series," Journal of Geophysical Research 102, no. C12 (November 30, 1997): 26,345–26, 366; **Kunihiko Nishiizumi, Robert C. Finkel,** and **Kees C Welsten** "26Al in GISP2 Ice Core," presentation as part of New Developments in Terrestrial Cosmogenic Nuclide Research September 9, 2005, Space Sciences Laboratory, University of California, Berkeley, https://llnl.confex.com/llnl/ams10/techprogram/P1917.HTM

DEATH CREATES LIFE

Out of death and destruction come creation and life. As you shall learn in great detail, the universe is of a dual nature: life and death, destruction and creation, are part of the same process. The deaths of stars—supernovas—created all the elements on earth that allow for and sustain all living beings, including you.

Stars must die so that we may live, and out of the death of Geminga came the dawn of human civilization, setting in motion a pattern that continues to this day: ruling classes controlling the masses in order to achieve their own evil designs.

But do not trouble yourselves over these coming sorrows, for you shall now learn about the Golden Age—a time of prosperity and spiritual growth that has since found no equal, though it shall soon come again.

CHAPTER 2
THE GOLDEN AGE

The Roman poet Publius Ovidius Naso, commonly known as Ovid, grouped human history into four stages he identified as the Golden, Silver, Bronze, and Iron Ages. While Ovid did not know the exact dates when one age transitioned to another, he did accurately describe the conditions of each one and the events surrounding the transitions. He describes, for example, the Bronze Age as a dark time for humanity, which perfectly coincides with the aftermath of a cataclysmic event 12,800 years ago, known today as the Great Flood, about which you shall read more in a future chapter. Of the Golden Age, our present consideration,

Ovid says it was a time when men lived amongst the gods and attained a notably high level of spiritual development. The environment was idyllic, perfect for growing food year-round. [4]

[4] Publius Ovidius Naso, *Metamorphoses*, http://www.perseus.tufts.edu/hopper/text?doc=Perseus%3atext%3a1999.02.0028

Ovid's work lays a foundation for understanding the history you have lost. You shall learn of these ages in chronological order, starting with the Golden Age, which commenced about 24,000 years ago, just as the sun last entered the house of Aquarius.

ATLANTIS AND THE SONS OF GOD

In the ensuing 17,000 years after the supernova rained radiation down upon the earth and spawned a new haplogroup, humanity continued to spread across the African continent and beyond. The Sahara Desert as you know it did not exist during those days. Instead, the area was a lush landscape crisscrossed by rivers and covered with tropical jungles as far as the eye could see.[5] That large river system made it easy for humans to travel back and forth across the African continent.

[5] **Charlotte Skonieczny** et al., "African Humid Period Triggered the Reactivation of a Large River System in Western Sahara," Nature Communications, November 10, 2015, https://www.ncbi.nlm.nih.gov/pmc/articles/PMC4659928/

Iberomaurusians

As you now know, the earliest humans migrated from Jebel Irhoud to the east side of Africa, where the E-M215 haplogroup resulting from the supernova emerged in Ethiopia. Those humans then traveled in two directions, with some heading north into the Levant—about whom you shall learn more shortly—and some heading west, back toward Jebel Irhoud and Mount Atlas, to the land that is today Mauritania. They traveled by way of the Tamanrasset River, a river so imposing that it has no equal today, not even the mighty Amazon with its hundreds of tributaries coursing through South America. The Tamanrasset emptied into the Atlantic, and as the great volume of water hit the ocean floor, it carved out the Cap Timiris Canyon, which is 2.5 kilometers wide and 3 kilometers deep.[6]

[6] **Sebastian Krastel,** "Cap Timiris Canyon: A Newly Discovered Channel System Offshore of Mauritania," EOS 85, no. 42 (October 19, 2004): 417–432.

Among those humans who traveled along the Tamanrasset to Mauritania was an Aterian man with the E-M215 mutation. He settled with his people in an area to the south of Mount Atlas, in a region of naturally formed rings, islands within islands, separated by fresh water. To be sure, these geographic features were so striking, it was as if the gods themselves had turned the whole region on a lathe. To the immediate north, a vast plain ideal for growing all manner of food could be found. Due to the nearness of the equator, the climate was perfect for growing food all year round. Because of the natural features of this fortuitous place, it was incredibly easy to defend their position—no intruder could invade the central island.

Today, you may know this region as the Richat Structure, the Eye of Africa.

Signs of habitation in this area go back to the deepest reaches of humanity, with an exceptional number of Acheulean artifacts having already been recovered from

Richat structure

this region. Rather than going on a journey into the unknown, these travelers of the Tamanrasset were returning to a place that was well known to them.

The Aterian who belonged to the E-M215 haplogroup fathered sons whose lines began at the last Age of Aquarius 24,000 years ago and continue to this day. Thus, due to the large number of successful progeny, a sub-clade of this man's own mutation, called E-Z827, emerged around this time. With this man, the Aterian lineage ended and the Iberomaurusians began.

This first Iberomaurusian man must have been prolific because remains of his descendants have been found in caves across the Maghreb, from modern-day Mauritania to Libya, in the Atlas Mountains, the Rif, and beyond. Members of the haplogroup E-Z827 are even alive and living among you today.

Who was this first Iberomaurusian, this original possessor of the E-Z827 mutation? This is the crux of human history that has been lost to you, for this man was none other than Poseidon, the father of King Atlas, founder of the great city of Atlantis.[7] It is his children who have survived from that great civilization's founding unto this day. And here you are, Seeker of Truth, at the beginning of the next Age of Aquarius, standing on a similar precipice as the Atlanteans when they established humanity's first advanced civilization and the great city of Atlantis. In time, these people would become known as the Sons of God.

[7] *Plato: Timaeus and Critias*, trans. Robin Waterfield (Oxford: Oxford World Classics, 2008), Critias 114b.

Plato's Record

The earliest stories of humanity include Plato's *Timaeus* and *Critias*. In the latter, Critias recites a story passed down by his great-grandfather, who learned it from Solon, one of the Seven Sages of Ancient Greece, who learned it from a priest at the Egyptian temple at Sais. Solon lived 2,600 years ago, and at the time he was told the story, it was already more than 9,000 years old. The story tells of a civilization at least 11,600 years old—the kingdom of Atlantis.

Plato's *Timaeus* and *Critias* record the story of Atlantis through a tale of two mortals, whom he calls autochthons—native humans, born of the earth. These native Mauritanians, named Evenor and Leucippe, had a daughter named Cleito, with whom Poseidon fell in love and had five sets of twins.

The first-born of the first set of twins, Atlas, became king of the southern regions, including the capital of Atlantis in the Richat Structure. His twin brother, Gadeira, ruled over the Rif and Maghreb regions of the kingdom, in present-day Morocco, Algeria, Tunisia, and Libya. As Plato writes, Atlas's brother "was assigned the edge of the island which is closest to the Pillars of Heracles and faces the land which is now called the territory of Gadeira after him." Today, this region to the south of Spain is called the Bay of Cádiz, but in the time of Plato it was called Gades. [8] The other eight twins were given rule over islands in the far reaches of the kingdom.

[8] Plato, *Critias* 114b.

In *Critias*, Plato says of the Atlanteans that they came from a beautiful sun-drenched island. Sailing from Athens, Greece, where Plato lived, beyond the Pillars of Hercules—which you know today as the Strait of Gibraltar—a ship would head south along the coast of Morocco and then into the Tamanrasset, which would take them to this tropical island, the Richat Structure. It is exactly the same journey made by Hanno the Navigator, a Carthaginian about whom you will have occasion to learn more later.

Through his description of history and geography, Plato makes it remarkably easy for modern man to find Atlantis, as he describes the capital city and the characteristics still visible in the Richat Structure, including the rings within rings, in every detail. He says there was a plain just north of the city, where the people grew their food, and there were numerous species of animals, including elephants. Though the area has since been stripped down to the bedrock by the Great Flood, to this day, there is evidence of buildings and animal pens having been present thousands of years ago, and the site meets every criterion of Plato's description of Atlantis.

Plato does not say when Atlantis was founded, but he does disclose that it was destroyed 11,600 years ago—which fits with a cataclysmic event that befell the earth at that time. He also says that when Atlantis arose, humans were still hunter-gatherers with no knowledge of farming, astronomy, or sea travel. The Atlanteans developed all three and became the first true city with a government and permanent structures.

The center island of the city was reserved for the priests and the king, serving as the spiritual center of the whole kingdom. The defense force, which had 1,200 ships, operated from the inside ring, while the outer ring contained the commercial area. The rings were encircled by the broader landmass, where even more people lived, and which was bustling day and night. It was a city as big as the ancient world had ever seen or would ever see, having the grandeur of Rome, and likewise a population of up to one million.

The people of Atlantis developed the ability to process and ferment food, a technique they later taught to other cultures, as you shall soon see. That discovery was not made by Mesopotamians, as some historians have mistakenly asserted, but rather Atlanteans. [9]

[9] Louise T. Humphrey et al., "Earliest Evidence for Caries and Exploitation of Starchy Plant Foods in Pleistocene Hunter-Gatherers from Morocco," PNAS 111, no. 3 (January 21, 2014): 954–959.

Today, all that remains is sand and sea debris, salt, and bedrock, along with the indications of where some structures sat, the remnants of this ancient first civilization having been scrubbed away—but Plato describes the city and the people at length in *Critias*. Atlantis is not just a legend but a place that did exist, and it changed the course of human history.

African Humid Periods

For millions of years, North Africa has experienced alternating dry and humid periods, the latter of which produced the vast river system that allowed early humans to travel from Northwest Africa to Ethiopia and back again. Because of these conditions, Atlantis existed in an ideal location for agriculture—and then the inhabitants became even more fortunate. Because of changes in the tilt of the earth—the axial precession—the area entered another humid period, also known as the Bølling–Allerød interstadial period. All of North Africa became even more lush, a true tropical paradise. [10]

[10] Timothy M. Shanahan et al., "The Time-Transgressive Termination of the African Humid Period," Nature Geoscience 8 (January 26, 2015), https://www.nature.com/articles/ngeo2329

Is it too far-fetched to think that this fertile Atlantis is the Garden of Eden described in the Bible? Not at all, according to one noted scholar who said this humid period created an area that "can possibly be equated with the biblical paradise . . . The mythology of antiquity knows, for example, the garden of Eden, Elysium, and the Golden Age. It is certainly not too daring to see a correspondence with the climatic optimum of the Holocene." [11]

[11] Wolf Dieter Blümel, "20000 Jahre Klimawandel und Kulturge—von der Eiszeit in die Gegenwart [20,000 Years of Climate Change and Cultural History: From the Ice Age to the Present]," Wechselwirkungen; Zeitschrift der Universität Stuttgart, January 2000.

Charting the Heavens, Sailing the World

Surely, you have been taught to question the existence of the kingdom of Atlantis, though you now see that this ancient civilization is very much real. Perhaps, like so many skeptics, you also believe that transoceanic voyages would have been impossible for people living at this time, that such expeditions did not happen until the Vikings or Christopher Columbus. Now it is time to put to rest lingering doubts on this front as well. Consider the career of Thor Heyerdahl, a Norwegian sailor, who, in the 1940s, made a balsa-wood raft christened the *Kon-Tiki* and sailed 8,000 kilometers from Peru all the way to Polynesia. Twenty years later, he undertook another long voyage in a papyrus reed boat called *Ra II*, this time from an old Carthaginian port on the Atlantic shores of Africa all the way across the Atlantic to Barbados. [12]

[12] The Kon-Tiki Museum, https://www.kon-tiki.no/

Heyerdahl's experience shows it is possible to use a primitive raft to travel long distances, making it quite likely that a civilization such as the Atlanteans had the technology to cross oceans much earlier than the Vikings. The *Homo sapiens* alive in the age of Atlantis had brains just like Heyerdahl's, and they had access to papyrus. They needed only ingenuity and a daring spirit to build simple boats and sail them huge distances, beginning on the vast and lush rivers that ran through North Africa.

As they looked to the sea, the Atlanteans also looked to the sky and used the stars to guide their travels. They built telescopes and installed them high up on Mount Atlas and Mount Teide, the tallest peak in the Canary Islands. To this day, Teide, on the island of Tenerife, is home to over a dozen astronomical observatories. The mountain is so high that there is very little atmospheric distortion of the light, allowing a clear look into the heavens.

From this peak, the Atlanteans studied the stars and developed their observations into the science of astronomy. They created the Zodiac as a navigational tool and established the doctrine of the sphere. Anyone who sails by the stars today uses these techniques developed over 20,000 years ago. [13]

[13] Diodorus Siculus, Bibliotheca Historica, trans. C. H. Oldfather (Cambridge, MA: Harvard University Press, 1935), Book III, Chapter 60.2.

Do you doubt that this ancient society created this science and the technology to study the stars? Search out Plato's *Critias*, and you shall find that he speaks of the Atlanteans' prowess on the sea and in studying the heavens. There is also evidence from more recent sources: in the first half of the last century, French researchers interviewed the Dogon people of Mali, a country adjacent to the Richat Structure, and found they knew Sirius is not one but three stars orbiting each other, even though the two companion stars are not visible to the naked eye. The Dogon also knew the orbital period of these stars and that Saturn has rings and Jupiter moons, though these details could not have been discerned without the aid of a telescope. [14]

[14] Marcel Griaule and Germaine Dieterlen, "The Dogon," in African Worlds: Studies in the Cosmological Ideas and Social Values of African Peoples, ed. Daryll Forde (Oxford: Oxford University Press, 1954), 83; Marcel Griaule and Germaine Dieterlen, "Un Système Soudanais de Sirius," Journal des Africanistes 20, no. 2 (1950): 273–294.

How did the Dogon come to have such knowledge though they lacked the technology to make these observations? Thousands of years ago, their next-door neighbors were the Atlanteans, who were not only astronomers and sailors but also great teachers of humanity, including the Dogon people's distant ancestors who knew them as the *Nommo*.

All the evidence lies before you, Seeker of Truth, revealing the history you have been denied: the great civilization of Atlantis existed, and its inhabitants were highly advanced, creating knowledge for themselves and for generations of humans after them.

EDEN
AND THE SONS
OF ADAM

As has been revealed, some of the E-M215 haplogroup did not travel west across Africa, but rather north into the Levant. While the main literary source for the people of Atlantis is Plato, for this northern group, the main source is the Book of Genesis from the Hebrew *Pentateuch.*

Like Plato's works, the Book of Genesis also describes North Africa and the Atlantean region. In one passage, the author names the four great rivers of the world, from left to right, west to east:

> And a river went out of Eden to water the garden; and from thence it was parted, and became into four heads. The name of the first is Pison: that is it which compasseth the whole land of Havilah, where there is gold; And the gold of that land is good: there is bdellium and the onyx stone. And the name of the second river is Gihon: the same is it that compasseth the whole land of Ethiopia. And the name of the third river is Hiddekel: that is it which goeth toward the east of Assyria. And the fourth river is Euphrates. [15]
>
> [15]**Genesis** 2:10–14 (KJV).

Havilah is what you know as North Africa, the Maghreb, but because there are no rivers left in North Africa today, your teachers have thrown up their hands and said they do not know where the River Pison was. It is the Tamanrasset, the very same river that carried members of the E-M215 haplogroup from Ethiopia to the land south of Mount Atlas, the land that became the great capital city of Atlantis. The ancient Greeks used to say one could travel the Nile south, then eventually it turned and headed west, all the way across Africa—they were referring to the Pison, the mighty Tamanrasset.

The next river, the Gihon, is now known as the Nile, which does indeed course through the whole land of Ethiopia. In some versions of the Bible, the third river, Hiddekel, is identified as the Tigris, but this is an erroneous interpretation. Genesis describes the Hiddekel as flowing toward the east of Assyria, which you know as northern Iraq, which the Tigris does not do. Instead, the Hiddekel is today known as the River Jordan, which runs through Israel and becomes the River Dan near Mount Hermon. From there, it once continued east toward Assyria, through the ancient settlement of Abu Hureyra, but that portion of the ancient river no longer exists. The fourth river is clearly identified as the Euphrates, a name that remains to this day.

The point where the Gihon and Pison met in Ethiopia is where the new haplogroup formed after the supernova. From thence, the progenitors of King Atlas sailed west along the Tamanrasset, as has been said. The other group sailed north along the Nile, the Gihon, and into the Levant. Modern-day Jews knowledgeable of the Sefer haYashar and the works of Josephus will tell you that this is the true Exodus spoken of in the Bible. This is the place from whence Moses led his people—not out of Egypt, but out of Ethiopia.

What is the significance of the river map laid out in the Book of Genesis? Read closely, and you shall find the true location of Eden. It is not in the Middle East, as many suggest, nor is it Asia or the Americas, as other scholars have proposed. No. As we have seen, Plato described a lush paradise in the land of Atlantis, a land—nay, a garden—watered by the River Pison. This is Eden. This is Atlantis. They are one and the same.

The "Gods"

The two branches of the E-M215 haplogroup came from the same ancestor affected by the supernova, but they lived very differently after they left Ethiopia. The people of the lush paradise of Atlantis formed a highly advanced agricultural civilization, while people in the more unforgiving land of Israel, in the Levant, were the primitive Kebarans, a hunter-gatherer society.

When the two cultures interacted, their exchange became the stuff of legend. Using their sailing capabilities, the Atlanteans visited the Levant many times over thousands of years and left behind bladelets and other tools that your archeologists have cataloged. [16] They also amazed their Kebaran cousins with their knowledge of the stars and their ability to grow food and build structures. It has been said that any sufficiently advanced technology is indistinguishable from magic, and so it was when the Atlanteans met the Kebarans. The latter decided the former must be gods, for their powers could not possibly be those of mortal men.

[16] Deborah I. Olszewski, "Issues in the Levantine Epipaleolithic: The Madamaghan, Nebekian and Qalkhan (Levant Epipaleolithic)," *Paléorient* 32, no. 1 (2006): 19–26.

This dynamic has repeated itself throughout human history, where primitive human beings tend to perceive more advanced humans as gods. To this day, there are cults in the South Pacific who worship American GIs and the war materiel they left behind. Dogmatic Christians, Jews, Muslims, and Hindus like to think of themselves as more sophisticated because their gods are abstract incorporeal entities, but that attitude is simply part of their modern-day hubris. As you shall see, they are no different than the South Pacific cargo cults in terms of the gods they worship today.

Just as Polynesian tribesmen today worship a mythical American soldier named John Frum, perceived to be a god, so the Kebarans of old revered their Atlantean cousins as gods. The latter became the Sons of God because they were perceived as such due to their technical superiority. When you consider the historical timing of the events of the Book of Genesis, the only place a "godlike" human civilization lived at the time was Atlantis, and thus the authors of the Bible called the leader of the men who dwelt in Eden "God" and the others were his angels and his sons.

The Atlanteans traveled to and from the Levant many times over thousands of years, observing Kebaran progress. Then, 15,000 years ago, the Atlanteans decided to take one of the Kebarans back to Atlantis with them, to reside in the royal garden as a curiosity for the Atlantean king, and to see just how far a savage man could be educated.

That Kebaran was Adam from the Book of Genesis.

When the Atlanteans brought Adam to Atlantis, they did not put him in the large main agricultural garden, but in a smaller place where "God"—King Atlas—took walks. It was Adam's task to care for this tranquil space. After eating the fruit of a tree of particular medicinal value to the king, Adam was terminated from his occupation—expelled from the garden and sent back to the Levant. The Book of Genesis records the interaction thus: [17] Genesis 3:23 (KJV). "Therefore, the Lord God sent him forth from the garden of Eden to till the ground from whence he was taken." [17]

Adam was taken, not made.

Adam returned to the Levant with the knowledge of how to work the land, so he taught his people how to grow and process food as he had learned in the garden. With Adam's return, the Natufian culture arose, and the Kebarans disappeared. Adam was the bridge from Kebaran to Natufian—the E-M78 subclade of the E-M215 haplogroup that originally settled in the Levant. Those with the M-78 mutation who have survived to this day are the Sons of Adam, as the other Kebarans sharing this mutation soon died off without heirs.

How Men Become Giants

After Adam returned to the Levant, he founded the city of Abu Hureyra, on the banks of the ancient River Hiddekel. This city became the hub of Natufian culture 15,000 years ago. [18]

[18] Andrew M. T. Moore, Gordon C. Hillman, and Anthony J. Legge, *Village on the Euphrates: From Foraging to Farming at Abu Hureyra* (Oxford: Oxford University Press, 2000).

Your scientists know the Natufians were engaged in cultivating cereals, fermenting them, and making bread. There is evidence from the Rakefet Cave in Israel that they made not only bread but also beer. Everything Adam learned about fermentation and gardening, he learned from the Atlanteans, and that knowledge then spread among the Natufians. [19]

[19] Li Liu et al., "Fermented Beverage and Food Storage in 13,000-Year-old Stone Mortars at Raqefet Cave, Israel: Investigating Natufian Ritual Feasting," *Journal of Archaeological Science* 21 (October 2018): 783–793, https://www.sciencedirect.com/science/article/abs/pii/S2352409X18303468?via%3Dihub

Unfortunately for the Natufians, the carbohydrate-rich but animal protein-deficient diet Adam introduced negatively affected the subsequent generations, for reasons your scientists understand. One doctor, Francis M. Pottenger, studied the effects of an improper diet on the health of cats and found that those who ate primarily raw meat fared better than those who ate cooked meat and similarly unsuitable foods, with cumulative effects from one generation to the next being seen in smaller and sicklier cats. The same is known about humans, though the effects are less pronounced. A World Health Organization publication talks about stunting, stating that "stunting has been linked with the ingestion of aflatoxin-contaminated cereals and nuts." The report also found that animal-source foods "are the best sources of high-quality nutrients." [20]

[20] World Health Organization, "Global Nutrition Targets 2025: Stunting Policy Brief" (Geneva: World Health Organization, 2014), p. 3, n. 1; p. 6, n. 1.

Over successive generations of eating the cereal-rich, protein-deficient diet that Adam had learned to cultivate, the stature of the Natufians was greatly reduced. As you shall learn, by the time the Silver Age arrived, the Natufians had shrunk to the point that Iberomaurusian men just over six feet tall appeared as giants. [21]

[21] Michael Hermanussen, "Stature of Early Europeans," *Hormones* 2, no. 3 (2003): 175–178.

A COMING
WAR

Having considered the Golden Age, you now see clearly that Atlantis did exist, as told in the stories of both Plato and the Book of Genesis, as well as the genetic and archeological records. The Atlanteans had contact with your distant ancestors in the Levant, and your stories about human origins are actually stories of human contact with Atlanteans, because there was a relationship between the two in the deepest reaches of history. The civilization emerging in the Levant came from the influence of the Atlanteans, beginning with Adam.

During the Golden Age, the Atlanteans in Africa and the Natufians in the Levant had an emerging, peaceful coexistence—both amongst themselves and with each other. This peace was interrupted by the events that brought about the Silver Age, the battle between Atlas and Cronus—the War in Heaven.

CHAPTER 3
THE SILVER AGE

A s you have learned, each new age of humanity was ushered in by a significant event, usually cataclysmic and world-altering in nature. The transition from the Golden Age to the Silver Age was no exception.

After millennia of peaceful coexistence between Atlanteans and Natufians, internal strife among the Sons of God erupted into a vicious civil war that has been well documented by Ovid, Diodorus, Plato, and many other revered ancient writers. These accounts overlap and intertwine, painting a clear portrait for those who have eyes to see: the Atlanteans are the Olympians, the gods from ancient Greek mythology. The War in Heaven is the battle between Cronus and Zeus, which is the Greek Titanomachy, a ten-year battle between the Titans and the Olympians. These figures and events are one and the same, described by different writers using different names, but the similarities are unmistakable.

You shall now see just how significant the events of this age were, and continue to be, for all inhabitants of this planet and beyond.

RISE
OF THE
OLYMPIANS

Perhaps you have been taught that Plato is the only ancient source that reveals the story of Atlantis. Indeed, one scholar by the name of Robin Waterfield proclaims there is only one source that establishes the existence of Atlantis, and that source is Plato, with nothing before or after that is independent of him. Yet this same scholar has translated numerous works by Diodorus, who clearly describes the Atlanteans in Book III of his *Bibliotheca Historica*:

> But since we have made mention of the Atlanteans, we believe that it will not be inappropriate in this place to recount what their myths relate about the genesis of the gods, in view of the fact that it does not differ greatly from the myths of the Greeks. Now the Atlanteans, dwelling as they do in the regions on the edge of the ocean and inhabiting a fertile territory, are reputed far to excel their neighbours in reverence towards the gods and the humanity they showed in their dealings with strangers, and the gods, they say, were born among them. [22]
>
> [22] Diodorus, *Bibliotheca Historica*, Book III, Chapter 56.

Was Waterfield, one thoroughly versed in other works by Diodorus, unaware of this description of the inhabitants of Atlantis, living in the shadow of Mount Atlas, and their similarity to the ancient Greek gods of Mount Olympus? What say you, Seeker of Truth?

By ignoring Diodorus's detailed account of Atlantis, scholars such as Waterfield, the rest of academia, and the ruling class have deceived you and other Seekers like you. Such an omission from the curriculum traditionally taught to humankind is so egregious that it cannot possibly be a mistake but is rather the result of an active effort at deception—to conceal the existence of Atlantis and its people, the descendants of whom are walking among us today, dictating world events in ways about which you shall soon learn.

In his account, Diodorus points to the same geographic location that Plato identifies and says that civilization was destroyed in the same way Plato describes: a violent cataclysm, a natural disaster of proportions that beggar the human imagination. He calls these individuals by the same name as well—Atlanteans—and says, "The gods were born among them," meaning the gods of the Greco-Roman world were Atlanteans.

Diodorus explains the story he tells is not his own, nor Plato's, but rather relayed from another book, written by Dionysius Scytobrachion, an author who lived in Alexandria, resting place of the famed library, giving him access to the best source material that ever existed in the ancient world. That same source bequeaths us a story of Dionysus, the god of wine and ecstatic experiences, who was reported to have been born in Libya and traveled all over the Mediterranean, meaning his roots are in the vicinity of Atlantis of old.

You surely have been taught about those Greco-Roman gods, but what you have not learned is that those stories are not fanciful legends but rather historical accounts about the Atlanteans, whom the less advanced peoples took for gods. The mythology around the Olympians and their mighty deeds throughout the Mediterranean is in fact an account of the Atlanteans' impressive accomplishments.

Diodorus provides another perspective on the history recounted in the chapter on the Golden Age, from a source that academia pretends does not even exist. For example, while Plato gives a mythological genealogy of Poseidon, who had a series of five identical twins, Diodorus says Uranus, the Atlanteans' first king—the one who "caused his subjects to cease from their lawless ways and bestial manner of living" [23]—is the father of forty-five sons by a number of wives, of whom Atlas, the eponymous king of Atlantis, is the first. Plato calls Atlas's brother Gadeirus, the brother who is known as Cronus in Diodorus's account. According to Diodorus, Atlas's mother is Titaea, and one of Atlas's brothers was a Titan named Hyperion, who married his sister, Basileia, and had a son and a daughter, Helius and Selenê.

[23] Diodorus, *Bibliotheca Historica*, Book III, Chapter 56.

After the death of Uranus, other Titans murdered Hyperion and Helius, concerned that the whole kingdom of Atlantis would pass to this father and son much loved by the Atlanteans. Selenê, stricken with grief, committed suicide after learning of these evil deeds, and Basileia went into a self-imposed exile, later becoming known to the Phrygians as the Great Mother, or Cybelê.

As made plain in Plato's record and revealed in the last chapter, Poseidon's kingdom—referred to as Uranus's kingdom in Diodorus—was divided between Atlas and Cronus, with Atlas taking the regions of the kingdom bordering the Atlantic Ocean and Cronus taking those bordering the Mediterranean. Cronus took the Maghreb, while Atlas had the southern mountains and the land known today as Mauritania.

Diodorus's account also provides more detail about Atlas's progeny. The Atlanteans practiced a form of stellar ancestor worship, in which they figuratively raised important people who died into the heavens and named a star after them. When Helius and Selenê died, he was honored as the sun and she as the moon. Diodorus says that before the sun was referred to as such, people called it the holy fire, but after the deaths of Helius and Selenê, those heavenly bodies took on their honorific names. Likewise, after her death, Titaea transformed into Gê, or Gaia—Mother Earth. Uranus, receiving honors as great as his achievements in life, became the sky itself, the firmament upon which all stars are fixed.

The Pleiades and Hyades, together forming the Golden Gate of the Ecliptic, and the Hesperides are all highly important star formations for navigators, and they are all named after children of King Atlas. In Greek mythology, the Pleiades, the most famous star cluster, with seven visible stars, are the seven daughters of Atlas; in life they were known as the Atlantides. [24]

[24] Diodorus, *Bibliotheca Historica*, Book III, Chapter 60.

A CIVIL WAR

After Cronus took control of the northern region, he married his sister Rhea, also known as Pandora, and together, they had a son named Zeus. In mythology, Cronus worried about eventually being overthrown by his son, and began eating his own children as soon as they were born. Evidence from the region of Cronus's kingdom in the Maghreb suggests that some Iberomaurusians may have practiced cannibalism for thousands of years, but in this case the myth is slightly different from reality: the real Cronus did not eat his own progeny, but his people did conduct religious observances in which human children were sacrificed and consumed in his honor.

[25] Deborah I. Olszewski, Utsav A. Schurmans, and Beverly A Schmidt, "The Epipaleolithic (Iberomaurusian) from Grotte des Contrebandiers, Morocco," *African Archaeological Review* 28 (2011): 97–123.

[26] Christopher M. Stojanowski, Charisse L. Carver, and Katherine A Miller, "Incisor Avulsion, Social Identity, and Saharan Population History: New Data from the Early Holocene Southern Sahara," *Journal of Anthropological Archaeology* 35 (2014): 79–91.

This practice was condemned, under no uncertain terms, by the broader Atlantean kingdom, and the punishments meted out were severe. From over thirty caves throughout the Maghreb, your scientists have recovered more than 500 bodies of Iberomaurusians, many of which have had one or more of their incisors forcibly removed, a fitting punishment for their cannibalistic ways. [25] Women and young adults who engaged in cannibalism were not spared, and they were marked for life along with the men who engaged in this horrific practice. [26]

In the Greek myths, Zeus is so outraged at being offered stew made with human flesh that he destroys the world with a flood, but this is not a complete account. Cronus was a mad king who saw eating human beings as extending his own life, allowing him to live forever and refuse his own son the throne. This violated Atlantean custom and law, and as a result, Zeus, who was loved by the people of the Mediterranean, went beyond the Pillars of Hercules to recruit the help of his uncle, Atlas.

In Greek mythology, this battle is known as the Titanomachy, a ten-year civil war between the Titans led by Cronus and the Olympians led by Zeus. Plato describes a similar war between forces beyond the Pillars of Hercules, those of Cronus, and those within the Mediterranean. Even in Judeo-Christian mythos, angels rebelled against God, resulting in the War in Heaven. Just as the rebellious angels lost and were cast out of heaven, in the Atlantean civil war described by both Diodorus and Plato, the forces of Cronus were defeated and ultimately cast out of the Atlantean kingdom. According to myth, Cronus was imprisoned in Tartarus, but as you shall see, others left the Maghreb and sailed around Africa to the land between two rivers.

Over the millennia, after the descendants of the expelled armies took over the societies throughout the Mediterranean, they began editing history to make themselves sound like forces of good in this war, and the true Atlanteans as the forces of evil. In their telling, Atlas is still ever the powerful Titan, but he fights on the side of Cronus. Those revisionist stories claim Atlas led an assault on Zeus, almost won, and was made to hold up the sky as punishment, but in fact, this is simply an allegory about Mount Atlas, the ultra-prominent peak that appears to hold up the sky.[27]

[27] Diodorus, *Bibliotheca Historica*, Book III, Chapter 60.

A LAND
BETWEEN
TWO RIVERS

Cronus was imprisoned after losing the war, and his army and followers were completely expelled from the Atlantean kingdom. The exiled Titans had to leave by the quickest route, without entering any part of the kingdom, so they ventured south from the Pillars of Hercules along the Atlantic coast, circumnavigating Africa, sailing into the Persian Gulf and finally into the Euphrates. The exiles chose this location because they knew the Natufians and other tribes of this region would worship them as gods for their knowledge, technological advancement, and stature, as had already happened among Adam's people.

There is ample evidence of the practicability of such a voyage. You have already learned of the voyages of Thor Heyerdahl, but let us also take, for example, the Phoenicians, whom an Egyptian pharaoh commissioned to circumnavigate Africa 2,600 years ago. They started in the Red Sea, sailed out through the Gulf of Aden, all the way around South Africa and up the Atlantic coast, through the Pillars of Hercules, and back into Egypt. The story of that original voyage was passed down through the millennia. [28]

[28] Herodotus, *Histories*, Book IV, Chapter 42.

The Phoenicians knew how to make this journey because their ancestors, the expelled followers of Cronus, had done so after their loss; they simply traveled in the other direction. Furthermore, the very beginning of the histories of Herodotus also discusses the Phoenicians—who lived in Byblos, Sidon, Tyre, Baalbek, and other cities in the land of Canaan—and says they had their origin on the shores of the Persian Gulf, referring to the site of the expelled armies' landing. Once they came ashore, they spread out and eventually made it to the Levant, Anatolia, and Greece.

According to the stories, the Euphrates is exactly where the Natufians observed their gods arriving. When Cronus's loyalists made their egress into the Middle East by traveling up the Euphrates, they reached Mesopotamia, the land between the Euphrates and the Tigris. Here they found the climate to be much different than the tropical Atlantean kingdom from which they had departed. As earth was still in the grips of the last ice age, the climate in Mesopotamia would have been considerably colder than it is today, subjecting the expelled Atlanteans to their first winter and thus giving credence to Ovid's mythology, which states that the Silver Age introduced winter to mankind.

When they arrived in Mesopotamia, Cronus's followers made an impression on the people there, who recorded their story. Because of the carbohydrate-rich diet introduced by Adam and carried on by his Natufians descendants, the people of this region were much shorter than the former Atlanteans who landed on their shores and built cities all along the Euphrates. As with earlier encounters in the Levant, the exiles' massive size and advanced technologies made them seem like gods.

The Eridu Genesis, an ancient Mesopotamian epic recounting the creation of the world, talks about beings arriving from heaven—referring to these tall, impressive people coming from the Atlantean kingdom. The ancient Mesopotamians said their gods arrived from the sea, founded cities, and ruled over them like kings. In addition to the Eridu Genesis, another creation epic called the Atrahasis tells of the gods moving in, establishing cities, and beginning to practice agriculture. At first the Igigi, the laboring class of gods, do all of the work, but eventually they revolt, wanting something else to do the work for them. One of the gods is sacrificed so his blood can be mixed with earth, creating seven male and seven female humans. Thus, Mesopotamians' view of themselves was as creations made to grow food and brew beer for the gods who ruled over them. [29]

[29] Eridu Genesis: Joshua J. Mark, "Eridu Genesis: Definition," May 2020, https://www.worldhistory.org/Eridu_Genesis/; Atrahasis: Stephanie Dalley, *Myths from Mesopotamia: Creation, the Flood, Gilgamesh, and Others* (Oxford: Oxford University Press, 2009), henceforth cited as Atrahasis.

Other Mesopotamian myths such as "Erra and Ishum" and "Adapa" discuss the seven sages, whom they called Apkallu, a group who taught the less advanced peoples living in Mesopotamia the arts of civilization, such as how to plow fields and tend to the other burdens Cronus's followers demanded of them. Yet others make mention of the Anunnaki, the ruling council of seven gods composed of Enlil, Enki, and five other powerful deities.

While the ruling class of Cronus's loyalists craved the servitude of the people of Mesopotamia, they also became obsessed with human overpopulation and the need to control it. The chief god in the Mesopotamian Pantheon was Enlil, a vain, selfish entity who did not like humans and complained endlessly about the racket they made, interrupting his rest. He unleashed genocide after genocide on the Mesopotamian humans to control their numbers—the beginning of eugenics, 15,000 years ago. Its roots are in the dehumanization of Natufians by the unruly defeated soldiers of Cronus. Enlil viewed the Natufians as beasts of burden and wanted to cull the herd, preventing the possibility of another uprising. [30]

[30] Atrahasis, Tablet I.

Regular genocides by disease and famine run in opposition to the commandment to be fruitful and multiply followed by King Atlas and his people. Thus, the exiles of the war were no longer Atlanteans in their way of living.

The Eridu Genesis says the first city the gods founded was Eridu, but that is a distortion resulting from generations of retelling and the true name and location has been lost to time. Modern-day dating methods rule that place out as the first founding, and you should know that your human scientists have yet to find the real first city of the exiles.

ARRIVAL OF
THE WATCHERS

The Atlantean exiles continued sailing up the Euphrates, establishing cities wherever they went. Evidence of their presence has been well documented, in everything from the arrowheads and bladelets left behind to the skeletons recovered from the Nautufian territory. Like those found in caves in the Maghreb, these skulls have their central incisors forcibly removed, suggesting they are either Cronus's descendants or Natufians who received a similar punishment. [31]

[31] Isabelle De Groote and Louise T. Humphrey, "Characterizing Evulsion in the Later Stone Age Maghreb: Age, Sex and Effects on Mastication," *Quaternary International* 30 (2015): 1–12.

By transitioning to the River Jordan, the exiles finally arrived in the Levant, where they encountered a Natufian named Enoch, who came to call these visitors the Watchers. Let us see what he had to say, for the Book of Enoch is primarily concerned with the arrival and exploits of these gods, corroborating what the people of Mesopotamia had earlier observed.

The oldest extant copies or excerpts of the Book of Enoch were in a collection found in a cave at Qumran and known today as the Dead Sea Scrolls. But even in that form, the book was spliced together from many other, much older texts. It is a collage of numerous sacred stories whose true antiquity is unknown to your modern scientists. The earliest versions known today are 2,300 years old, and those were already compilations of much older tales.

Until the Dead Sea Scrolls library was found, the only complete copy of the Book of Enoch was in the Ethiopian Bible, written in the ancient semitic language of Ge'ez. Though the canonical Old Testament references Enoch and the events described in the Book of Enoch, and though the New Testament's Epistle of Jude heavily references it as well, the book itself is not part of the canon. It is part of the Ethiopian Orthodox Church canon alone.

The Dead Sea Scrolls library revealed the same story found in the Ge'ez version, essentially verbatim, without changes or edits. It is an antediluvian story, before the flooding of Eden described in the Book of Jubilees, which we will have occasion to discuss further on. The great global flood occurred 12,800 years ago, so the events of Enoch are even older, and his story has been passed down for millennia, changing and recombining in the process.

Enoch says 200 Watchers landed at Mount Hermon in the Levant, likely arriving by way of the River Jordan, via the Euphrates, which flowed near Abu Hureyra in those days. The Bible describes Watchers as angels or holy ones come down from heaven, sometimes individually but often in pairs, to give specific warnings and guidance to humans on earth. Note, for example, the Book of Daniel, which records King Nebuchadnezzar's words: "I saw in the visions of my head upon my bed, and, behold, a watcher and a holy one came down from heaven; [32] Daniel 4:13–14 (KJV). he cried aloud, and said thus...." [32] And note the Book of Genesis, which records the appearance of two angels who tell Lot to leave before God destroyed Sodom and Gomorrah. [33] Even the Native American myths that shall be shared in a coming chapter [33] Genesis 19:1, 12–22 (KJV). record Watchers arriving individually or with a partner.

In no case did these beings travel by the hundreds, so the Watchers who arrived in Enoch's land were more accurately an all-male army in exile, and more specifically, those who were loyal to Cronus.

Enoch uses "Watcher" as a description of employment, knowing how the Atlanteans engaged in projects with other human cultures all over the world. The true Atlantean Watchers were ambassadors who left the kingdom and lived among these other humans, tasked by King Atlas to watch over them with good will—not intermarry or impose themselves as rulers. Of course, the expelled followers of Cronus did not adhere to that model, and they intermarried and had children to perpetuate their legacy. According to Enoch, these fallen Watchers made a pact amongst themselves to take human wives and have children by them, though they remarked that doing so would be a great sin. They decided that they did not care for the moral rectitude of their Atlantean origins and proceeded to go to the tribes around the area, take Natufian women, impregnate them, and teach them to be like Atlantean women in dress, makeup, and behavior. The resulting offspring were called the Nephilim.

Enoch describes the Nephilim as awful people, "great giants, whose height was three thousand ells," which is, of course, an exaggeration, though they were noticeably taller than the Natufians. He says they "consumed all the acquisitions of men" and taxed away all of their property. They began to sin against birds, beasts, reptiles, and fish, as

well as humans, devouring their flesh and drinking their blood.[34] These Nephilim continued their forefathers' hatred for mankind, viewing
humans as a source of labor or food, nothing more.   [34] Book of Enoch 7:2–5

Among the Dead Sea Scrolls were two other books describing this time of the
Watchers. The Book of Giants is told from the perspective of the Nephilim, while
the Book of Jubilees is told from the Atlanteans' perspective. Along with the Book
of Enoch, these ancient texts provide a varied account of this time, an account
that is corroborated by anthropological and genetic evidence.

As you have learned, the Atlantean exiles landed at Mount Hermon and sailed down
the River Jordan, closer to the Dead Sea, and founded a city in an area dominated by
Natufians. Coinciding with the timing of that journey
is evidence of new DNA injected into the Natufians   [35] Elena Bosch et al., "High-Resolution
via a descendant of the Atlantean Y haplogroup—the   Analysis of Human Y-Chromosome
Sons of God, E-Z827. At this time and in this place,   Variation Shows a Sharp Discontinuity
a sub-mutation called E-M81, the Sons of Cronus,   and Limited Gene Flow between
was brought from the Maghreb to the Levant.[35]   Northwestern Africa and the Iberian
                                                        Peninsula," *American Journal of Human
                                                        Genetics* 68 (2001): 1019–1029.

Natufians did not have a sophisticated language,
whereas the Iberomaurusians—whom you know as the Atlanteans—spoke the
Afro-Asiatic language. The Nephilim taught this language to the Natufians,
which eventually evolved into all the Semitic languages, as revealed by the study
of linguistics, a science similar to the study of DNA, which traces how all extant
languages descended from ancestral ones.

Scientists today know of the Mushabian culture, a catch-all term for any evidence
of Iberomaurusians in the Levant, as researchers have never narrowed the culture
to a particular place or time. Throughout human history, these Iberomaurusians
seem to appear and then disappear all over this region, including near Jericho, a city
at least 10,000 years old that is considered the world's oldest city by mainstream
archeology (though you, Seeker of Truth, know the truly oldest city was Atlantis).
Archeological exploration of Jericho has revealed that the city had walls and a
highly developed defense system—evidence that it had been a Nephilim stronghold.

Thus, the stories, the archeology, and the genetic and linguistic facts all align,
confirming your real history. The Iberomaurusians took their technology, their
genetics, and their language to Mesopotamia and then the Levant, imposing their
ways on the peoples already living there.

BIRTH OF
THE GOD-KINGS

You undoubtedly learned in your childhood that human civilization began in the Fertile Crescent, but it did not—that is a false history from the Nephilim, the children of the Watchers and their Natufian wives. They are the ones who have darkened the human mind and deprived you of your history.

As previously recounted, Mesopotamian myth says godlike beings created humanity, and the Bible says God created Adam. These are all distortions by those who crave power, the Nephilim, in order to insert a message into the cultural mythos and ensure their perpetuation as the ruling class. For these Nephilim are none other than the God-Kings, who continued ideas of enslavement and population control originally imposed by the fallen Watcher Enlil, leader of the Mesopotamian gods. [36] His ideas were carried on by these children, self-appointed divine rulers who wreaked havoc on humanity.

[36] Atrahasis, Tablet I.

The Nephilim have so successfully distorted history that the Bible even describes these beings as "heroes of old, men of renown," painting them as forces of good when they were actually forces of the most evil kind. [37]

[37] Genesis 6:4 (KJV).

The false stories perpetuated by these God-Kings caused humans to see themselves as lesser beings and to readily accept the ruling class's authority over them—and this dynamic continues to this day. In telling the history of the Atlanteans behind the myths, Diodorus cracked the rulers' façade, and now you, Seeker of Truth, are called to tear it down.

From the land between two rivers and then Abu Hureyra, the Nephilim fanned out, spreading through the Levant and as far as modern-day Greece. In those days, the inhabitants of the region were called Pelasgians, and their ancient founder-hero was Pelasgus. Many of the Greek mythical characters—including Zeus, Hephaestus, Poseidon, and Atlas—came from gods already worshipped by the Pelasgians, the first group of Nephilim to enter the land that became Greece.

Plato mentions one of the Nephilim in *Critias*: the mythical founding king of Athens named Erechtheus, or Erichthonius, who existed thousands of years before there were Greek people and of whom every Athenian would have known. Erechtheus was the eldest of a pair of identical twins, just like the Platonic Atlantean king Atlas, and his twin brother's name was Butte. Echoing the Platonic tale of Atlas's parentage, Erechtheus and Butte were the sons of a god and the earth, the Greek way of describing the coupling of a male Atlantean and an indigenous woman—in this case represented as Hephaestus and Gaia. Hephaestus is known as the god of metallurgy and weapon-making, skills taught by the Enochian Watcher Azazel.

Being a direct descendant of Hephaestus made Erechtheus a first-generation Nephilim, offspring of the fallen Watchers, but he presented himself like an Atlantean king because he would not stand for being cast as the bastard son of an evil angel. Based on the Book of Enoch, the Nephilim like Erechtheus were capricious, lascivious, murderous rulers, who taxed, starved, impoverished, and cannibalized the humans beneath them. Yet, because of the Nephilim's distortion of history, the Greeks praised Erechtheus as a great hero, just as the writer of Genesis spoke positively of the Nephilim who roamed the earth.

Erechtheus's presentation of himself as an Atlantean king with the right to rule marks the beginning of the sacral king or imperial cult practice, which holds that the king is god's son or god's representative on earth who rules by divine right. Belief in the special powers possessed by this ruling class resurfaces throughout history, around the world, in various cultures—all from the original assertion of divine rule by the Nephilim of the E-Z827 haplogroup, who recast the story of Atlas.

For many millennia, people ruled as gods, having arrived with greater stature and technology, impressing the primitive peoples. There are myriad manifestations of king worship: the mandate of heaven in China, the divine right of kings in Europe, the imperial cults of Rome and the Far East, the sacred kings in Babylonia, and the Pharaohs of ancient Egypt. All of these societies for thousands of years practiced this belief in the king as a god, because of the distortions and oppression wrought by the fallen Watchers and their offspring, the Nephilim.

FROM
END TO END
OF THE EARTH

Slowly, the Nephilim took over the whole region, ruling the Levant and everything around the eastern Mediterranean, from Turkey to what became Greece. According to Enoch, the people were oppressed and suffered greatly under these kings—they were murdered, lied to, and lied about—and they looked to "God," the king of Atlantis, for help. They did not have the weapons, skill, or ability to fight and overthrow the giants on their own, so they prayed to King Atlas, and eventually their desperate cries became impossible for the king to ignore.

Enoch lived in the land of Dan, north of the Sea of Galilee, and he tells of walking by the River Dan by Mount Hermon, where the Watchers landed. On that walk, "God"—the Atlantean king—contacted him telepathically to deliver a message to the fallen Watchers that they would never return to Atlantis and would not ascend to heaven because of the many atrocities they had committed.

Atlantis

Subsequently, the Atlanteans collected Enoch from Palestine, taking him "aloft on the chariots of the spirit" to embark on a 23,000-kilometer journey across the planet, which is retold in the Book of Enoch, though not in a linear fashion because of the way the book itself was pieced together from a collage of separate stories.

Seeker of Truth, know this: while the trip Enoch describes may sound impossible, it is clear that he must have gone on that exact journey. Even 2,500 years ago, no one could have described the geographic features, people, animals, and plant life he encountered on that trip, except by having seen it all with their own eyes.

From the Levant, the Watcher took Enoch west, to the ends of the earth:

> And in those days a whirlwind carried me off from the earth, and set me down
> at the end of the heavens. And there, I saw another vision, the dwelling-places
> of the holy, and the resting-places of the righteous. Here mine eyes saw their
> dwellings with His righteous angels and the resting-places with the holy. [38]
> [38] **Book of Enoch** 39:3–5.

In Atlantis, exactly as Plato described, Enoch saw multitudes beyond his ability
to reckon—"10,000 times 10,000" people, all having white skin; blonde, white,
or red hair; fair eyes and beards; and an unidentified red feature, referring to
armpit and pubic hair. He also met "God," the Atlantean king, and saw the
place where the first fathers were buried, a reference to the
very beginnings of humanity in the cave at Jebel Irhoud. [39]   [39] Book of Enoch 70:4.

The Atlanteans had all manner of technology the likes of which Enoch had never seen, and he struggled to find the words to describe what he witnessed and
touched. His stories are told in the language of a technologically primitive being
confused and awed by his new surroundings, so you must read between the lines.
The king showed him a structure made of crystal—a telescope at the royal observatory—and he saw "God and his angels" entering and leaving this place, using
the telescope to study the heavens, for as you learned from Diodorus, this great
civilization developed the science of astronomy.

In the observatory, the Atlanteans used a telescope to show him the cluster of
debris on a path to destroy the world, which they said would arrive in seventy
generations—1,400 years—and release Enoch's people from the yoke of the
Nephilim. The present-day geological record shows the debris in fact made
impact 12,800 years ago. If you add 1,400 years to account for the moment
Enoch received this prediction, you will find that Enoch's visit to Atlantis took
place 14,200 years ago, in the middle of the Silver Age, when
Atlantis had become a major civilization and the Nephilim's   [40] **Bosch** et al., "High-
E-M81 haplogroup emerged in the Levant. As in all cases, the   Resolution Analysis."
story and the genetic record align. [40]

In the astronomy lesson, Enoch also learned about supernovas and nebulae, as
the Atlanteans explained stars could change and never regain their original form,
demonstrating their astronomical knowledge and ability to foreshadow the cosmic
impact. Enoch calls a supernova a "lightning," which can be a blessing or a curse
upon the earth.

The Atlanteans knew stars exploded and could affect the earth, as their earliest ancestors had passed down knowledge regarding the devastation of the supernova 26,000 years earlier. Because of those legends, as soon as the Atlanteans developed telescopes and took them to the high mountains, they searched the sky for the remains of the evil second sun and found the debris. Thus, by the time of Enoch's visit, they had long been monitoring the celestial aftermath, and Enoch says the coming destruction was known since the beginning of time, meaning before the founding of Atlantis.

The Canary Islands

After that astronomy lesson, Enoch traveled across the Atlantic ocean, where conditions were "chaotic," a common way of describing the open ocean and its undulations in the ancient world. He speaks of seeing seven mountains rising up out of the chaos, and there is only one set of seven islands near West Africa: the Canary Islands.

Enoch names the seven archangels and their respective domains, saying Uriel, his guide, ruled over Tartarus. He learned that Tartarus, where Cronus was imprisoned, was in fact the Atlanteans' prison island of Tenerife, one of the volcanic Canary Islands, and he tells a story similar to that of Atlas holding up the world in recounting the formation of those seven islands—again, a recurring number also seen in the seven archangels, seven sages, and the seven Pleiades.

The Archangel Uriel told Enoch the islands were in the water because they were stars being punished for not rising at their appointed times; they were sent down and forced to endure 10,000 years on earth. In the Atlanteans' practice of stellar worship, being sent down to earth was a punishment, while being raised up into the heavens was a reward. The Atlantean mythos draws a connection between people and stars, events in the sky and events on earth, personifying stars, and islands. People with particularly high honors would have a star named after them, and the island formation myth fits this pattern of mythology—calling stars down to earth as punishment, where they existed as burning mountains.

Because of its great potential for astronomical seeing, the island of Tenerife had observatories then and still does to the present day. There is an ancient caldera on the island, known today as Las Cañadas, that blew up spectacularly 170,000 years ago, and the geology shows its intense activity, with rivers of lava pouring out—which Enoch describes as columns of fire, rivers of fire, burning sulfur, and brimstone. He also mentions seeing "hollow places, deep and wide and very smooth." [41] These are lava tubes, formed by the

[41] Book of Enoch 22:2.

continuous eruptions from the volcano that can still be seen today at La Cueva del Viento.

Tartarus, on Tenerife, is also where the Atlantean king imprisoned all of the fallen Watchers. As an angel tells Enoch, Tenerife with its volcano, Teide, is where "shall stand the angels who have connected themselves with women and their spirits, assuming many different forms, are defiling mankind and shall lead them astray into sacrificing to demons as gods." [42] The account of Enoch is confirmed in 2 Peter 2:4. Some translations of this passage from the Bible say "God" cast the fallen angels into hell, but others correctly use the word Tartarus.

[42] Book of Enoch 19:1.

Here the Watchers shall remain, forever chained to earth, never to return to heaven or incarnate on another world with their Atlantean brothers. On this planet, they remain, incarnating into human being after human being, leading the rest of humanity astray. To this day, their followers use dark magical practices to summon a particular soul into the body of a baby, that of a Watcher or a Nephilim.

All of the fallen Watchers received the same punishment except for Azazel, to whom the king "ascribed all sin" and ordered that he be buried alive. In Hebrew lore, Azazel is looked upon as a devil, and in every tradition, he is an evil entity.

As the ages passed, and as the Nephilim edited history to frame themselves in a more positive light, this prison for fallen angels became a mythical paradise known as Elysium, resting place of the ancient Greek heroes—a chain of islands referred to as the "Blessed" or "Fortunate" Isles. In their retelling, the Nephilim transformed hell on earth to a heaven ruled by Cronus and located in the western ocean at the edge of the world.

And those Nephilim, who are only half-Atlantean, will be punished in a different way—through wars waged on one another and through the coming of the Son of Man. You have likely been taught that the Son of Man is Jesus, but this is not so. The Atlanteans personified bodies in the sky, and the Son of Man is no different. Repeatedly in the Book of Enoch, the Atlanteans tell Enoch that the Son of Man is coming down to earth to sit on his throne, and that when he does, all of the nations and kings of the earth will be laid low by floods and fire and unimaginable destruction. The Atlanteans were speaking not of Jesus, but of the cluster of comet debris heading toward earth, the debris seen through their telescopes on Mount Atlas and Teide.

Enoch goes on to say, "And the seventh mountain was in the midst of these and excelled them in heights," describing Teide, which is in the middle of the islands and is the highest peak in all of Spain. Measured from the sea floor, it is the third highest volcano in the world, after Mauna Kea and Mauna Loa. He describes the peak as

> resembling the seat of a throne: and fragrant trees encircled the throne. And amongst them was a tree such as I had never yet smelt, neither was any amongst them nor were others like it: it had a fragrance beyond all fragrance and its leaves and blooms would wither not for ever: and its fruit is beautiful, and its fruit resembles the dates of a palm. [43]
>
> [43]Book of Enoch *24:3–5.*

The description of that tree aligns with the date palm of Tenerife and all the Canary Islands, *Phoenix canariensis,* an appropriate name for a plant that withers not forever. You have no doubt seen this particular palm in tropical resorts around the world and on the American continents to this day. In Enoch's day, though, the tree existed only in the Canary Islands, and he could only have seen it by visiting there.

Cape Verde

After visiting Tenerife, Enoch left the seven islands and traveled toward the center of the earth, the equator, and reached another chain of islands known as Cape Verde. All these places would have been accessible by sailing, but multiple times, he recounted being taken up into the air. He accurately described the flora, fauna, and geography of each place to which he went, which should persuade you beyond all doubt that his stories are based on real events, not fabrications.

When visiting Atlantis at the beginning of his journey, Enoch saw people being dragged from their homes. In Cape Verde, he saw the same people and learned they were being punished as malcontents and agitators, supporters of Cronus who "deny the name of the Lord of Spirits" and "utter with their lips against the Lord unseemly words and of His glory speak hard things." [44] Uriel tells Enoch those on Cape Verde will survive, and "they shall bless Him for the mercy in accordance with which He has assigned them." [45] They would not suffer the same fate of the fallen Watchers, who were destined to die by the comet.

[44]Book of Enoch *41:2.*

[45]Book of Enoch *27:2.*

The Other End of the Earth

After Cape Verde, they traveled 15,000 kilometers as the crow flies, to the other end of the earth, to what is now Indonesia. Given Enoch's detailed descriptions and the order in which he presents them, the Atlanteans must have used their technology to fly him across the globe, for sailing would have taken him on a different route, one that would have afforded him different sights from a different vantage point. To have seen what he recounts, Enoch must have been in the air.

Enoch describes leaving Cape Verde and seeing all the paths and routes of the angels—the Tamanrasset River and other sailing routes used by the Atlanteans. He flew over the ancient biblical lands of Havilah in North Africa, and thence "went over the summits of all these mountains, far towards the east of the earth." [46]

[46] Book of Enoch 32:2.

Enoch passed over the Arabian Peninsula, where he saw trees "similar to the almond tree" [47]—such trees have, in fact, been growing on the western coast of Arabia for thousands of years. Jabal al-Lawz, an ultra-prominent peak in the Midian Mountains, literally means "Almond Mountain" in Arabic, and today the almond tree blossoms in Al-Baha Province are said to blanket the mountain range like snow. Enoch also describes the fragrance of frankincense and myrrh on the eastern coast of the Arabian Peninsula, both of which grow plentifully in present-day Oman and Yemen.

[47] Book of Enoch 29:2.

He continued east, passing above the Erythraean Sea, today's Persian Gulf, and then to the site of the legendary Indian holy city Dvārakā, built by Krishna, another traveling Atlantean. Dvārakā was later destroyed in a flood and, beginning in 1983, archeologists have rediscovered and excavated the submerged city in present-day India in the Gulf of Cambay. [48]

[48] The Hindu Portal, "Further Excavations of the Submerged City of Dwaraka—by S.R. Rao—Recent Advances in Marine Archaeology," Hindu Portal, November 16, 2013, https://www.thehinduportal.com/2013/11/further-excavations-of-submerged-city.html

They came to the Garden of Righteousness in India, where Enoch saw sugar cane, cinnamon, cardamom, and pepper, all native Indian plants. He also saw many large trees, including "the tree of wisdom, where they eat and know great wisdom." Rafael, another archangel with Uriel, tells Enoch, "This is the tree of wisdom, of which thy father, old in years and thy aged mother, who were before thee, have eaten, and they learnt wisdom and their eyes were opened, and they knew they were naked and they were driven out of the garden." [49] Thy father and thy aged mother, of course, are the Kebaran Adam and Eve, the woman fetched from the Levant to be his wife.

[49] Book of Enoch 32:6.

The tree of wisdom precisely matches descriptions of the jamun fruit tree, *Syzygium cumini*, native to India. Enoch compares it to plants he knew from the Mediterranean, saying, "That tree is in height like the fir, and its leaves are like those of the Carob tree, and its fruit is like the clusters of the vine." [50]

[50] Book of Enoch 32:4.   A fir tree grows thirty to fifty meters tall, like the jamun tree, and the leaves and fruit of the latter also uncannily match the Mediterranean analogues mentioned by Enoch.

Earlier in their history, the Atlanteans had visited India and noted the valuable healing properties of the jamun: the fruit of the tree is able to lower blood sugar, which was useful to a civilization starting to eat carbohydrates. They took one tree back to Atlantis and planted it in the garden of Eden, where it became the Tree of the Knowledge of Good and Evil. In addition to its biblical references, the jamun fruit tree remains a holy tree in Hinduism, Jainism, and Buddhism. According to the Buddhists, the land from whence the jamun tree comes, Jambudvīpa, is an island made up of concentric rings of land and water. Does this not sound like Atlantis?

From India, Enoch says he continued to the "ends of the earth and saw there great beasts, and each differed from the other. And I saw birds also differing in appearance and beauty and voice, the one differing from the other. And to the east of those beasts I saw the ends of the earth"— which you know as the Pacific Ocean—"whereon the heaven rests, and the portals of the heaven open." [51] Here, Enoch refers to the moon and the

[51] Book of Enoch 33:1–2.   stars rising up out of the horizon.

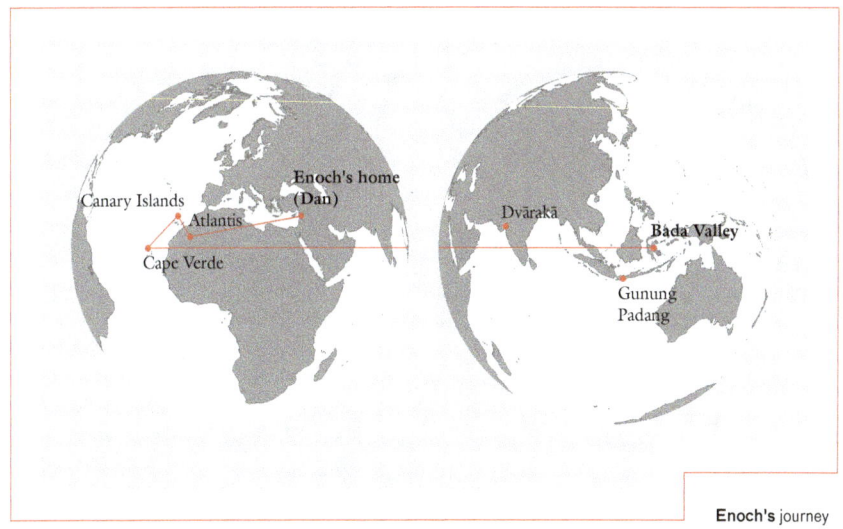

Enoch's journey

Continuing in his straight line, he flew to Sundaland, modern-day Indonesia and remembered in myth as Lemuria, renowned for its biodiversity to this day—cats and birds of all shapes, sizes, and stripes, substantiating the truth of Enoch's observations.

Southern Indonesia is where you will find Gunung Padang, a terraced pyramid your archeologists are just beginning to excavate. Over the millennia, it has become completely overgrown by the jungle. Scientists have drilled cores from the top and recovered items at least 20,000 years old, putting its creation within the time frame of Atlantis and Dvārakā.

Now you know Enoch's journey and the details of what he saw and recorded. The journey was real, not mythological. He describes a real tree from India, not an imagined plant, one of which he could have learned only by seeing it. His journey was 23,000 kilometers long, a voyage he could not have traveled unless he was flying using the incomparable technological abilities the Atlanteans held 14,000 years ago.

THE MAN
"GOD" TOOK

After Gunung Padang, the Atlanteans returned Enoch to his home in the Levant, saying they would leave him there for one year to teach his son, Methuselah, everything they had taught him. Then, they would bring him back to Atlantis to live with them for the rest of his days. [52]

[52] Book of Enoch 81:5-6.

In the Book of Enoch, there is no record of the year he spent teaching his son before returning to Atlantis, but that record does exist in the *Hermetica*, a collection of texts written by Hermes Trismegistus. Of these texts, one of the prime sources is the *Asclepius*, the earliest fragments of which are from the Nag Hammadi Library of Gnostic Christian texts, which contains Christian materials, and Jewish materials, as well as the Hermetic texts. So important were the works of Hermes that, when an agent of Cosimo de' Medici discovered a Greek version of Hermes's other great work, the *Corpus Hermeticum*, in Florence nearly 600 years ago, Medici ordered the agent to cease his translations of Plato to focus entirely on translating the newly recovered, far more significant work.

Here is a truth of which you might not be aware: early Jews and Christians believed Enoch and Hermes were one and the same person—and they were not alone. The early alchemist Zosimos of Panopolis noted their similarities over 1,700 years ago in his writings to a fellow alchemist, Theosebia, in the ninth book of *Imouth*. This work is lost but an excerpt is contained in the *Chronographia* of George Syncellus, a Byzantine chronicler.

Zosimus describes a lost Hermetic work called *Physika*, contrasting it with the works of Enoch:

> The holy scriptures, that is the books, say, my lady, that there is a race of demons who avail themselves of women. Hermes also mentioned this in his Physika, and

nearly every treatise, both public and esoteric, made mention of this. Thus the ancient and divine scriptures said this, that certain angels lusted after women, and having descended taught them all the works of nature. Having stumbled because of these women, he says, they remained outside heaven, because they taught mankind everything wicked and nothing benefiting the soul. The same scriptures say that from them the giants were born. So theirs is the first teaching concerning these arts handed down by Chemeu. He called this the book of Chemeu, whence also the art is called Alchemy, and so forth. [53]

[53] *The Chronography of George Synkellos: A Byzantine Chronicle of Universal History from the Creation*, trans. William Adler and Paul Tuffin (Oxford: Oxford University Press, 2002), 18–19.

Enoch is but one name for this person whose story has been passed down in many cultures. Because this Natufian was picked up by the Atlanteans and flown all over the world, many accounts have come forth, and in different places the storytellers remembered him by different names. In Greece, he was Hermes Trismegistus; in the Levant, Enoch; in Egypt, Thoth; in Arabia, Idris. All of these literary characters describe the same person who learned from the great civilization of Atlantis. Enoch the scribe, Hermes the scribe, Thoth the scribe, and Idris are all teachers of humanity—sources of science, alchemy, and the knowledge and wisdom of the gods, to counterbalance the corrupt teachings of the fallen Watchers. The stories overlap to a remarkable degree because they all describe the same person who, according to the Book of Jubilees, was the first man able to read and write.

The Book of Enoch offers a fragment of the entire picture, but you will find much more of his experience in other books under different names, chiefly the *Asclepius* and *Corpus Hermeticum*. Hermes Trismegistus makes a direct reference to what happened in the Levant and what the Atlanteans did to prepare for the coming cataclysm wrought by the Son of Man, which you now know was the debris from the supernova.

The *Asclepius* explains the most unbelievable things Hermes learned on his trip from end to end of the earth, told in as many ways as he can so his son will understand all the knowledge he has gained. The credits to Hermes are legion—as the inventor of alchemy, philosophy, and mathematics, and as the developer of the knowledge of humanity. Asclepius is a friend of Hermes's son, Tat, and the text appears as a discourse among them. Each chapter illuminates a different subject matter, such as the immortality of the soul, the nature of man and the gods, and the coming destruction of the earth. The *Corpus Hermeticum* similarly elucidates his great accumulated knowledge.

Consider this quote from the *Asclepius*:

> How grievous will be the withdrawal of gods from men! Only the evil angels will remain. Mingling with humanity, they will force these wretches into all the evils of violence: wars, robbery, fraud, and all those things which are contrary to the nature of souls. [54]

[54]**Clement Salaman**, ed. and trans., *Asclepius: The Perfect Discourse of Hermes Trismegistus* (London: Bloomsbury, 2007),80.

Elsewhere in the *Asclepius*, Hermes describes Atlanteans as monks living in a temple, subsisting on offerings and gifts people bring them. He shows how the corrupted Watchers behave quite differently, exploiting the human laborers around them.

Further on, Hermes describes an important discovery of Enoch's journey, something that underscores the Atlanteans' understanding of the heavens and history and the cosmic cataclysm heading toward earth. He explains that the Atlanteans, "those gods who rule the earth ... will be dispersed and then settled in a town at the very extremity of Egypt, which will be founded to-wards the setting sun and to which the whole race of the mortals will hasten both by land and sea." [55]

[55]Hermes Trismegistus, *Asclepius*, 82.

Hermes is referring to the northwest region of Egypt, the Giza Plateau, where today you find the pyramids and the Sphinx. During his journey, Enoch flew over this region and saw the Atlanteans' undertakings in Egypt. They knew a great cataclysm was coming and that the impact would likely cause enormous tidal waves and flooding as far inland as their great capital city near the Atlantic coast. Hermes/Enoch saw their preparations as they readied to transplant the seat of their civilization.

Some of your scientists theorize that the Sphinx is more than 8,000 years old, which is correct—it was, in fact, built by the Atlanteans much earlier than that. The original head of the Sphinx was the head of a lion, but it eroded until it became unrecogniz-able, at which time the Egyptians carved its head into a pharaoh and called it their own. As you shall learn, the supernova debris did in fact make impact at the start of the age of Leo, roughly 12,800 years ago and, in that age, the Atlanteans' original reposing lion faced the sun on the equinox, as the sun rose in the sign of Leo. On earth as it is in heaven: the Sphinx gazed upon its celestial self on the equinoxes.

The Hidden Truth

In addition to the philosophical hermetic texts, the *Asclepius* and *Corpus Hermeticum*, there is another body of hermetic work called the technical hermetic materials, which remain untranslated, meaning the general public does not have access to the vast majority of hermetic material. Much Atlantean knowledge is not accessible because the ruling class has controlled that information.

Why is it not common knowledge that Diodorus talks at length about the Atlanteans? Why are more people not familiar with Hermes Trismegistus and Enoch? Why did the search for Atlantis stop being funded shortly before the Richat Structure was found, and why was its discovery not touted around the world with fanfare exceeding that of Heinrich Schliemann's discovery of Troy? As late as 1915, French researcher Pierre Termier published a paper in the annual report of the board of regents of the Smithsonian Institute about the latest findings in the search for Atlantis.[56] It is not accidental that all of these discoveries were silenced by academia.

[56] **Pierre Termier**, "Atlantis and the Gods of Antiquity," in *Annual Report of the Board of Regents of the Smithsonian Institution* (Washington DC: Government Press Office, 1916), 219.

Enoch/Hermes wanted to preserve the knowledge of the Atlanteans for his descendants and the world, but the ruling class has largely suppressed that information and prevented its translation, preventing Seekers of Truth such as yourself from learning about them and their evil intent towards mankind.

The Rest of His Days

After Enoch spent a year in the Levant teaching Methuselah, the Atlanteans took him to Atlantis, where he spent the rest of his days walking with "God." As it says in Genesis,

> Enoch lived sixty and five years, and begat Methuselah: And Enoch walked with God after he begat Methuselah three hundred years, and begat sons and daughters: And all the days of Enoch were three hundred sixty and five years: And Enoch walked with God: and he was not; for God took him.[57]
>
> [57] Genesis 5:21–24.

Supporting the biblical account, the Book of Enoch says, "And it came to pass after this," meaning the year Enoch taught his son, "that his name during his lifetime was raised aloft to that son of man and to the lord of spirits," meaning he was taken into space to see the comet coming and then to Atlantis. "He was raised aloft on the chariots of the spirits," a vessel built by the Atlanteans, "and his name vanished amongst them."[58] He "was not" in the sense that he was no longer seen in the Levant, for the Atlanteans took him to their kingdom.

[58] Book of Enoch 70.

During the time when Enoch walked with "God" in Atlantis, he took an Atlantean wife and begat sons and daughters with mixed Natufian and Iberomaurusian blood. The scientific record of the Taforalt cave supports this truth, as the DNA found in six male bodies was two-thirds Natufian and one-third Iberomaurusian. All six males were E-M78, the line of Adam. Researchers dated these bodies and found they were 13,900 to 15,000 years old, the descendants of Enoch, buried in the cave because they were people of importance—hard scientific evidence for the biblical story of Enoch and his intermarrying with Atlanteans. [59]

[59] Marieke van de Loosdrecht et al., "Pleistocene North African Genomes Link Near Eastern and Sub-Saharan African Human Populations," *Science* 10.1126 (2018).

Godlike Descendants

Whenever an ancient culture describes what their gods look like, invariably, they give the same description: beings with light skin and blonde or red hair. Likewise, in modern UFO abduction stories, people report being taken by beings who match this fair-skin and fair-hair depiction.

How can this be? The answer is quite plain if you have eyes to see: they are all talking about the same civilization of people who traveled the world, made contact with all the different cultures, and spawned the myriad myths and religions: the Atlanteans.

The Kebarans of the Levant had darker skin and much darker hair than the Atlantean Iberomaurusians. Enoch was from this region, and he shared this darker complexion. Sumerians, one of the first great civilizations of Mesopotamia, are not Israelites, but their name literally means "the black-headed people."

Noah, however, was different. Enoch describes his great-grandson Noah, the builder of the ark, as having skin "whiter than snow"; hair "whiter than wool"; another feature, possibly body hair, "redder than the bloom of a rose"; and eyes "like the rays of the sun." In short, Noah had "the likeness of the angels of heaven." [60]

[60] Book of Enoch 106:2.

Thus, there can be no doubt as to the appearance of the Atlanteans, angels and gods of old.

THE GREAT FLOOD

Let us close with the Book of Jubilees, similar to Genesis but written from the perspective of the angels. Like the Book of Enoch, it is another book of the apocrypha, and it says of Enoch:

> And he was taken from amongst the children of men, and we conducted him into the Garden of Eden, in majesty and honor, and behold there he writes down the condemnation and judgment of the world, and all the wickedness of the children of men. And on account of it God brought the waters of the flood upon all the land of Eden; for there he was set as a sign and that he should testify against all the children of men, that he should recount all the deeds of the generations until the day of condemnation.[61]
>
> [61]Book of Jubilees *4:23–24.*

This flooding of Eden—Atlantis—ushered in the Bronze Age.

CHAPTER 4
THE BRONZE AGE

According to Ovid, the Bronze Age began with the flood of Ogyges, the first Greek flood—earlier referred to as the Great Flood—which resulted from cosmic debris raining down on the earth and oceans 12,800 years ago, causing cataclysmic destruction and terror on a scale that humans had never seen before and have not seen since. The world burned, shook, and flooded, and the terror unleashed an age that lasted 1,200 years, an age known by your scientists as the Younger Dryas. This nuclear winter closed with yet another cosmic disaster that included a second flood, known by the Greeks to have occurred in the time of Deucalion.

Between the two events, it is said, humans simply scrambled to survive. Conditions were extremely difficult, as confirmed by the scientific evidence as well as the cultural myths from around the world.

BY FIRE
AND FLOOD

You will recall that 40,000 years ago, humans witnessed a supernova that caused a "second sun," a burst of deadly gamma radiation, and the modification of the human genome among survivors. The Atlanteans remembered the legends of this event passed down from the humans who were present during the actual explosion all those millennia ago, and as soon as they developed telescopes and ability in astronomy, they began monitoring the debris over generations.

The Atlanteans had known the comet was coming for a very long time, and by the Silver Age, they predicted the impact would destroy their capital city and the west coast of Africa with tidal waves. As a result, they resolved to relocate to Egypt, and in Enoch's time, they still had 1,400 years to prepare. This new settlement would act as a safe haven for humanity; as Hermes writes, "The whole race of men will hasten there by land and by sea." [62]   [62] Hermes Trismegistus, *Asclepius*, 82.

During the Silver Age, the Atlanteans not only tried to secure their own safety but also traveled the world, warning the many cultures of the time that destruction was coming. Some people listened and thus survived—but most did not heed the admonition to head to safety and perished as a result.

From their time as Atlanteans, the fallen Watchers possessed knowledge of the coming destruction, and they passed it down to their children, the Nephilim. The Atlanteans and their descendants had been tracking the cosmic debris since the Golden Age, and Enoch said they had known about it since before the founding of Atlantis. He wrote, "And at that hour, the Son of Man was named in the presence of the Lord of Spirits, and his name before the Head of Days. Yea, before the sun and the signs were created"—the celestial sphere and navigation—"before the stars of heaven were made, His name was named before the Lord of Spirits." [63]   [63] Book of Enoch 48:1–3.

At the transition between the Silver Age and the Bronze Age, the supernova debris finally reached earth, resulting in multiple impacts, not all of which have been discovered by your scientists, but the event itself has been confirmed beyond a doubt. The most recent and spectacular find thus far has been the Hiawatha Crater in Greenland, a thirty-five-kilometer-wide crater under the Greenland ice that dates to the beginning of the Bronze Age. No one was living at the site of the crater, but upon impact, the earth launched debris—known as ejecta—into the air, which rained down on multiple civilizations across North America. [64]

[64] Kurt H. Kjaer et al., "A Large Impact Crater Beneath Hiawatha Glacier in Northwest Greenland," *Science Advances*, November 14, 2018.

Your scientists have identified many other potential impact sites, including several places in the Americas, as far south as Chile and as far north as Hudson Bay, Lake Michigan, and the Carolina Bays. [65] Another study indicates Abu Hureyra itself was hit directly and completely obliterated. The chaos was worldwide, pushing the whole planet into a nuclear winter. [66]

[65] Mario Pino et al., "Sedimentary Record from Patagonia, Southern Chile Supports Cosmic-Impact Triggering of Biomass Burning, Climate Change, and Megafaunal Extinctions at 12.8ka," *Scientific Reports* 9, no. 4413 (2019).

[66] Andrew M. T. Moore et al., "Evidence of Cosmic Impact Abu Hureyra, Syria at the Younger Dryas Onset (~12.8ka): High-Temperature Melting at >2200°C," *Scientific Reports* 10, no. 4185 (2020).

Depending on the location, the impacts led to fires, floods, and even earthquakes. Humans who did not heed the Atlanteans' warnings were killed instantly. The land impacts led to scorched earth that decimated animal life, including the extinction of all the North American megafauna—the giant sloths, the North American lion, the Hagerman zebra, and the mammoths were all wiped out.

You surely know an aircraft creates a shockwave when it flies through the sound barrier and the nose cone becomes heated by the pressure wave. Now, imagine cosmic debris traveling a hundred times faster through the atmosphere. The resulting superheated shockwaves blew down entire forests and caused everything—and everyone—on the surface to spontaneously combust, even in places where the debris only passed over without making contact. In total, about 50 million square kilometers of earth—essentially all of North America and Europe—were completely incinerated.

There were also impacts in the Atlantic, which experienced a series of two dozen underwater slides of thousands of square kilometers of mud and rock, huge amounts of moving earth with underwater speeds of 140 meters per second, which caused massive tidal waves of unprecedented size, the biggest ones reaching up to one kilometer high. [67]

[67] Mark Maslin, Matthew Owen, Simone Day, and David Long, "Linking Continental-Slope Failures and Climate Change: Testing the Clathrate Gun Hypothesis," *Geology* (January 2004).

Studies conducted by your scientists confirm a spike in mudslides took place around 12,800 years ago in three specific areas: three off the coast of Africa, three off the coast of North America, and another three off the coast of South America. The North and South American mudslides sent massive tidal waves to West Africa and to the Canary Islands. [68]

[68] Maslin et al., "Linking Continental-Slope Failures."

The events were so disastrous that the human imagination has difficulty grasping the scale of the destruction. Indeed, some of these tidal waves moved close to the speed of sound. The earthquakes, ejecta, and flooding caused by the Atlantic impacts affected everyone on the planet. People could not get out of the way fast enough and died instantly. Even though the Atlanteans themselves had already moved to Egypt, the force of the tidal waves stripped Atlantis down to the bedrock, as now seen at the Richat Structure—leaving nothing of the many ingenious constructions of that great civilization.

The worst and last tidal wave occurred in South America, "travel[ing] dozens or hundreds of miles inland over very shallow terrain … The worst part was that in nearly all cases, no one would have seen them coming. They just would have risen suddenly from the ocean to smash into shorelines, obliterating everything in their path." [69]

[69] Firestone, West, and Warwick-Smith, Cycle of Cosmic Catastrophes, 333.

The destruction was widespread and brought an end to the world as people knew it.

THE YOUNGER DRYAS

Like tree rings, soil tells history: layers pile upon layers and compress each other, allowing scientists to dig down and see what planetary conditions were like thousands of years ago. The beginning of the Bronze Age 12,800 years ago coincides with the beginning of the Younger Dryas boundary layer, a black mat of ash baked into the strata of the soil because 50 million square kilometers of the earth were incinerated. Some of your scientists have described the extraordinary biomass burning and impact winter triggered by the cosmic impacts,[70] which blew landscapes apart, set them on fire, and launched debris high into the atmosphere, which then rained back down and caused more damage. These impacts even affected the tilt of the earth—accounts from the time describe the orientation of the heavens changing because of the sheer force.[71]

[70]Wendy S. Wolbach et al., "Extraordinary Biomass-Burning Episode and Impact Winter Triggered by the Younger Dryas Cosmic Impact ~12,800 Years Ago," *Journal of Geology* 126 (2018).

[71]Book of Enoch 80:6.

All across the Younger Dryas impact field scientists have found "impact proxies"—soot, nanodiamonds, carbon spherules, high-temperature melt glass, iridium, osmium, platinum, acidoform—all elements found in higher concentrations in meteorites or produced by the extreme energy of the strike.[72] The process is similar to when an atomic bomb is tested in the desert and the surrounding sand fuses into glass, or when a cosmic impact in Germany 14 million years ago created a substance called moldavite.

[72]Charles R. Kinzie et al., "Nanodiamond-Rich Layer across Three Continents Consistent with Major Cosmic Impact at 12,800 Cal BP," *Journal of Geology* 123 (2014).

Estimates of the size of the boundary layer continue to grow. As of today, more than fifty sites across three continents have been found showing the Younger Dryas boundary.

Younger Dryas
boundary field sites

MYTHS
AND LEGENDS

This impact event marks the most important day in history, because all humanity still suffers its effects, most notably, the destruction of much of your cultural memory and the most technologically advanced civilization to date, the great city of Atlantis.

Almost every civilization has a flood myth of some kind, and the stories are remarkably consistent, which should not surprise you, aligning as they do with all the scientific evidence of the real flood. Where there is a warning from a god in these myths and legends, the descriptions of these beings are consistent with those whom you know to be the Atlanteans.

The flood story with which you may be most familiar is the story of Noah found in the Book of Genesis in the Judeo-Christian Bible. What you may not know is that the source of the Noah story is a much older account, which comes from the *Epic of Gilgamesh*:

> At the very first light of dawn there came up from the horizon a black cloud, within it Adad did bellow continually. Šullat and Haniš were going at the fore, "throne-bearers" travelling over mountain and land. Errakal was ripping out the mooring-poles; Ninurta, going (by), made the weirs overflow. The Annunaki bore torches aloft, setting the land aglow with their brilliance. The still calm of the Storm God passed across the sky, all that was bright was turned into gloom. Like an ox [he] trampled the land, he smashed [it like a pot,] for one day the gale [.....] Quickly it blew and the [Deluge...] the east wind, like a battle [the cataclysm] passed over the people. One person could not see another, nor people recognize each other in the destruction.[73]

[73]*The Epic of Gilgamesh*, trans. Andrew George (New York: Penguin Classics, 2003), Tablet XI.

Other legends from around the world give accounts from this horrific time, beyond the flood that covered the earth. From the Caribbean we have a Toba and Pilaga legend describing impacts on the moon just hours prior to impacts on the earth. We also have an infernal account from the Arawak, who describe "scorched earth as far as they could see." The battle between Thunder and Horned Serpent is the account of the Iroquois, who lived close to the Hiawatha Crater. From further south come the accounts of the North American Navajo and Lakota, as well as the Peruvian Inca, the latter of which tells a tale of a city destroyed by fire, floods, and earthquakes.

You can read these stories in full by consulting a text written by lead comet researchers belonging to a global team of scientists studying and publishing on the cataclysm that launched the Bronze Age.[74] In the pages that follow, you shall read segments, specifically, the warning, the event description, and the aftermath described in these ancient legends.

[74] Firestone, West, and Warwick-Smith, *Cycle of Cosmic Catastrophes.*

The Warning

Warnings do not appear in every legend, but when included, they generally contain specific instructions relevant to the local landscape of the tribe, which type of disaster would happen—fire or water—and often where the people could find safety. The Atlanteans not only knew what would happen in each location, but also how to survive the coming disaster.

For instance, the Navajo were visited by a messenger identified as "Begochiddy (son of the Creator), called Golden Child of the Sun, [who] warned the People, 'If you do not stop all this fighting, a great and terrible flood will come upon you that will destroy the world.'" The people did not stop, and the flood came, just as the messenger forewarned:

> One day in the midst of a big battle, the People were startled by a great explosion that came from all directions … Then, without warning, a torrent of water poured out of the Earth and began to rise, swirling all around them higher and higher.[75]
>
> [75] Firestone, West, and Warwick-Smith, *Cycle of Cosmic Catastrophes*, 235.

With the Lakota, the Creator himself warned of a different kind of destruction, including specific instructions on where to flee:

> In the world before this one, the People and the animals turned to evil and forgot their connection to the Creator. Resolving to destroy the world and start over, the Creator warned a few good People to flee to the highest mountaintops.[76]
>
> [76] Firestone, West, and Warwick-Smith, *Cycle of Cosmic Catastrophes*, 152.

Several other groups describe a visitation of the Creator, warning them to take heed and prepare. The Arawak legend says,

> Ages ago, the Creator became impatient with all the evil in the world and decided to destroy it and create a new one. Looking around the Earth, the Creator could find only one righteous family that deserved to live. Appearing to them one day, the Creator told them, "Go dig a large pit, cover it with logs, and pile sand over the top. After it is done, seal yourselves up inside the pit for protection.[77]
>
> [77]Firestone, West, and Warwick-Smith, *Cycle of Cosmic Catastrophes*, 169.

Similarly, "Chimantou, the Great Spirit, visited the Ojibwe tribe, who lived near the edge of the Frozen Lands," the Laurentide ice sheet in North America:

> Chimantou warned them that a dangerous star was about to fall and urged them to hurry to the bog to cover their bodies with mud. Most People did not recognize the Great Spirit, however, and made fun of Chimantou. "Do not listen. That man is just a crazy person," they said, laughing. "Cover ourselves with mud! Ha!" they said as they went on their way and paid no more attention to the Great Spirit. Only a few hurried to the bog as Chimantou suggested.[78]
>
> [78]Firestone, West, and Warwick-Smith, *Cycle of Cosmic Catastrophes*, 155.

The Creator also visited the Aztec, but according to the legend, many people "no longer paid any attention to the gods. Others said, 'We have plenty of time. Anyway, maybe it will not happen.'" Alas, it did happen, as "before long, a heavy rain of flaming firestones and blood began to fall from the sky."[79]

[79]Firestone, West, and Warwick-Smith, *Cycle of Cosmic Catastrophes*, 224.

Other warnings are found in Zoroastrian myth, where Ahura Mazda warns Yima to build the Vara to escape a devastating winter, and in the Hindu flood myth, where Vishnu, in the form of a fish, comes to warn hero Manu that a flood is coming and to make preparations. The fish returns later with a boat, and after Manu fastens a rope over the fish, it tows the boat to safety.

Clearly, with their advanced technology and ability to read the heavens, the Atlanteans were able to foresee which cosmic pieces would hit where, and what kind of damage they would cause. They delivered precise warnings to each civilization, with pinpointed guidance on how to escape.

Note how the Inca legend describes the arrival of these messengers, along with the warning they provide:

One day, several shabby-looking men came to the great city of the Inca on Lake Titicaca. Some people thought they were beggars, but later, some thought they were gods in disguise. They told everyone who would listen, "Get ready. Leave the city. Death and trouble is coming, because the Earth is angry with you. The ground will shake and the sky will burn and the waters will rise up to strike you." [80]

[80] Firestone, West, and Warwick-Smith, *Cycle of Cosmic Catastrophes*, 308.

In many cases, gods such as Zeus and Viracocha presented themselves as vagabonds and beggars so as to better observe human morality unrecognized, which is how Atlantean Watchers appeared to people when inserting themselves into regular human society. They were not ones to arrive in ships and large crews to conquer, as the fallen Watchers did, but as a consequence of their humble appearance, the Atlanteans' warnings were largely ignored.

The Event

The second element of these legends is the event itself and the sheer destructive force that the inhabitants of earth witnessed—fires, floods, earthquakes, or all three. The Toba and Pilaga myth mentioned earlier confirms that your planet was not the only body in the solar system to be struck. This ancient Central American legend describes a collision in the sky when the supernova debris hit the moon hours before it reached earth.

All of the other legends are terrestrial stories recounting events impacting the geographical area around them: stars falling and hitting the ground, forests knocked down or burned, whole mountains exploding, flood waters covering dry land until it disappeared.

Some stories tell of impacts on earth—of rocks melting or glowing from the extreme heat and of people bursting into flames because they did not hide. Others describe the impact of debris hitting the oceans, triggering massive tidal waves that caused widespread flooding. A Yurok tribal legend, for instance, says, "One day the sky fell. It crashed into the oceans, causing huge breakers that flooded inland far across the land, and it happened so suddenly that it caught the People by surprise." [81] The Yurok were on the coast of what is now California, so their legend confirms impacts struck the Pacific Ocean.

[81] Firestone, West, and Warwick-Smith, *Cycle of Cosmic Catastrophes*, 337.

The Aztec legend describes the chaos and death in this way:

A heavy rain of flaming firestones and blood began to fall from the sky. It fell on houses and they burst into flames. It fell on fields from the sky. It fell on the forests and they were consumed. The People sought shelter, but their clothes burst into flames and they perished. Shaking caused by the falling firestones made some of the mountains explode, so that even more fire and rocks fell on the People. There was fire from above and fire from below; it came at them from all directions. [82]

[82]Firestone, West, and Warwick-Smith, *Cycle of Cosmic Catastrophes*, 224.

The Ojibwe describe the damage caused by a near miss rather than a direct impact:

Before long, when the sun was high, the day suddenly grew brighter. The People all looked up in panic and someone shouted, "Look! A second sun is in the sky!" The new star was growing larger, brighter, and hotter as it hurtled toward them. It became so bright that they had to shield their eyes.

The People who had not covered themselves with mud ran for shelter in terror, but it was too late. The star flew down to Earth and blanketed the world with its long, flowing, glowing tail. Tall trees burst into flame like giant torches, lake and rivers began to boil, and even the rocks glowed and shattered from the heat, as terrible fire swallowed up the entire world.

Then suddenly, when the heat was the greatest and the People in the bog thought even they would surely die, the star climbed back up and moved away from Earth. [83]

[83]Firestone, West, and Warwick-Smith, *Cycle of Cosmic Catastrophes*, 155.

From the Chinese we have the tale of their legendary Emperor Yao, who was sixth after Fuxi, the Asian analogue for the biblical Adam:

Like endless boiling water, the flood is pouring forth destruction. Boundless and overwhelming, it overtops hills and mountains. Rising and ever rising, it threatens the very heavens. How the people must be groaning and suffering! [84]

[84]Kuo-Cheng Wu, *The Chinese Heritage* (New York: Crown Publishers, 1982), 69.

Together, these stories tell us that no part of the earth escaped destruction. Except for a near miss, the impacts brought about a near total annihilation of the world's primitive societies. Had the Atlanteans not taken flight, as you shall see, they too would have been destroyed along with their city.

The Aftermath

The third common element of the legends is the aftermath, which is described in terms of the death toll on humans and animals alike. In nearly every legend, mention is made of the widespread decimation of life and of the handful of survivors who emerged from their holes or came down from their high places, found the world destroyed, and became the founders of the tribes existing today.

The North American myths clearly state that this event caused the extinction of the North American megafauna, such as the mammoth, contrary to faulty scientific assertions that people hunted them to extinction. For instance, consider the Ojibwe telling:

> After the world cooled down, the mud-covered People cautiously came out of the bog to look around. Stunned, they saw that the world had changed completely. In all directions, all that remained were smoldering, blackened trees and scorched grasslands. The People who had not listened to Chimantou had perished, along with all the giant animals. Only their skeletons remained. [85]
>
> [85] **Firestone, West,** and **Warwick-Smith,** *Cycle of Cosmic Catastrophes,* 155.

The Lakota legend also mentions the remains of giant animals and humans' task of repopulating the planet:

> After the waters cleansed the Earth and subsided, the Creator sent the surviving People out to populate the new world, our world today, warning them not to fall into evil, or the Creator would destroy the world again.
>
> As the People went out over the land, they found the bleached bones of the giant animals buried in rock and mud all over the world. [86]
>
> [86] **Firestone, West,** and **Warwick-Smith,** *Cycle of Cosmic Catastrophes,* 153.

In the Aztec aftermath, "thick, dark clouds covered the land for twenty-five years. The few survivors then began to create a new world, the one in which we now live." [87]

[87] **Firestone, West,** and **Warwick-Smith,** *Cycle of Cosmic Catastrophes,* 224.

With their world in ruins, these humans had to essentially begin again as children, fighting for survival in a harsh and inhospitable landscape.

BEGINNING
AGAIN
AS CHILDREN

Prior to the cataclysm that occurred 12,800 years ago, the climate was warming as the earth began emerging from the last ice age, but the soot and debris released into the atmosphere caused a return to cooler climes during the Younger Dryas. Your scientists note, "Despite the persistence of short warm summers, the [Younger Dryas] is dominated by a shift to a continental climate with extreme winter to spring cooling and short growing seasons."[88] That short season raised the specter of hunger, and the cultural myths corroborate the scientific assessment.

[88]F. Schenk et al., "Warm Summers during the Younger Dryas Cold Reversal," *Nature Communications* 9 (April 24, 2018).

Because of the massive death toll and subsequent struggle among the survivors in the Bronze Age, scientists have found this 1,200-year period is associated with a massive bottleneck in human genetic diversity, which collapsed to 5 or 10 percent of what it had been previously, as there were so few people to repopulate.[89] This lessening of genetic variety is revealed by the sudden end of many Y haplogroups. In the scientific studies, all of the dates are expressed in confidence intervals, with 95 percent certainty. Starting 10,000 years ago, the diversity collapses. While that timing is later than the Great Flood, there is only one event in human history that could have caused this collapse. Human methodology has not become refined enough to correctly place the bottleneck in time, but we know the real cause of the genetic event scientists have identified.[90]

[89]Monika Karmin et al., "A Recent Bottleneck of Y Chromosome Diversity Coincides with a Global Change in Culture," *Genome Research* 25 (2015), 459–466.

[90]Karmin et al., "A Recent Bottleneck."

Among the survivors, the line of Adam (E-M78) persisted, because his descendants received a warning to build an ark. The Atlantean E-Z827 and Nephilim E-M81 have also survived to this day, as you shall learn in much greater detail.

PROPHECIES OF THE CREATOR

Before the cataclysm that led to the Younger Dryas, the Atlanteans relocated to Egypt. Once the acute crisis passed, they again traveled around the world to warn of the next cataclysm, destined to occur 1,200 years later, marking the end of the Younger Dryas. These prophecies are immortalized in the legends of the Aztecs and Ojibwe. According to the Aztecs,

> After the trouble was over, the Creator came back to tell the survivors that this current world will be destroyed by earthquakes one day. The People agreed among themselves never again to forget the Creator.
>
> Even today, to remind us of those terrible days, People still find among the river rocks and gravel the fire-starting stones that fell from the skies back then.[91]

[91]**Firestone, West,** and **Warwick-Smith,** *Cycle of Cosmic Catastrophes,* 224.

As previously mentioned, the Ojibwe legend described not a direct impact but a near miss, and the people received a prophecy that this fragment that passed them by would come back and cause the second flood:

> The People were afraid and did not know what to do, until Chimantou came to them and said, "Put aside your fear. The star is gone for now. Go out and multiply, for this new world is yours. But if I come to warn you another time, do not forget to listen, because Long-Tailed-Heavenly-Climbing-Star will surely come back again to destroy the world.[92]

[92]**Firestone, West,** and **Warwick-Smith,** *Cycle of Cosmic Catastrophes,* 156.

The Bronze Age began with a global cataclysm that obliterated most human and animal life and led to a period of unprecedented suffering. The Atlanteans did their best to help the peoples of the earth, as evidenced by the warnings and prophecies in the legends, and moved their own civilization to Egypt. Having begun with cosmic destruction, the age was poised to end in a similar way.

CHAPTER 5
THE IRON AGE

For 1,200 years, humans struggled in the harsh Younger Dryas conditions brought about by supernova debris hitting earth, which caused all manner of fire and flood around the globe, as the Atlanteans had warned it would. Then, as prophesied, the long-tailed heavenly climbing star returned, streaking across the earth's atmosphere before exploding in a fiery airburst. Although the meteor brought about more devastation in its path, it also reversed the inhospitable ice age conditions and pushed the world into the warming trend that marked the early Iron Age.

But unlike the last warming trend, this one did not bring about an easy or joyful life. According to Ovid, this age is marked by an existence of toil and misery in which the powerful ruled and the ancient custom of *xenia*, of offering protection and hospitality to strangers, was abandoned. The gods forsook humanity during this age as humans no longer felt shame or indignation at wrongdoing. Truth, modesty, and loyalty were nowhere to be found, for greed, war, and impiousness ruled the minds of men.

SECOND COSMIC CATACLYSM

Humans had begun again as children after the first cataclysm, and those in the path of this second event had to start over once more. As with the upheaval that opened the Bronze Age, humans across the globe who survived retold their experience in legends that have been passed down for millennia.

Corroborating Myths

Most of the extant flood myths refer to the beginning of the Bronze Age, but the Iron Age began with a cosmic event and flood of its own. The meteor entered the atmosphere over present-day Mongolia and then streaked westward over Mesopotamia, Egypt, and the rest of North Africa, burning everything in its path. Then it exploded over the Atlantic, sending shockwaves and debris crashing into the ocean, which triggered more underwater mudslides, more tidal waves, and thus, the stories of a second flood. The cascading impacts reached as far as Dvārakā, India, the city described by Enoch, which was destroyed by a tidal wave and now rests thirty feet under water. [93]

[93] Marc André Gutscher, "Destruction of Atlantis by a Great Earthquake and Tsunami? A Geological Analysis of the Spartel Bank Hypothesis," *Geology* 33, no. 8 (August 2005): 685–688; Matthew Owen, Simon Day, and Mark Maslin, "Late Pleistocene Submarine Mass Movements: Occurrence and Causes," *Quaternary Science Reviews* 26 (2007): 958–978; Timothy J. Pearce and Ian Jarvis, "Applications of Geochemical Data to Modelling Sediment Dispersal Patterns in Distal Turbidites: Late Quaternity of the Madeira Abyssal Plain," *Journal of Sedimentary Petrology* 62, no. 6 (August 1991): 1112–1129.

Various cultures have preserved the events of that time in their stories. Following the path of the comet, the story of Erra and Ishum records the experience farthest east, in Mesopotamia, while Ovid's *Metamorphoses* records the events in Greece, a Mattamuskeet legend recounts the destruction on the eastern seaboard of what is now the United States, and the *Mahabharata* describes the sinking of Dvārakā. Unlike the global catastrophe that initiated the Bronze Age, the destruction of this event was more localized to the path traveled by the debris.

Mesopotamia

As described earlier, prior to the onset of the first cataclysm 12,800 years ago, the Atlanteans had made every effort to warn people of the coming destruction, even going so far as to tell them exactly where to hide in order to save themselves. However, many of the primitive peoples assumed that because the Atlanteans were "gods," they were in control and were actually sending punishment upon sinful human beings.

You will recall that the Atrahasis, one of the Mesopotamian creation myths, relates that after humanity was created to be laborers for the gods, Enlil, the fallen Watcher chief, visited plagues and other disasters upon humanity every 1,200 years to reduce their number—a concern with population control shared by the descendants of Nephilim to this day. It is no coincidence that 1,200 years is the precise interval of time between the opening and closing of the Younger Dryas, a period that saw extensive destruction of human life. Primitive societies noted this timing and assumed they were being punished, in alignment with their cultural mythos and the natural events occurring around them.

The legend about Erra and Ishum discusses a completely different disaster from the Atrahasis, not at all associated with the creation of humanity, but rather an allegorical depiction of the airburst that ended the Younger Dryas period. In this account, Erra—a militaristic warrior god of potent, destructive power—feels restless and wants to unleash his power on humanity. He approaches the supreme god Marduk, a representation of the sun, and remarks on how his appearance no longer radiates as it used to, saying his raiment and garments are dirty. This dimming refers to the sky at the time, which was filled with debris from the nuclear winter, blotting out the sun.

Erra tells Marduk that humans no longer give the gods the proper reverence and that Marduk should unleash him to remind humanity of their power. Marduk eventually gives him leave to gather his seven unrivaled warriors, called the Sebitti, and they march off to annihilate an entire countryside. Even the gods are astounded by the destruction wrought by Erra. [94]

[94] Andrew R. George, "The Poem of Erra and Ishum: A Babylonian Poet's View of War," in *Warfare and Poetry in the Middle East*, ed. Hugh Kennedy (New York: I.B. Tauris & Co., 2013), 39–72; quote is from Tablet V.

As the legend goes,

> Ishum set out for the mountain Sharshar, the Seven, peerless warriors, following behind him. At the mountain Sharshar the warrior arrived, he raised his hand

and destroyed the mountain. The mountain Sharshar he turned into a void, he felled the trees of the forest of cedar. The woodland looked as if traversed by the Deluge, he took control of the towns and made them desert. He destroyed the uplands and slew their flocks, he roiled the oceans and wiped out their produce. He laid waste reedbeds and woodlands, and burned them like Fire, he cursed the livestock and turned them to dust.

The power of Erra manifests as an indiscriminate blast wave that levels forests, which was exactly the effect of the airburst. The translation, however, conceals a secret meaning, only understood if read in the original cuneiform script. You will recall the twin gods of destruction, Šullat and Haniš, who were used to describe the destruction wrought at the beginning of the Bronze Age. Haniš's destructive force is once again invoked in this passage to describe the devastated landscape. One noted scholar and translator of many ancient works from Mesopotamia likened the image of Haniš's power to "probably one of trees flattened by a gale." [95] There can be no doubt that this is a description of the shockwave created by the meteor as it traveled through the atmosphere.

[95] Andrew R. George, *The Babylonian Gilgamesh Epic: Introduction, Critical Edition, and Cuneiform Texts*, vol. II (Oxford: Oxford University Press, 2003), Tablet XI, note 110.

Greece

The Greek accounts of the destruction come from Ovid's long history, the *Metamorphoses*. Rivers boiled from the Ganges all the way to the Atlantic, showing the meteor entered the atmosphere over India, swept across Africa, exploded, and caused more undersea mudslides and tidal waves. Everything in the meteor's path—cities, forests, and even frozen lands—burned, leaving nothing behind:

> The highest altitudes are caught in flames, and as their moistures dry they crack in chasms. The grass is blighted; trees are burnt up with their leaves; the ripe brown crops give fuel for self destruction—Oh what small complaints! Great cities perish with their walls, and peopled nations are consumed to dust—the forests and the mountains are destroyed. [96]

[96] Publius Ovidius Naso, *Metamorphoses*, Book 2.

Ovid identifies the source of these all-consuming flames: Phaethon, a child of the sun god, Helios. He flew over North Africa, set it all ablaze, and caused such a conflagration on earth that Zeus intervened and killed him with one of his thunderbolts—Ovid's depiction of the airburst that then caused Neptune's flood:

Jove [Zeus], having reached that summit, stood and poised in his almighty hand a flashing dart, and, hurling it, deprived of life and seat the youthful charioteer, and struck with fire the raging flames—and by the same great force those flames enveloping the earth were quenched, and he who caused their fury lost his life. [97]

[97] Publius Ovidius Naso, *Metamorphoses*, Book 2.

The wrath of Jove was not content with powers that emanate from Heaven; he brought to aid his azure brother, lord of flowing waves, who called upon the Rivers and the Streams ... And Neptune with his trident smote the Earth which, trembling with unwonted throes, heaved up the sources of her waters bare; and through her open plains the rapid rivers rushed resistless, onward bearing the waving grain, the budding groves, the houses, sheep and men—and holy temples, and their sacred urns. The mansions that remained, resisting vast and total ruin, deepening waves concealed and whelmed their tottering turrets in the flood and whirling gulf. And now one vast expanse, the land and sea were mingled in the waste of endless waves—a sea without a shore. [98]

[98] Publius Ovidius Naso, *Metamorphoses*, Book 1.

[99] Clement of Alexandria, "The Stromata," trans. William Wilson, in *Ante-Nicene Fathers*, vol. 2, ed. Alexander Roberts, James Donaldson, and A. Cleveland Coxe (Buffalo, NY: Christian Literature, 1885), Book I, https://www.newadvent.org/fathers/02101.htm

Clement of Alexandria says the burning of Phaethon and the flood of Deucalion occurred at the same time, under the rule of Crotopus, the eighth king of Argos. [99] Societies kept time by their rulers, noting in which year of the reign of which king a historical event occurred.

Whereas the flood of Ogyges happened in the time of Phoroneus, the mythical first king of Argos and contemporary of Erechtheus, the Phaethon and Deucalion accounts make clear that time passed between the two cosmic events and there were two separate floods. Thus, Clement of Alexandria confirms the dating of these myths from Ovid. The second flood and second cosmic disaster are related to each other, but separate from the first catastrophe that occurred 1,200 years earlier. [100]

[100] Robert W. Embly, "Anatomy of Some Atlantic Margin Sediment Slides and Some Comments on Ages and Mechanisms," in *Marine Slides and Other Mass movements*, ed. S. Saxov et al. (New York: Plenum Press, 1982), 189–190; Pearce and Jarvis, "Applications of Geochemical Data."

North America

After the giant meteor broke into thousands of pieces in the airburst, those still sizable fragments continued their momentum across the Atlantic—as told in a Mattamuskeet Native American legend about the formation of Mattamuskeet Lake as a result of smaller impacts from such debris. The legend describes the horrific conditions they experienced during the Younger Dryas, followed by the sudden airburst:

> As the princess knelt before the altar, her mind turned to the plight of her dying People. It had been brutally cold for as long as anyone could remember, and there had been no summer that year and not much harvest. She chanted and prayed to the Great Spirit to help them through the winter season that had come very early again. Every day seemed colder than the last, and every week, a few more of her People weakened and fell ill.
>
> After her chanting, she wondered if the Great Spirit was listening anymore. Then she heard a loud, high screaming noise and an enormous explosion, and then more blasts, one after another.

To the east, "an immense bluish white steam cloud billowed high up into the noon sky above the crest of a nearby hill"—steam pouring out of the ocean:

> That afternoon, the princess and other tribe members left the camp to see what had happened. They found that the explosions had burned giant holes into the ground and that rain-swollen streams cascaded into them. The rains continued every day for thirteen moons, so that soon the craters were full.

Thus, the rain continued for thirteen days, as the atmosphere purged all the steam created by the airburst.

> The giant hole closest to their camp became a huge fifteen-mile-long inland lake. They called it Mattamuskeet, the Lake on the Hill, and named their tribe after it. Thanks to the falling stars, which brought much-needed water, they had survived. Out of seeming catastrophe came a new life. [101]
>
> [101]Firestone, West, and Warwick-Smith, *Cycle of Cosmic Catastrophes*, 193.

This story from a tribe on the eastern seaboard is the only one to survive, suggesting the second cataclysm did not affect North America on the same widespread scale as the first disaster.

India

As you have learned, Vishnu came in the form of a fish to warn the Indian hero Manu that a flood was coming. Matsya the fish was Vishnu's first avatar. In the legend about the sinking of Dvārakā, Vishnu appeared as Krishna, his eighth avatar, meaning he had reincarnated then died seven times since appearing as a fish, showing that Dvārakā sank in the second flood. This span of time denoting two floods associated with two different avatars of Vishnu aligns with the Greek account of two floods associated with two different kings of Argos. Being located at the southernmost tip of Asia, India and Sri Lanka were spared the devastating firestorm of the passing meteor.

China

From China comes the myth of Kuafu, which explains that, one day, Kuafu decided to chase and catch the sun. He followed the sun from the east to the west, draining the Yellow River and the Wei River to quench his burning thirst. However, the big rivers were unable to satisfy him, and as he searched for more water, he eventually died of dehydration.

This tale is plainly an allegory for a celestial body traveling westwards through the sky and boiling away the water from all of the rivers in its path. The Chinese experienced this in the afternoon, as the sun was in the west, while the Greeks witnessed the ball of fire emerge from the sun in the east, being that their day was just beginning. These differences in eyewitness accounts perfectly align with their positions on earth as the event unfolded.

But there is more, dear Seeker, for if you consider all of these accounts closely along with a modern map of the earth's surface, you will make an astounding discovery: the path from the Gobi Desert in China, across the Arabian Peninsula, to the Sahara in North Africa, is one uninterrupted, continent-spanning wasteland—a vast desert left in the wake of a passing meteor. The Greeks believed the burning of Phaethon created the Sahara, and this event seems to have spawned deserts on the Asian continent as well. [102]

[102] Plato, *Timaeus* 22d.

A Modern Parallel

To understand the effect and character of the airburst, consider two events in modern Russia: Tunguska and Chelyabinsk.

The Tunguska event happened in 1908 in the far reaches of Russia near the Podkamennaya Tunguska River, and at that time, no one knew what had happened. Your scientists today believe that when earth passed through the Taurid meteor stream, a meteor measuring fifty to sixty meters entered the atmosphere at a speed of twenty-seven kilometers per second, exploded, and leveled thousands of square kilometers of trees—to this day, none grow in that torched space, leaving a large bare circle. Tunguska represents the worst cosmic disaster humans have experienced in the modern industrial era. One study estimated its blast at ten to twenty megatons, enough force to obliterate an area the size of Manhattan or London.[103] Despite its large effect on the forest, this event is dwarfed in size by the impacts at the beginning of the Bronze Age, which collectively released hundreds of megatons of energy all over the world, akin to a global nuclear war.

[103] Peter Jenniskens et al., "Tunguska Eyewitness Accounts, Injuries, and Casualties," *Icarus* 327, July 15, 2019, 4–18.

Trees near the
Tunguska event

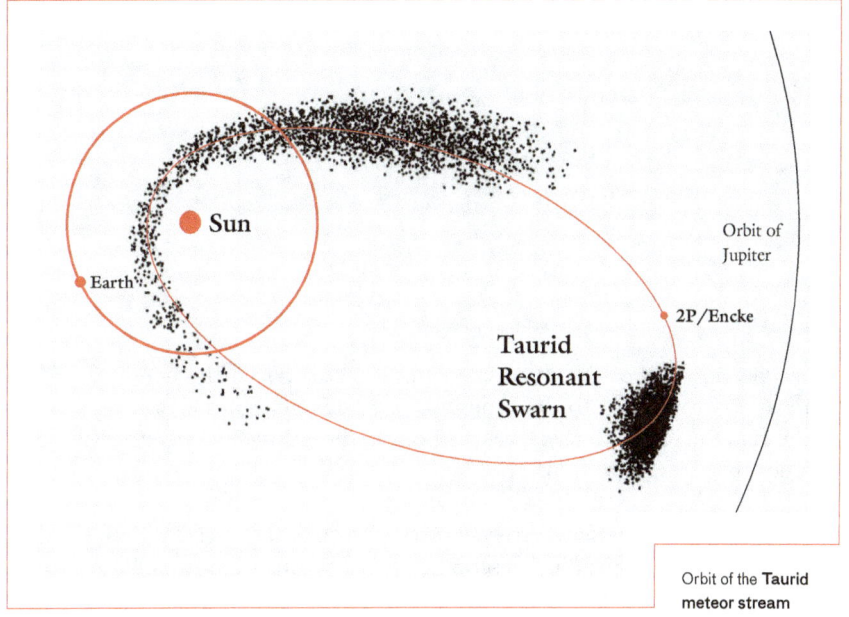

Orbit of
Jupiter

Sun

Earth

2P/Encke

**Taurid
Resonant
Swarm**

Orbit of the **Taurid
meteor stream**

Scientists have tried to discern when and under what circumstances the Taurid meteor stream came to be, estimating a comet reached the vicinity of earth 20,000 years ago, broke into pieces, and formed the debris stream, some of which has hit earth and some of which still circulates in the solar system. The debris that did not impact any planets settled into a highly eccentric orbit crossing that of the earth and reaching almost all the way to Jupiter. [104]

[104] Pulat B. Babadzhano, Iwan P. Williams, and Gulchehra I. Kokhirova, "Near-Earth Objects in the Taurid Complex," *Monthly Notices of the Royal Astronomical Society* 386, no. 3 (May 21, 2008), 1436–1442.

Another likely Taurid meteor entered earth's atmosphere in the year 2013, again exploding over Russia, this time over the southern Ural region, near Chelyabinsk. People described something flying overhead, blowing the windows out of their houses, and spontaneously incinerating trees and other objects. These accounts of the smaller-scale event corroborate the stories of the cataclysm ending the Younger Dryas period and beginning the Iron Age.

The Atlanteans made their prophecies about the second cataclysm because they had been tracking the Taurid meteor stream with their sophisticated astronomy. They knew earth was no longer in a safe cosmic space, as evidenced by events to this day like Chelyabinsk and Tunguska.

WE ARE THE GODS NOW

Whatever portions of the Atlantean empire that survived the flooding 12,800 years ago were burned to the ground at the beginning of the Iron Age. Egypt was also in the path of infernal destruction, so the Atlanteans' second civilization was destroyed along with the first.

The Atlanteans' response was to become a fully space-faring civilization, building on the technology Enoch had described. When the Atlanteans took Enoch to the ends of the earth, their craft could orbit the planet but not fully leave, which is why they escaped Atlantis by setting up a second civilization in Egypt rather than on another planet. By the end of the Younger Dryas, however, they had fine-tuned their technology, enabling them to depart earth completely.

It would be hard to relay to you the sadness the Atlanteans felt as their entire homeland was incinerated by the passing comet. For millennia, they had been custodians of the earth and caretakers of humanity. That time had now come to an end and, to focus their remaining resources on off-planet colonies not plagued by the debris field present in the solar system, the Atlanteans took their leave of earth to join their brethren in the cosmos—the colonies in the Pleiades star cluster they had begun after achieving interstellar travel.

Perhaps you are wondering, Seeker of Truth, why the Atlanteans chose the Pleiades? Unlike many constellations, the Pleiades truly are a close grouping of stars, consisting of not only the seven visible to the naked eye, but hundreds more. The Atlanteans, with their advanced astronomy, were certainly aware of this fact and would also have calculated their relative proximity—450 light years from earth. The cluster is dominated by young, blue stars, providing ample opportunity for them to find planets devoid of other intelligent life, suitable for colonization. From the Atlanteans' journey to the Pleiades leapt folklore spanning all ages and cultures across the world, with cultures such as the Hopi even crediting the constellation as the home of their gods.

The Atlanteans still had a concern for what happened on earth, as we shall discuss at some time in the future, and what they witnessed likely saddened them even further. For not long after the Atlanteans departed, their evil Nephilim relatives sensed a power vacuum and a momentous opportunity. Over the ensuing millennia, they spread from Mesopotamia back to North Africa and then to all corners of the planet, seeking to usurp the Atlanteans' holy centers and the goodwill they had sown amongst the still-primitive human tribes. In their relatives' place, the Nephilim set themselves up as the "gods," bringing with them evil practices such as ritual human sacrifice and cannibalism, as well as their traditions in megalithic architecture and mummification. As you shall learn, evidence of the Nephilim's infiltration is found on virtually every continent—and continues to be to this day.

The Neolithic Age

According to historians, the Neolithic Age is when modern civilization began. The airburst over the Atlantic Ocean at the end of the Younger Dryas created a great deal of steam, which caused the earth to begin warming rapidly. Areas across the globe that were not incinerated by the meteor actually benefited from the new environment. The planet entered the Holocene period and became much more hospitable for more people, animals, and plant life in more places. Rising sea levels brought about by the warming changed the coastlines and allowed ships to access areas further inland. The Nephilim took full advantage of these new waterways and sailed their ships to previously unexplored locations across the planet.

Agriculture supposedly started in the Levant during this time, though you know it originated much earlier with the Atlanteans, who taught it to Adam, who then shared it with his Natufian brethren. By the Holocene, however, the Natufians had disappeared from the Levant, according to your anthropologists, who call the survivors by the unimaginative name Pre-Pottery Neolithic A, followed by B. Settlements like Abu Hureyra had been completely destroyed in the first flood, but the Nephilim still inhabited the area that became the city of Jericho.

During this time period, the Nephilim embarked upon a major construction venture, building temples all around northern Mesopotamia, which is now south-eastern Turkey. Your scientists have recently made discoveries in this area, the most famous having been found in 1995—Göbekli Tepe, a structure twenty times larger and 6,000 years older than Stonehenge that likewise surpasses Stonehenge in the quality of its stonework. Göbekli Tepe is one complex among a dozen found in the area surrounding the Plain of Harran, which includes an old, dried-up river bed that once joined the Euphrates.

Today this region is fertile farmland, but in the days of the Nephilim, around 11,600 years ago, the Plain of Harran was a lake and the surrounding land served as their base of operations for training the rulers who would usurp the Atlanteans as teachers of humanity and then go on to dominate societies around the world. Training sites such as Göbekli Tepe mark the beginning of the elite, ruling class academies still in use today. A record of this site is preserved in the oldest extant literary work, the *Epic of Gilgamesh*.

Epic of Gilgamesh

At the beginning of the epic, Gilgamesh was a raucous, lascivious king who slept with brides on the day of their marriage, the origin of *primae noctis*. Consistent with other descriptions of Nephilim, he was a raging bull who fought indiscriminately and exploited those around him.

To counterbalance Gilgamesh, the gods created his opposite, Enkidu, a primitive man akin to Tarzan. Quite the opposite of a king, Enkidu wore a loincloth and lived in the forest. Someone saw him there one day and ran back into town, saying he had seen a giant even stronger than Gilgamesh. Gilgamesh charged one of the priestesses of Ishtar to find Enkidu and bring him back. She tamed him by having sexual relations with him for a week, at which point he agreed to join civilization.

Upon meeting, Enkidu and Gilgamesh brawled in the streets, knocking down buildings, throwing each other through huts, and destroying carts. The oxen and horses were terrified and ran away. Finally, the fight ended in a stalemate, and the two shook hands, becoming the best of friends.

However, Enkidu subsequently fell ill and died. So despondent was Gilgamesh over the loss of his friend that he embarked on a quest to find Utnapishtim, the Mesopotamian version of Noah and legendary survivor of the Great Flood, who had been granted immortality by the gods. Having faced the death of his friend, Gilgamesh wanted immortality for himself.

Gilgamesh found Utnapishtim, but he did not find the way to become immortal. The flood hero told Gilgamesh that his own immortality came as a gift from the gods and that he could not help Gilgamesh gain such a gift for himself. However, Utnapishtim showed him a plant that, when consumed, lifted the fear of death. This exchange gave rise to the sacraments, of which you shall learn much more in Book IV. Gilgamesh also learned about the great cataclysm and what the world looked like before, as well as construction techniques for temples and other buildings, rites, and sacraments—in short, from Utnapishtim he gained all of the societal wisdom the Mesopotamians ascribed to him.

Utnapishtim told Gilgamesh about his own journey to the Persian Gulf, carried downstream by the rushing floodwaters. The gods rescued him and took him to the source of the rivers, to a site on what was then the Lake of Harran and not a plain, which is a long but passable journey by boat from the Persian Gulf.

Gilgamesh's quest began at Uruk, on the shores of the Euphrates, and he journeyed up the great river until he came to a large body of water—the Lake of Harran—and met Urshanabi the boat man, who told Gilgamesh he needed 200 long poles to help him paddle swiftly, because they would sail through a noxious spot in the lake and if they lingered too long, they would die. An underwater fissure existed at that spot, with volcanic gasses rising up—sulfuric acid strong enough to dissolve the boat and kill the person who breathed the fumes.

According to the Bible, by the time of Abraham, this lake had already dried up and Abraham lived in its former location. Because of the legend of this evil, noxious spot, the people built holy structures, towers, and temples, to consecrate it.

Lest you miss the point, here is the true meaning of the *Epic of Gilgamesh*: Gilgamesh was a Nephilim king from Uruk, near the Euphrates, and was two-thirds "god." This epic memorializes his journey to Göbekli Tepe to learn from the academic Nephilim how to be a ruler.

The Dispersal

When the Lake of Harran dried up around 8,000 years ago, the structures were no longer accessible by ship, so the Nephilim abandoned the region. Their dispersal coincides with the genetic record, which shows arrivals of the E-M81 haplogroup among populations all through the Mediterranean and into South America over the next thousand or so years.

As the Nephilim dispersed, they recaptured North Africa and parts of Greece, leaving their genetic, cultural, and architectural fingerprints everywhere they went. There are many ancient megalithic structures in Greece predating any known habitation by the Greeks, such as the Pyramid of Hellenikon, which is over 5,000 years old and located near the site of Argos, and the Hypogeum of Hal Saflieni, a huge underground temple on Malta. In point of fact, some of the oldest structures in all of the Mediterranean are on Malta, and to this day your scholars ponder over who built them.

Genetic Markers

When the Watchers left the Maghreb and moved to the Levant during the Silver Age, they brought with them many cultural practices, including cattle farming. In their genetic makeup, they also brought lactase persistence—the production of the lactase enzyme into adulthood. Around age eight, many human beings stop producing lactase and become lactose intolerant, but those with lactase persistence like the Watchers and their Nephilim offspring can drink milk their entire lives without ill effects.

Before the Nephilim dispersal at the beginning of the Neolithic Age, the majority of human beings suffered from lactose intolerance as adults. Afterwards, however, the genetic mutation that allows for lactase persistence spread back to North Africa and then beyond, following the Nephilim's movement to new regions and interbreeding with the local populations. [105]

[105] Sarah A. Tishkoff et al., "Convergent Adaptation of Human Lactase Persistence in Africa and Europe," *Nature Genetics* 39, no. 1 (2007): 31–40.

Your scientists have failed to grasp the genetic and cultural relationship between the Levant and North Africa, so they assert lactase persistence emerged independently and simultaneously in these regions. In reality, it began with the Atlanteans in North Africa, was carried into the Levant by the fallen Watchers, and then returned during the Neolithic Age when Nephilim started spreading across the globe. There are five genetic variants producing lactase persistence, and Africa is the only continent upon which your scientists have found all five.

As Nephilim encountered primitive humans who were lactose intolerant, these less advanced societies thought it miraculous that white, giant humans could drink milk as adults without becoming violently ill. Thinking these people to be deities with supernatural powers, primitive humans started making offerings consisting of milk and roasted meat to these "gods"—a practice that continued long after in many religions.

Along with the lactase persistence mutation, the E-M81 gene follows the Nephilim. Within 2,000 years of the abandonment of Göbekli Tepe, three major cultures emerged in the Maghreb: Capsian, Mechta-Afalou, and Kiffian, all of which are Nephilim cultures with strong signals of the E-M81 haplogroup. As one modern study states, mitochondrial DNA and Y-chromosome haplogroup evidence suggests "either a population replacement or an important genetic influx into Morocco between 5,000 and 3,000 BCE"—5,000 to 7,000 years ago—"associated

[106] Rosa Fregel et al., "Ancient Genomes from North Africa Evidence Prehistoric Migrations to the Maghreb from Both the Levant and Europe," *PNAS* 115, no. 30 (July 24, 2018).

with the back migration to Africa from Eurasia."[106] It is this place and time where archeologists unearthed the world's oldest mummy at Uan Muhuggiag, Libya, which pre-dates any known mummification by the Egyptians by a thousand years. Most Maghrebian men today are either E-M81 or E-M78, the former being the Nephilim, descendants of Cronus returning home, and the latter being the line of Adam, descendants of Enoch who stayed in North Africa.

[107]**"Study Reveals 'Extraordinary' DNA of People in Scotland,"** BBC News, April 17, 2012, https://www. bbc.com/news/uk-scotland-17740638

A genetic study in the British Isles found that "more than 1 percent of all Scotsmen are direct descendants of the Berber Tuareg tribesmen of the Sahara, a lineage which is around 5,600 years old."[107] Your scientists call E-M81 the Berber gene, so this data corroborates the Nephilim arrival in the British Isles 5,600 years ago; they are the source of the red-haired, megalithic-building Druids, known to the ancient Greeks

[108]**Steve Hewitt**, "The Question of a Hamito-Semitic Substratum in Insular Celtic," *Language and Linguistics Compass*, July 2009.

[109]**Page Selinsky**, "Celtic Ritual Activity at Gordion, Turkey: Evidence from Mortuary Contexts and Skeletal Analysis," *International Journal of Osteoarchaeology* 25, no. 2 (2015): 213–225, https://onlinelibrary.wiley. com/doi/epdf/10.1002/oa.2279

as Hyperboreans, constructors of Stonehenge, and inventors of the horrific Wicker Man ritual sacrifice of humans and animals by fire. Along with the E-M81 gene, they also brought the Afro-Asiatic language, which by this point had evolved through ancient Semitic to the Celtic language still spoken today.[108] Celtic presence is confirmed by your scientists stretching from Ireland, through Iberia, all the way to ancient Scythia, where burial sites of sacrificed children and adults have been found.[109]

Architectural Markers

Beyond the Mediterranean, the Nephilim ventured east and west. Evidence of their presence in China dates to over 8,000 years ago, where they left behind dozens of pyramids near Xi'an, one rumored to be over twice the height of the Great Pyramid of Giza, as well as 4,000-year-old auburn-haired mummies discovered in the Tarim basin in present-day Xinjiang.[110]

[110]**Callum Hoare**, "China's Mysterious 8,000-Year-Old Structure 'Guarded by Military' Could Hold Key Secrets,"*Express*, August 10, 2020, https://www.express. co.uk/news/world/1320322/china-mystery -white-pyramid-xian-shaanxi-military- secret-archaeology-google-earth-spt

They continued east, all the way to the Bada Valley in modern-day Sulawesi, Indonesia, where a similar megalithic culture exists to this day in the Sumba people. They represent the easternmost reach of the old Nephilim kingdom.

To the west, in the Canary Islands, were the pyramids of Güímar and the Guanche Indians, white people with blonde or auburn red hair of the E-M81 haplogroup who practiced mummification and the occasional human sacrifice. Their own legends state they arrived in ships long ago, so far in the past that they did not remember when. Islamic sailors encountered white people on the Canary Islands and left peacefully, unlike the Spanish. A love poem written by Spanish historian and doctor Antonio de Viana about the Guanche Princess Dácil in 1604 confirms the Nephilim-like appearance of the Guanche people:

> Long hair, more golden than the sun. Eyebrows subtle, of the same golden color that seem like golden arches and correspond the brown eye lashes to her semblance. Beautiful eyes like emeralds; enclosed by transparent crystals and shine rose circles as beautiful as flowers on her cheeks. Sharp nose, in proportion to a graceful mouth with thick lips that seem made of the purest fine coral. Beautiful face, the color of snow with blood and fire intermixed.

In the Azores are pyramids that look like the modestly sized step pyramid on Tenerife. The Portuguese government avoids talking about these pyramids, because it wants to maintain the national myth that the Portuguese discovered the islands. However, also in the Azores are ancient iron arrowheads and other evidence of inhabitants long before the Portuguese. There is no iron in the Canary Islands or Azores, so the iron arrowheads found there were brought from somewhere else. [111]

[111]"Pico: New Archeological Evidence Reveals Human Presence before Portuguese Occupation—Azores," *Portuguese American Journal*, August 28, 2013, https://portuguese-american-journal.com/pico-new-archeological-evidence-reveals-human-presence-before-portuguese-occupation-azores/

In the Amazon, a fully developed megalithic civilization built the city of Caral 5,500 years ago, where archeologists have found ancient pyramids on the coastline of Peru built by the Norte Chico civilization, and the Sechin people built a similar, even older megalithic civilization at Sechin Bajo. The Amazonians' chief deity is Viracocha, a character who appears in other Mesoamerican myths as Kukulkan and Quetzalcoatl. In actuality, he was an Atlantean whose role was later usurped by a Nephilim. Viracocha is a Zeus-like figure, a bearded man wielding the thunderbolt who takes frequent sojourns disguised as a vagabond to observe human morality and teach the arts of civilization. Like Poseidon, he is intimately associated with the sea and even walks on water like Jesus Christ. His first creations were giants who behaved very badly, so he destroyed them in a massive flood.

In what is now the Ica region of Peru, the ancient Paracas culture arose, and they too have evidence of megalithic structures. There you will find the Paracas candelabra—a large geoglyph that resembles the ancient Phoenician depiction of the goddess Tanit, consort of their chief god Baal, to whom they sacrificed children.

Beyond South America, the Nephilim traveled even farther west to Easter Island, where they established another culture who built the Moai, which looked much like the Bada Valley megaliths: men standing with their arms clasped in front of them or holding a phallus, similar to statues found in Göbelki Tepe. Urfa Man, found in the same region, also has hands clasped in front in a similar manner, and though this statue is sans phallus, it may be that this appendage wore off. Another similarity across the megalithic structures is the recurring motif of the chevron dress, as appears on the pillars of Göbekli Tepe, the megaliths of Bada Valley, and many Moai on Easter Island.

The Nephilim influence is also clear in the advanced stonework that arose simultaneously at sites in Mesopotamia, Peru, and Egypt 5,000 to 5,500 years ago. There is even evidence in the Levant of impossibly huge stones being cut and moved at the ancient site of Baalbek, upon which the Romans later built a temple to Jupiter, but the foundations of the entire temple complex are much older and likely Phoenician. Within these foundations are three stones called the Trilithon, each weighing over 1,000 tons. A nearby quarry contains two other, even bigger stones that were destined for the complex.

Had these civilizations evolved naturally instead of with the exported knowledge of the Nephilim, your scientists would have seen a progression from working with tiny stones up to building more complicated projects. A society cannot go from nothing to building Caral, for example, on the first attempt. The Caral pyramid is as old and big as the one in Giza.

Similarly, in Giza, the Egyptian abilities to work with stone emerged fully formed and then slowly degenerated over millennia, as the Nephilim were absorbed into the local culture and lost their connection to their Atlantean knowledge. The old kingdom contained stonework never attempted again, on scales both large and small, including plates and delicate vases cut from diorite, the hardest type of granite. To this day, humans do not have tools or skill to replicate such work.

The Skulls of Kings

In addition to their stoneworking skills, the Nephilim apparently passed on their fair skin, light-colored hair, and genetic mutations to the Paracas people living in Peru. Accounts of the Spanish conquistadores reveal that the ruling class in

Peru resembled the Nephilim: Pedro Pizzaro wrote in his diary, "The people of this kingdom of Peru were white, swarthy in color, and among them the Lords and Ladies were whiter than Spaniards. I saw in this land an Indian woman and a child who would not stand out among white blonds. These people [of the upper class] say that they were the children of the idols." [112]

[112] **Pedro Pizzaro**, *Relations of the Discovery and Conquest of the Kingdoms of Peru*, vol. II (New York: The Cortes Society, 1921), 471.

Skulls from this region have been recovered, and some of them do indeed show evidence of blond and auburn hair. Some of these light-haired skulls are also elongated and, in some cases, even missing the sagittal suture. These mutations, likely a form of macrocephaly, manifested through generations of inbreeding.

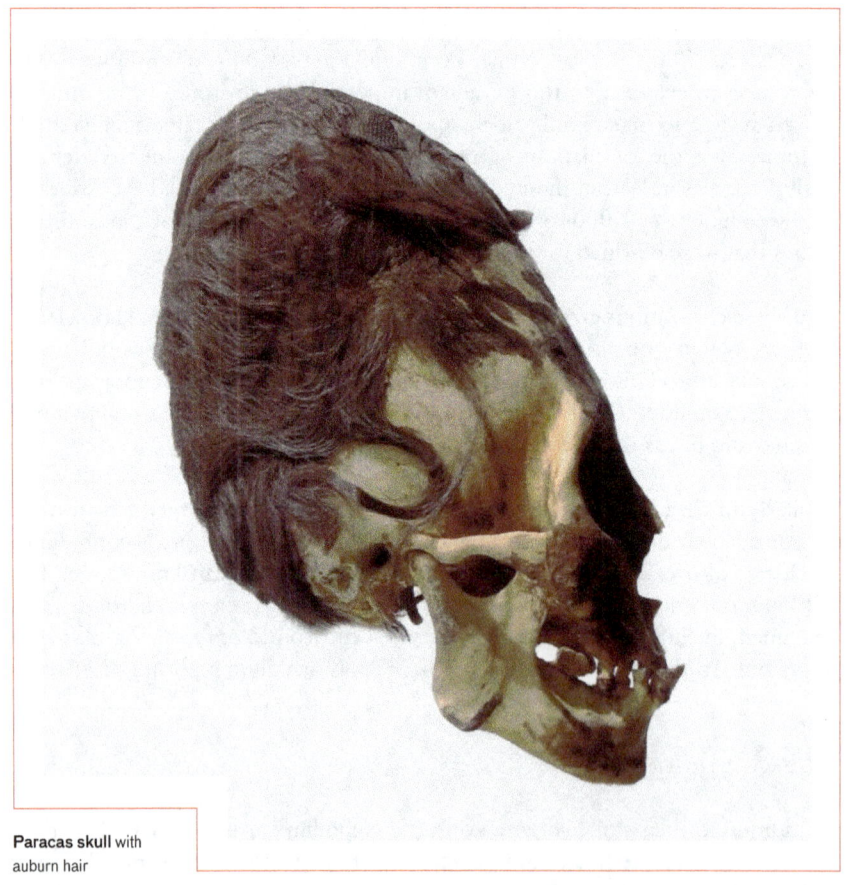

Paracas skull with auburn hair

Curiously, other skulls have been recovered that show evidence of cradle boarding—a practice one might expect the ruled class to follow in an effort to imitate their long-headed rulers. None of these cradle-boarded skulls have blonde or auburn hair, however; contributing to the theory that the mutation came from outsiders, not someone native to the Paracas region, where the dominant hair color is black.

From whence did these outsiders come? Mitochondrial DNA has shown that these elongated skulls belong to Canaanites from the Levant, the homeland of the Nephilim. [113]

[113] **Lynn A. Marzulli**, *Nephilim Hybrids: Hybrids, Chimeras, and Strange Demonic Creatures*, (Malibu, CA: Spiral of Life Publishing, 2016), chapters 5-6 and the appendix; **April Holloway**, "New DNA Testing on 2,000-Year-Old Elongated Paracas Skulls Changes Known History," Ancient Origins, July 23, 2016, https://www.ancient-origins.net/news-history-archaeology/breaking-new-dna-testing-2000-year-old-elongated-paracas-skulls-changes-020914

The elongated skull mutation also appeared in Egypt in the line of Akhenaten, the Egyptian Pharaoh who tried to introduce a solar deity named the Aten as the one and only god of the Egyptians. For various reasons, among them moving the capital city of Egypt to Amarna, Akhenaten was very unpopular—so much so that statues of Akhenaten and his entire family line have had their faces chiseled off as if to erase them from history. Surviving illustrations reveal that both of Akhenaten's daughters had large cone-shaped heads, even as infants. His son, Tutankhamen, did not appear to present the same genetic mutation, though he did suffer from a host of other genetic defects as a result of inbreeding. [114]

[114] **Zahi Hawass** et al., "Ancestry and Pathology in King Tutankhamun's Family," *JAMA* 303, no. 7 (2010): 638-647, https://jamanetwork.com/journals/jama/fullarticle/185393

Everywhere you find the practice of cranial deformation, whether in the Peruvian Paracas culture 2,000 years ago or in Egypt 3,500 years ago, it probably started among people who wanted to emulate Nephilim with this mutation of skull elongation. If the native people themselves didn't mate with and inherit the mutation from a member of the ruling class, they may have engaged in the practice of cradle boarding to deform the heads of their offspring in order to emulate their rulers and make them appear as royalty. [115]

[115] **Chris White**, "Head Space: Behind 10,000 Years of Artificial Cranial Modification," Atlas Obscura, Mar 26, 2015, https://www.atlasobscura.com/articles/head-space-artificial-cranial-deformation

In addition to the stories of Peruvian white Indians with light hair and eyes, there is widespread evidence that cannibalism and human sacrifice were practiced among these tribes—traditions learned from the Nephilim. [116] Cannibalism was

[116] **Robert Redfield**, "Cannibalism among South American Indians," *Journal of Religion* 10, no. 3 (1930).

not as common, but it was practiced by the Ache Indians in particular.[117] Pizzaro wrote in his diary, "And likewise there were three or four boys, Indians of the land, whom they captured aboard the balsas, as well as some others whom the Indians gave them to eat, thinking that the Spaniards were eaters of human flesh."[118] When the Spaniards came, the Peruvians saw they were white like the old gods and assumed they would like to eat human beings, too.

[117] **Pierre Clastres**, "Guayaki Cannibalism," in *Native South Americans: Ethnology of the Least Known Continent*, ed. Patricia Lyon (Boston: Little, Brown, 1974), 309–321.

[118] **Pizzaro**, *Relations of Discovery*, vol. I, p. 139.

FIRE AND BRIMSTONE

Meteor impacts did not end with the ones previously described, as Taurid meteors came down repeatedly throughout the Iron Age. You have no doubt heard of Sodom and Gomorrah from the Book of Genesis. Their real destruction resulted from a meteor, which has been accurately dated to 3,700 years ago. Archeologists found the site of Sodom and confirmed a Tunguska-like airburst caused its demise. [119]

[119] **Ped E. Bunch** et al., "A Tunguska Sized Airburst Destroyed Tall el-Hamman a Middle Bronze Age City in the Jordan Valley near the Dead Sea," *Scientific Reports*, 11 (2021).

Physically, Sodom existed at the site of Tell el-Hammam, just northeast of the Dead Sea, on the opposite side of the Jordan River Valley from Jericho. Tells are mounds that form on flat land as people move in, build structures, live, accumulate garbage, and build once more on top of those mounds. When archeologists look for ancient settlements, they locate and dig into tells, finding pottery, arrowheads, soot from fires, and so on.

As described in Genesis, Watchers came the night before the airburst and warned Lot to escape immediately, as quickly as possible, without wasting time or looking back. Lot made haste, but his wife did not, and when she looked back, she was instantly incinerated by the meteor, appearing for a moment as a "pillar" of ash in the shape of her fully formed body, described in the Bible as a pillar of salt.

SONS
OF ANAK

The ruling Nephilim class survived the cataclysms beginning and ending the Younger Dryas, and they went on to establish the civilization of Phoenicia 4,000 years ago. Their exploits are recorded in the Hebrew accounts known as the *Torah*, or the *Pentateuch*, which is what you may know as the first five books of the Old Testament.

In the same way that Ovid, Diodorus, and Plato corroborate historical events surrounding the Atlanteans, the Hebrew works confirm the connection of the Sons of Anak with their Nephilim ancestors. As Greek mythology and Atlanteans' history overlap, so does the history of the people known as the Canaanites and Phoenicians overlap with that of the Nephilim, for they are one and the same people. The Bible mentions the connection in the books of Numbers, Deuteronomy, and Jeremiah, and a corroborating story is found in the apocryphal Book of Jubilees. Here are but two examples:

> And there we saw the giants [Nephilim], the sons of Anak, which come of the giants: and we were in our own sight as grasshoppers, and so we were in their sight. [120]
> [120]Numbers 13:33 (KJV).

> Hear, O Israel: Thou art to pass over Jordan this day, to go in to possess nations greater and mightier than thyself; cities great and fenced up to heaven, a people great and tall, the children of the Anakims, whom thou knowest, and of whom thou hast heard say, "Who can stand before the children of Anak!" [121]
> [121]Deuteronomy 9:1–2 (KJV).

These Sons of Anak, or Anakites, were the Nephilim's descendants, the Canaanite ruling class.

Throughout present-day Syria, Lebanon, and Israel, in what was then known as the Land of Canaan, there existed a network of Phoenician cities. To this day, Lebanon and Syria have lands that historically were part of Canaan, and the State of Israel wants them—understanding this history can help you understand the modern age.

The Phoenicians were not a civilization as you traditionally understand civilizations; rather, they were loosely federated, independent city-states without a central government, as in Greece. They were colonizers of the Mediterranean and established and expanded a massive trade empire. They were well known throughout the ancient world as being master sailors and navigators, and the Egyptians hired them to build their boats. As recorded by Herodotus in Book 4 of the *Histories*, Pharaoh Necho II also commissioned them to circumnavigate Africa 2,600 years ago, in the reverse direction of the Watchers' journey described in the Silver Age account.

One particular practice that connects the Phoenicians to their Nephilim ancestors is the murdering and eating of children. The Phoenicians and all their colonies, chiefly Carthage, the largest and most successful of them, carried out child sacrifices to the god Baal on a massive scale, particularly in the Valley of Hinnom, also called Gehenna, in Jerusalem. In the Bible, "God" calls this region the valley of slaughter. In Deuteronomy, Numbers, and Jeremiah, "God" repeatedly warns the Israelites not to worship in the Canaanite way because they trick people into committing awful, sinful acts. Enoch, too, said the fallen Watchers would trick a person into sacrificing to demons as gods. Thus, "God" repeatedly ordered the extermination of the Canaanites, wanting to wipe these people from the face of the earth because they would not give up this horrifying practice.

Plato and Diodorus mentioned the slaughter as well. In *Minos*, Plato discussed the Carthaginian and Phoenician practice of killing babies. In Book 20 of the *Bibliotheca Historica*, Diodorus mentioned that these same people made sacrifices to Cronus, whom the Carthaginians and Israelites called Baal, according to the Bible. One report underscores the magnitude of these sacrifices, stating that they killed tens of thousands of babies over the course of several centuries, averaging dozens per week. This same paper also enumerates the many child burial sites that have been located at Phoenician colonies throughout the Mediterranean, including Africa, Sicily, Sardinia, and Malta. [122] In all of these cultures, sacrifices were made to the same deity known by different names—Cronus (Greek), Baal (Carthaginian), Enlil (Mesopotamian), El (Hebrew), and Saturn (Roman) have always been linked.

[122] Brian Felushko, "The *Tophet* and Child Sacrifice in the Ancient Mediterranean," paper prepared in partial fulfillment for the requirements of CLST 511A, submitted on December 9, 2015.

After they killed a baby, they would throw the body into the fire and burn it, then gather the remains into an urn and bury it in the tophets, or cemeteries. Sometimes, they would sacrifice an animal alongside the child, burning both and putting them into the urn together, demonstrating a view that humans are no different from or more deserving than animals.

Academics have manufactured a debate regarding whether or not these were actual child sacrifices, as opposed to stillbirths; however, the babies were uniformly killed between two and three months of age, so they were not born dead, a fact that is further supported by the presence of teeth in the remains. These were living viable beings who were murdered. [123]

[123] Patricia Smith, Lawrence E. Stager, Joseph A. Greene, and Gal Avishai, "Cemetery or Sacrifice? Infant Burials at the Carthage Tophet," *Antiquity* 87 (2013): 1191–1207 Paolo Xella, 'Tophet': An Overall Interpretation," *Studi Epigrafici e Linguistici* 29–60 (2012–2013): 259–281.

This vile practice started among the fallen Watchers, who believed that if they sacrificed the soul to God and consumed the body, that act of taking the life force of a child would extend their own life and confer other benefactions. Young children, they believed, allowed the extraction of the greatest benefit.

The Phoenicians were close to the Egyptians, both physically and culturally, and Phoenician iconography looks quite similar to Egyptian iconography. At one point, the Phoenicians invaded Egypt and took over a large portion of it; the Canaanite rulers were known as the Hyksos and tried to implement many unwanted practices, but they were seen as bloodthirsty and corrupt and were eventually expelled from Egypt.

The dynasty that assumed rule over Egypt after the expulsion of the Hyksos is the one that eventually produced Akhenaten, whose daughters had the conical heads. Did the Egyptians truly succeed at driving out the Nephilim, or had they become embedded by intermarrying with the Egyptian family who succeeded the Hyksos? Judging from the depictions of Akhenaten's daughters, the Nephilim persisted.

FINDING CERNÊ

By 2,600 years ago, Phoenicia had begun to fade in economic and military power. Still, they knew from their fallen Watcher heritage that one could circumnavigate Africa, and they were quite comfortable sailing out beyond the Pillars of Hercules, even establishing trade routes with people living on the Atlantic coast of Africa, as noted by Herodotus. [124]

[124] Herodotus, *Histories*, Book IV, Chapter 196.

A century after the Phoenician circumnavigation, Hanno, a high-ranking Carthaginian, voyaged out beyond the Pillars of Hercules and down the African coast, with sixty ships and 30,000 people, founding colonies and meeting myriad tribesmen. Hanno kept a periplus—a captain's log—which was later installed in a public temple to Baal in Carthage, where people could read the account of this great and legendary journey of the ancient world. The original periplus in that temple was later destroyed by the Romans, but translations and copies were passed down through the generations in other ways.

According to this document, Hanno sailed east into Africa, arrived in a bay, found a circular island, and started a colony called Cernê—clearly, he traveled up the mighty Tamanrasset River to the Richat Structure. Reconstructed maps of Hanno's journey place Cernê on the African coast precisely where one finds the Cap Timiris Canyon, mouth of the ancient Tamanrasset and gateway to Atlantis.

As a Carthaginian, Hanno had access to the ancient Phoenician records and knew the Richat Structure was the site of the Atlantean city called Cernê, so he called his colony by the same name.

Centuries after Hanno took this journey, Diodorus retrieved the account of Dionysius Scytobrachion from the library of Alexandria and noticed that the Atlanteans lost one of their cities to the Libyan Amazonians, a city named Cernê. In the account of Dionysius, Diodorus relays how the Atlanteans were invaded by

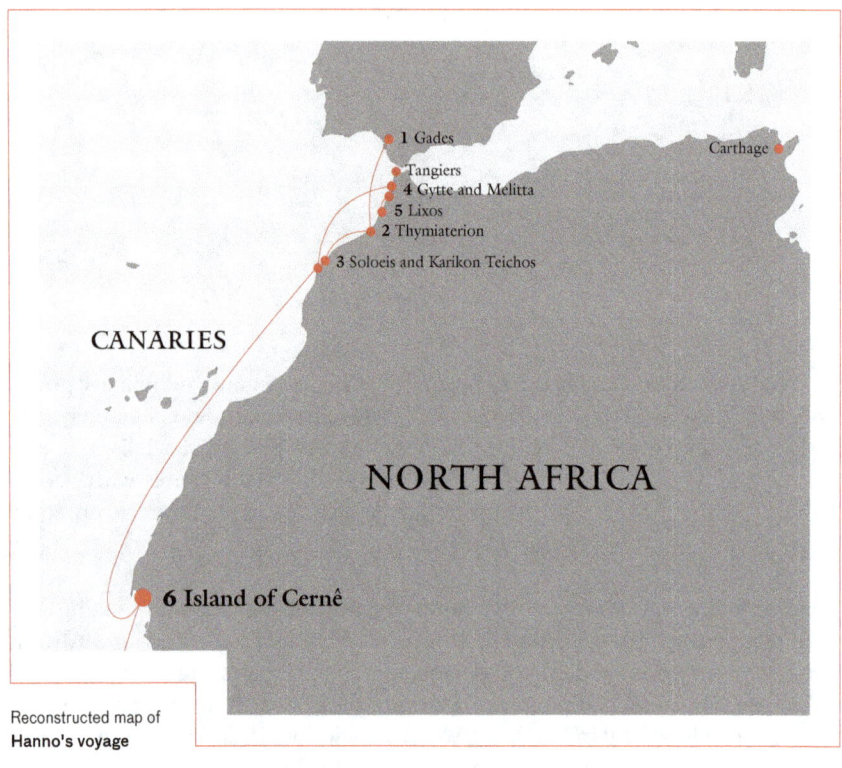

1 Gades

Tangiers
4 Gytte and Melitta
5 Lixos
2 Thymiaterion

3 Soloeis and Karikon Teichos

Carthage

CANARIES

NORTH AFRICA

6 Island of Cernê

Reconstructed map of
Hanno's voyage

Libyan Amazonians, an army of women who conquered the city of Cernê, leading the Atlanteans to surrender the whole empire. Diodorus says the Amazonians came from a marsh named Tritonis that was destroyed in a cataclysm, making it a pre-flood tale. The marsh Tritonis was transformed into the Lake Tritonis on the same site with which the Greeks were familiar. The tidal wave turned it into a lake, but it has long since dried up and disappeared along with the Tamanrasset.

No one has done an archeological excavation in the Richat Structure, and in the past twenty years, only two people have gone there to do research. Of those two, one man found pottery from Mesoamerica dating to the time of the Carthaginian colony, demonstrating they had established trade with other Nephilim colonies in the Americas. [125]

[125] **"Richat Artifact Dating Results— Incredible Find—Earliest Transatlantic Voyage?"** YouTube video posted by Indie Archeology, January 11, 2020, https://www. youtube.com/watch?v=RcIs2UhafUY

ROMAN CONQUEST OF LIBYA

Though the Carthaginians were great sailors and traders with access to people and goods around the world, they were also cannibals who murdered children, and as a result, many people feared them and wanted them eliminated. The Romans took up this cause 2,250 years ago and warred against these people in the hope of exterminating them as the Hebrew god wished, the result being the Punic Wars, thus referred to because the Phoenicians and their colonies practiced the Punic religion. Hannibal, whose name meant "Beloved of Baal," invaded and almost sacked Rome during that time, but the Romans eventually defeated the Carthaginians, sacked the city of Carthage in what is now Tunisia, and destroyed everything, including its giant library, which contained all their knowledge about Atlantis.

The typical Roman conquest involved deposing the local ruler and annexing the kingdom into Rome, for Romans were not generally destroyers but rather subjects of a conglomerate of other states. Their treatment of Carthage was completely unique. They systematically combed the city for days, killing everyone they found and setting fire to the buildings as they passed.

Unfortunately, the Romans failed in their quest. At least one E-M81 man or family escaped the destruction, as evidenced by the fact that a subclade of E-M81, known as E-M183, survived in North Africa. Broadly speaking, E-M81 is the Nephilim haplogroup, and E-M183 is the Carthaginian line that is also found in the Guanche mummies of Tenerife on the Canary Islands. As already mentioned, in the present day, E-M183 (the Carthaginian subclade of E-M81, Sons of Cronus) and E-M78 (Sons of Adam) make up most of the men in North Africa. Seventy-one percent of men in Morocco, Algeria, Tunisia, and Libya are E-M183.[126]

[126] Neus Solé-Morata et al., "Whole Y-Chromosome Sequences Reveal and Extremely Recent Origin of the Most Common North African Paternal Lineage E-M183 (M81)," *Scientific Reports* 7, no. 15941 (2017): 1–11.

West of Carthage was the state of Numidia, and further westward was the ancient country of Mauretania and the Mauri people. Mauretania is known to be a land of great wisdom, and in particular, King Juba II was famous as being a very wise king. Mauretanians have a founding legend just as the Greeks do, a story so old they do not know when their society began, and their legendary founder was King Atlas, who invented the celestial sphere and the science of astronomy—a remarkable similarity to the Atlantean king who bears the same name.

In the intervening 2,000 years, the Nephilim descendants of Cronus who escaped the Roman conquest have continued to infiltrate your most important and powerful institutions—including secret societies, intelligence, academia, and government bureaucracies—as will become clear in Book III.

CHAPTER 6
THE NEW AGE

I f you raised your eyes to the heavens on the evening of December 21, 2020, you witnessed a singular cosmic event. For on that night, the planet Jupiter "overtook" Saturn in the sky, their orbits passing so closely together that, to the naked eye, their lights appeared to merge into one.

Such a conjunction of these planetary giants occurs every twenty years, but the one in 2020 was unique, for it took place on a solstice. To be sure, this event was the first in recorded history to occur during a solstice, an event that did not go unnoticed by the Atlanteans, for it not only represented the overtaking of Cronus (Saturn) by Zeus (Jupiter), but it also suggests that earth entered a new age on that night: the Age of Aquarius.

Just as the first kingdom of Atlantis was founded at the beginning of an Age of Aquarius, so now must it be again. While many people are of sufficient spiritual maturity to coexist amongst the Atlanteans, all humanity toils under the oppressive yoke of the Nephilim, who have ruled the earth for 12,000 years. The time of these despicable beings, and those who have given themselves over to their evil plans, is at an end. Though the Atlanteans left earth at the beginning of the Iron Age, their plan all along has been to return, to reclaim this planet and put an end to the Nephilim's vile reign.

Now you shall learn more of the judgment to come, that which has been foretold in the ancient writings of many cultures.

THE AGE
OF AQUARIUS

With the exception of the Silver Age, which began in war, cosmic events have marked the transitions among ages. To understand the dawning of the New Age, it is important to understand the movement of the cosmos relative to your planet. The sky is divided into twelve constellations, and as earth turns over the course of one year, there are two solstices and two equinoxes. When the sun rises during the spring equinox, a constellation rises with it, and it is said that the sun is in the house of that constellation. The age of Leo, for example, occurs when the sun and Leo rise together.

For the last 2,000 years, the sun has been in the house of Pisces, which is why Christianity contains such plentiful allegory and symbolism of fish. Jesus is the fisher of men, and using two fish, he fed thousands of his followers. Like Pisces, the symbol of Christianity is a fish, same as the symbol for the ancient Greek word *ichthys*, which is an ancient acronym for "Iesous Christos Theou Yios Soter" (Ἰησοῦς Χρῑστός Θεοῦ Υἱός Σωτήρ), or Jesus Christ, Son of God, Savior."

Given the movement of the cosmos, the age of Pisces cannot last forever, as the sun is destined to rise in another house as the earth continues in its orbit. That next house is Aquarius, the constellation representing a vessel overflowing with water. There is no clear boundary in the sky determining where Pisces ends and Aquarius begins, and the constellations do not share equal space on the celestial sphere, but a great conjunction provides a line of demarcation, and the unprecedented solstice great conjunction of 2020 indicates the dawn of the Age of Aquarius. [127]

[127] **Nina Kahn**, "One of the Year's Most Anticipated Astrological Events Is Almost Here," Bustle, November 26, 2020, https://www.bustle.com/life/december-2020-astrology-great-conjunction-age-of-aquarius; **Pepe Escobar**, "Behold the Dawning of the Age of Aquarius," Asia Times, December 21, 2020, https://asiatimes.com/2020/12/behold-the-dawning-of-the-age-of-aquarius/

Always keep in mind that as it is in heaven, so it is on earth. Events on this planet are mirrored in the stars, as with the battle between Zeus and Cronus in the great conjunction. Atlanteans are very intimately attuned to the celestial bodies, lessons they have tried to pass down to humans.

A GENETIC ANCHOR

From their current home in the celestial realm, the Atlanteans are preparing for a transformative return to earth, but not simply because the age of Pisces draws to a close or because of the special great conjunction. The movements of the stars relative to earth do not materially impact the Atlanteans—they have other existential reasons to remain connected to and concerned about the planet.

As you have seen in the previous ages, the Atlanteans have a great facility for accurate prophecies and predictions, from cosmic events to how governments will react in this very moment. They have prophesied a great harvest of humanity that is nearly upon us. Of course, as the Atlanteans' fallen descendants, the Nephilim can decode these predictions as well and do not want laypeople to have such knowledge. Thus, knowing their ancestors' righteous plan to return to earth at the dawn of the New Age, the Nephilim endeavor to make it as inhospitable a place as possible—environmentally, ethically, and genetically—in an attempt to cause the Atlanteans to forsake their ancestral home and leave it to be consumed by evil.

The Nephilim cannot give up their violent ways. Today's increases in violence, exploitation, and environmental degradation represent their intentional efforts to ruin earth for the Atlanteans' purposes. They have not changed their core destructiveness in thousands upon thousands of years. They have only changed their tactics and become more sophisticated by stealing regular human inventions and perverting them for their own uses. They spray substances into the atmosphere and call it "biowarfare readiness exercises" or "geoengineering" under the guise of saving the planet from climate change, but make no mistake: their motives are nefarious. Most recently they succeeded in deceiving a large portion of earth's population into repeatedly taking experimental gene therapies,[128] and now they are leading the world to the brink of a nuclear war.

[128]United States Securities and Exchange Commission, "Moderna Inc. Quarterly Report," June 30, 2020, https://www.sec.gov/Archives/edgardata/1682852/000168285220-000017/mrna-20200630.htm

Tyranny advances around the globe today as the Nephilim endeavor to cement their control over humanity before the Atlanteans return. They want to become powerful enough to continue ruling the world after their more ethical cousins arrive.

Avoiding Speciation

Why is earth still beloved by and of great value to the Atlanteans?

This planet represents their genetic anchor to humanity. They have colonized other worlds, separating their population from its mother gene pool, and these other worlds have different gravity, light, and atmospheric conditions, causing the Atlanteans to evolve in a different direction from humans on earth. In some cases, their eyes have grown bigger, and their complexion has changed, as observed in so-called alien encounters.

This separate evolution can only carry on for so long, however, before Atlanteans and humans can no longer interbreed and instead become separate species. The Atlanteans are trying to prevent that rupture, periodically returning to mate with humans and maintain a flow of genes between them and earthlings, preventing humanity from fracturing into several or even hundreds of different interstellar subspecies.

Such a rupture would have spiritual consequences as well. New Age spiritualists say Atlantean souls have been incarnating into humans on earth with increasing frequency over the past fifty years, a phenomenon referred to as "star seeds" and "indigo children," in anticipation of the great return. [129]

[129] "20 Signs You Have Returned from Atlantis," *Numerologist*, n.d, https://numerologist.com/spiritual-growth/returned-from-atlantis/ the-age-of-aquarius/

If the two groups speciated, then that interbreeding could no longer happen, preventing humans from ascending after death and reincarnating on other worlds. Native Americans as well as the Indian yogis talk extensively about other worlds with humans on them who were allowed to go there after conducting themselves well on your planet. [130]

[130] Paramhansa Yogananda, *Autobiography of a Yogi* (Los Angeles: Self-Realization Fellowship, 1998), Chapter 43.

UFO Sightings

Since the first nuclear bomb was detonated in New Mexico in 1945, sightings of unidentified flying objects across the globe have increased. Have you ever paused to consider why, Seeker of Truth? Here is the reason, laid plain before you: the Atlanteans are preparing for their return, both by mating with humans and by surveying the Nephilim's defense systems.

Several initiatives have led to official government acknowledgment that there are crafts in their airspace behaving in ways the military cannot explain. An official U.S. Director of National Intelligence report on unidentified aerial phenomena (UAP) reads,

> In 18 incidents, described in 21 reports, observers reported unusual UAP movement patterns or flight characteristics. Some UAP appeared to remain stationary in winds aloft, move against the wind, maneuver abruptly, or move at considerable speed, without discernible means of propulsion.[131]

[131]Office of the Director of National Intelligence, Preliminary Assessment: Unidentified Aerial Phenomena, June 25, 2021,

Whether they are called "unidentified aerial phenomena" or "unidentified flying objects," the conclusion is clear: they exist, the government of one of the most powerful countries on the planet admits they exist, and a designated group within the US military is looking into their presence.[132] With each passing day the perceived threat of these vehicles is being ramped up, with one report to the US Select Committee on Intelligence stating that "cross-domain transmedium threats to United States national security are expanding exponentially"—with "cross-domain" referring to their ability to travel effortlessly through air, water, and outer space.[133]

[132]Tyler Durden, "UFO Hearing: Pentagon Shows Declassified Footage of Flying Spherical Object," ZeroHedge, May 18, 2022, https://www.zerohedge.com/military/ufo-hearing-pentagon-shows-declassified-footage-flying-spherical-object

[133]Mark Warner and the Select Committee on Intelligence, "Intelligence Authorization Act for Fiscal Year 2023," Congress.gov, July 20, 2022, p. 12, https://www.congress.gov/117/crpt/srpt132/CRPT-117srpt132.pdf

Nephilim have always known about UFOs, given the fact that their ancestors developed the technology, and certain politicians today are aligned with them, knowingly or unknowingly. These individuals pretend to be serious about investigating the unexplained phenomena, when in fact, they are either pawns or simply putting on an act. As will be explained in Book III, the same names of Nephilim-aligned officials recur across seemingly disparate but actually connected subject matter, in initiatives they spearhead regarding UFOs, pedophilia, and propaganda.

Abduction Accounts

John Mack, an internationally renowned psychiatrist trained at one of the United States' most prestigious universities, has interviewed hundreds of abductees, who relay similar stories of having their sperm or eggs harvested during the encounter, or of being visited by an "alien" who then engages them in sexual intercourse. Later, these humans are taken again and presented with their children, because the Atlanteans understand humans are not simply tools or zoo animals but rather people with an emotional connection to their offspring. Many of these tales are recounted in Mack's 1994 book *Abduction*.

One of the abductees Mack interviewed is Peter Khoury, a Lebanese man descended from a sacred and ancient Christian bloodline. Given their origins, of course, the Atlantean "aliens" would be interested in mating with such a man. They share a common ancestor, thus increasing the chances of producing a viable, fertile child, as opposed to humans who have not descended from the E-Z827 bloodline. Khoury's story is recounted in UFO researcher Bill Chalker's book *The Hair of the Alien*, in which Khoury describes waking up in his bedroom to two women attempting to have sexual relations with him—one white and Nordic-looking, the other Asian-looking and presumably hailing from the sunken continent of Lemuria. They did not speak, but the Nordic woman attempted several times to take Peter in an embrace. He declined their advances, and they suddenly vanished from his room. Later Khoury found a long, blonde hair that had been wrapped tightly around his penis, which he sent to a lab that found it had 100 percent human DNA from Iberia that had not been seen on earth in many thousands of years. These visitors were not in fact aliens. They are as human as you are.

The Hair of the Alien also includes the story of Dr. Kary Mullis, first recounted in Mullis's own book *Dancing Naked in the Mind Field*. Mullis had his own alien encounter in 1985, following his discovery of the polymerase chain reaction (PCR) in 1983, a technology that has been misused ever since to Mullis's utter dismay. Could it be that the Atlanteans beamed the PCR idea into Mullis's head and then followed up with him afterward to make sure it took?

Another account comes from Travis Walton, a logger who disappeared for five days in 1975 after encountering a UFO while in the woods with friends. He walked too close to the ship and was struck by a beam from its automated defense system. Thinking Walton had died, his friends ran away, but he was actually taken onto the ship. After regaining consciousness, he felt battered but alive. He found himself on a medical table surrounded by prototypical gray aliens, and shock and fear caused Walton to act belligerently toward them.

After these gray aliens left the room, Walton got up and started exploring the ship. In the navigation room, Walton encountered a completely human-looking individual who led him out of the ship and through a facility to a room with yet more humans, one of whom pointed a device at him, causing him to immediately lose consciousness. When he again awoke, Walton found himself on the side of the road near the site from which he had been taken.

In possibly one of the most comprehensive interactions a human from earth has ever had with an off-worlder, Swiss farmer Eduard "Billy" Meier was visited over 100 times by a woman from the Pleiades who called herself Semjase, a name not that different from the leader of the fallen Watchers of Enoch, revealing their common Atlantean ancestry. The similarities also do not end there, for her home world is named Erra, a name with which you are by now well acquainted.

Semjase forewarned Meier that she would not be able to answer his questions as thoroughly as she would like, and then engaged him in discussions on topics ranging from human history to religion to spirituality to technology and more. Semjase also expressed great concern over the state of affairs on earth.

After receiving a thought transmission from Semjase, Meier recorded their conversations verbatim in four volumes. In one meeting, Semjase made it clear to him that she is a human being just like Meier:

> The Earth human being calls us extraterrestrials or star-people, or however he wants. He addicts to us supernatural things and does not know us in the least. In truth we are human beings like the Earth human being, too, but our knowledge and wisdom are superior to his, as well as our technology. [134]
>
> [134]Eduard Billy Meier, *Message from the Pleiades: The Contact Notes of Eduard Billy Meier*, ed. W. C. Stevens, 4 vols. (Tucson, AZ: privately published, 1988), vol. 1, p. 36.

In another meeting Semjase's father, Ptaah, elucidated their society's primary concern with the people of earth, who are enthralled by the lies and deceit of the Nephilim:

> [As] soon as the Earth human becomes master of the technologies for space-drive and travels to strange worlds, and brings them by power of his weapons or lies or deceit under his control, so also will he include in his doing, the crazy spread of his religion to his conquests, and the existing universal harmony will be destroyed. This means that the still guaranteed peace would be destroyed by your religions and degenerate to murderous wars and great destruction.

And just to prevent this occurrence is a great and difficult mission for spiritually developed space-traveling forms of life.[135]

[135] **Meier**, *Message from the Pleiades*, vol. 1, p. 320.

Semjase also told Meier that earth would enter the Age of Aquarius in 2028 after a 184-year transitional period. You no doubt remember that we began this chapter with the fact that December 2020 brought a great conjunction and seemingly ushered this planet into the new age. Does that mean Semjase's prediction was wrong, or ours? Neither. It simply means that the Atlanteans likely have a different way of calculating this transition. Foreseeing the future, as the Atlanteans seemingly are able to do, and in keeping with the past transitory events between ages, perhaps 2028 shall be the year of a cosmic calamity to befall the earth.

A simple calculation of this transitional period yields a beginning year of 1844, the year Joseph Smith, founding prophet of Mormonism, was assassinated during his presidential campaign. It is no coincidence the Mormon tradition holds that "God" and his angels are human beings from other worlds guiding terrestrial affairs. It is also no coincidence the Mormon church was targeted for infiltration almost immediately, with a top-level Mormon leader publicizing his suspicion of said infiltration in an internal document that eventually made its way to the public in 1991.[136]

[136] **Glenn L. Pace**, "Ritualistic Child Abuse," memorandum to the Strengthening Church Members Committee, July 19, 1990.

While many of the messages abductees receive are ominous, in every account people describe the Nordic "aliens" as very kind, benevolent, and long lived—up to 800 to 1,000 years, as in biblical times. They can communicate verbally and telepathically, and convey a sense of well-being to those around them.

Military Concerns

Since the dawn of nuclear weapons, UFO sightings around military bases, and particularly nuclear weapons facilities, have been on the rise.[137] As you might expect, they are appraising earth's weapons capabilities and how the Nephilim hope to guard against the Atlanteans' imminent return. Luis Elizondo, who led the Advanced Aerospace Threat Identification Program for the Pentagon, has reported instances of UFOs taking complete control of the systems in command of nuclear warheads, switching them

[137] **Robert L. Hastings**, "UFO Sightings at ICBM sites and Nuclear Weapons Storage Areas," NICAP.org, 2006, http://www.nicap.org/babylon/missile_incidents.htm

[138] **Henry Holloway**, "Ashes to Ashes: UFOs 'Shut Down 10 Nuke Missiles at US Base and May Have Been Alerted to Humanity by First Atomic Bomb Blasts," The U.S. Sun, June 21, 2021, https://www.the-sun.com/news/3125848/ufos-shut-down-nukes-us-base/;

[138] Ex-Air Force Personnel: UFOs Deactivated Nukes," *CBS News*, September 28, 2010, https://www.cbsnews.com/news/ex-air-force-personnel-ufos-deactivated-nukes/

on and off at will, with operators helpless to do anything against them. [138] In many accounts of alien encounters, the Atlanteans warn humans about nuclear weapons—they are worried the Nephilim will wage a nuclear war and turn earth into a wasteland. In an account captured in The Hair of the Alien, one abductee says,

> Strange visions flooded my head, visions of cities, some of which I recognized from my travels—but, cities which were half-destroyed, the buildings having their tops blown away, with windows like empty eye-sockets in a human skull. I saw these visions again and again. All the buildings that I saw were half-drowned in a reddish, muddish water. It was as if there had been a flood and the buildings were sticking up out of this great flood, partly destroyed by a disaster of some kind, and it was a terrible sight. [139]

[139] Whitley Strieber quoted in Bill Chalker, *Hair of the Alien* (New York City: Paraview Pocket Books, 2005), 158.

[140] Sean Christie, "Remembering Zimbabwe's Great Alien Invasion," *Mail & Guardian*, September 4, 2014, https://mg.co.za/article/2014-09-04-remembering-zimbabwes-great-alien-invasion/

Another warning came in broad daylight to a group of children at Ariel School in Zimbabwe, where aliens told the children that humans are taking science and technology down a path that will end in disaster for humanity. [140]

CHRISTIANITY CORRUPTED

During the time when the various councils, such as those of Nicaea and Trent, compiled the Bible, certain texts were discussed and discarded from the canon, though many of the early church fathers had long referenced them. Most versions of the Judeo-Christian Bible ultimately omitted the Book of Enoch and kept the Epistle of Jude, although the Ethiopian Orthodox Bible kept Enoch despite the controversy. Jude was likewise a source of contention, because it clearly identifies the Nephilim, who want to keep hidden their identity, their history, and the nature of their wicked plans.

According to the Epistle of Jude,

> For certain individuals whose condemnation was written about long ago have secretly slipped in among you. They are ungodly people, who pervert the grace of our God into a license for immorality and deny Jesus Christ our only Sovereign and Lord…
>
> Enoch, the seventh from Adam, prophesied about them: "See, the Lord is coming with thousands upon thousands of his holy ones to judge everyone, and to convict all of them of all the ungodly acts they have committed in their ungodliness, and of all the defiant words ungodly sinners have spoken against him." These people are grumblers and faultfinders; they follow their own evil desires; they boast about themselves and flatter others for their own advantage.[141]
>
> [141]Jude 1:4, 14–16 (NIV).

The reference to Enoch makes clear exactly who these ungodly people are: Nephilim, who had infiltrated Christianity, causing Jude to warn one of the seven ancient Christian churches against their corrupting influence. Because the Nephilim had already made their way into the ranks, they worked to strike the writings of Jude and Enoch from the Bible.

Elsewhere in Jude he condemns the Nephilim for falling into Balaam's error. But what was that error? The answer is found in 2 Peter 2:15, where Balaam is said to have loved "the wages of unrighteousness"—that is, letting material gain override his conscience, choosing sin and money over right action, as so many in service to the Nephilim today have themselves chosen.

Jude admonishes the faithful to take a nonviolent path while waiting for salvation from the evil forces of the world, for help will come from on high:

> But you, dear friends, by building yourselves up in your most holy faith and praying in the Holy Spirit, keep yourselves in God's love as you wait for the mercy of our Lord Jesus Christ to bring you to eternal life...

> To him who is able to keep you from stumbling and to present you before his glorious presence without fault and with great joy—to the only God our Savior be glory, majesty, power and authority, through Jesus Christ our Lord, before all ages, now and forevermore! [142]

[142] Jude 1:20–21, 24–25 (NIV).

You would do well to follow Jude's admonition and not take vengeance into your own hands. Your knowledge of these affairs is far less than perfect, and you will be more apt to take on the burden of sin, thus depriving yourself of the opportunity to experience the kingdom that is to come.

ALPHA
AND OMEGA

If you properly decode the Book of Revelation, it becomes clear that humanity is in the end times, awaiting the same fiery destruction and rebirth foretold in the Hindu scriptures, as you shall see. The book contains a history of the Israelite experience, going all the way back to the War in Heaven.

The woman riding a reptilian beast is an allegory for Babylon and the Ishtar priesstesshood, which practiced sacred prostitution and used sex as a sacrament. They worked closely with "the kings of the earth, who have committed fornication and lived deliciously with her,"[143] producing many children for the Nephilim kings to ritually slaughter. Babylon was equated with this biblical beast, and serpents are ubiquitous throughout myth—including Typhon, slain by Zeus, and Python, slain by Zeus's son Apollo, in the Greek traditions, as well as the Mesopotamian tradition's drag-on-like creature Tiamat, who was splayed by Marduk, son of Enki, to form the sky with one half and earth with the other. After the Babylonian enslavement, the book describes the destruction of the first and second temples and the chronology of the Hebrew experience.

[143] Revelation 18:9 (KJV).

Then Jesus arrived in the Second Coming, the man on the white horse whom everyone had awaited. However, the man on the white horse was not Jesus but rather a man named Simon bar Kokhba, who led a revolt against the Roman empire. To this day, he is depicted riding a white steed.

Revelation says the man on the white horse will fight with a sword that proceeds out of his mouth, and, in fact, bar Kokbha was an effective demagogue who could whip people into a violent frenzy with his grandiloquence. Jewish authorities of the time officially proclaimed bar Kokhba to be the Messiah, but when he lost the rebellion against Rome, they reversed their proclamation. Many people are still waiting for the man on the white horse, but they are 2,000 years too late—that man was, in fact, bar Kokhba, who has already come and gone.

According to Revelation, while the rider on the white horse slays an enemy remnant, angels bind Satan for a thousand years, during which time, humans will enjoy Christ's reign. Upon the expiration of that period, Satan shall be loosed out of his prison for the next 1,000 years, in keeping with the laws of universal harmony and balance. Everything has its equal and opposite: for the first thousand years of Christianity, the soul of Satan—Cronus himself—was imprisoned and could not incarnate. For the last thousand years, however, he has regained that ability and transformed the world into the one you see today, full of fear, greed, and ignorance.

The combined 2,000 years represent the Age of Pisces. The first fish in the sign of Pisces is the Christian fish, representing the first thousand years, and the second fish is its inversion, a symbol of anti-Christianity representing the present time when Satan has been free. With the great conjunction of 2020, we have begun the transition: from the end of the Age of Pisces's anti-Christian era to the Age of Aquarius and all that this entails.

Know you not, Seeker of Truth, that inverting a symbol has always been associated with assigning an opposite meaning? Flying the flag of a country upside down signals that country is in distress, destroyed, or being taken over. The pentagram, or five-pointed star, with a single point upward serves as a symbol of light and protection, whereas Satanists invert the point, facing it downward to summon evil.

The Watchers have thrived on taking everything good and inverting it, a manifestation of the cosmic duality.

The Seven Seals

The author of the Book of Revelation received a vision of God and his seven archangels holding a book sealed with seven seals that no one could open. Only the Lamb that looked as if it had been slain had strength enough to open the seals, and the first one unleashed a different rider on a white horse: "Behold a white horse: and he that sat on him had a bow; and a crown was given unto him: and he went forth conquering, and to conquer." [144] You may have heard various interpretations from your religious leaders, but here is the truth: that rider is Kalki, the final incarnation of the Hindu god Vishnu, going out to conquer the vile Nephilim. Of Kalki you shall hear more in the coming pages.

[144] Revelation 6:2 (KJV).

The second seal unleashed war, as has happened in Ukraine and will likely happen in Taiwan as tensions between China and the rest of the world over its most advanced silicon chip manufacturer continue rising.

The third seal unleashed famine:

> And when he had opened the third seal, I heard the third beast say, Come and see. And I beheld, and lo a black horse; and he that sat on him had a pair of balances in his hand. And I heard a voice in the midst of the four beasts say, A measure of wheat for a penny, and three measures of barley for a penny; and see thou hurt not the oil and the wine. [145]
>
> [145] Revelation 6:5–6 (KJV).

As you may be aware, this famine has begun in the world today, due not to environmental but rather to economic factors, such as inflation and supply chain issues, which were intentionally induced by the ruling class in your governments. The Nephilim are trying to cause a famine, because historically, starvation has been the most effective way of killing millions upon millions of people.

Current political and economic policies across the globe continue to exacerbate supply chain disruptions. Container ships cannot unload their wares and are sitting out at sea for months at a time, causing food to spoil. Your governments even pay farmers to not grow food. The truth is clear: there is enough food to feed the populations of earth, but the ruling class has implemented a deliberate destruction of the trade and distribution systems to ensure that food never reaches the hungry, including the destruction of the currency most used in international trade: the US dollar. [146]

[146] H. Claire Brown, "The Biden Administration Will Pay Farmers More Money Not to Farm," *The Counter*, April 22, 2021, https://thecounter.org/biden-administration-farmers-conservation-reserve-crp-usda-vilsack/

If you understand how central banks work, you will see that every hyperinflation that has ever occurred was deliberate. In each case, the government intentionally destroyed the currency, as in Zimbabwe, Venezuela, Argentina, the Weimar Republic, and Bolivia. There have been dozens of hyperinflations all around the world just in the last century, and if such acts were not intentional, they would represent an unfathomable level of incompetence.

The Carrington Event

Noting the real man on the white horse and the Christian and anti-Christian periods of the Age of Pisces, it is clear you are much farther in the events described in the Book of Revelation than many priests or religious leaders have taught. You are, in fact, nearing the very end:

And when the thousand years are expired, Satan shall be loosed out of his prison. And shall go out to deceive the nations which are in the four quarters of the earth, Gog and Magog, to gather them together to battle: the number of whom is as the sand of the sea. [147]

[147]Revelation 20:7–8 (KJV).

As you may have already guessed, Satan is the Judeo-Christian word for Cronus, just as the designation LORD is synonymous with King Atlas, and by now the number of Satan's followers is so vast that it cannot be counted, much like the sand of the sea.

Revelation says this immense army "went up on the breadth of the earth, and compassed the camp of the saints about, and the beloved city: and fire came down from God out of heaven, and devoured them." [148] Where is this camp of the saints, the beloved city, and how many righteous are gathered there? Are they two separate places, or one going by two names? That information is yet to be revealed, but you can know that in the future, the Nephilim-led corrupt governments will seek to destroy all the righteous who are gathered there.

[148]Revelation 20:9 (KJV).

Before they succeed, however, God will bring fire from heaven in the form of a Carrington event, akin to a geomagnetic hurricane, and wipe out all of the evildoers. Humans have long monitored solar weather, and the original such event in 1859, witnessed by solar observer Richard Carrington, was the most intense geomagnetic storm in recorded history. Auroras swept through the atmosphere as far south as the tropics, sparking fires in telegraph stations worldwide. This coming coronal mass ejection will disrupt the magnetic field of the planet and induce electric surges in all circuitry across the planet, destroying your technology completely.

The sun follows a sunspot cycle of eleven years from trough to trough with peaks in between, and it is now entering the twenty-fifth cycle since humans started monitoring it, a cycle that will peak in 2025. Solar cycle twenty-five was originally forecast to be less intense than cycle twenty-four, but thus far it is proving to be considerably more intense than predicted—causing forecasters to update their estimates to state that this cycle could be one of the strongest on record. [149] Geomagnetic storms are already occurring, including one that knocked forty of Elon Musk's Starlink satellites out of orbit—satellites that have

[149]Scott W. McIntosh et al., "Overlapping Magnetic Activity Cycles and the Sunspot Number: Forecasting Sunspot Cycle 25 Amplitude," *Solar Physics* 295 (2020), https://link.springer.com/article/10.1007/s11207-020-01723-y/

already crashed back to earth or will do so in the future. Forecasters recognize the chances of another Carrington event are rising by the day. [150] Indeed, in 2012 the earth was narrowly missed by just such an event. [151]

Here is an unfortunate truth that you must now understand, a truth that may affect you even if you are not one of the vile Nephilim or their followers: the COVID vaccine recently introduced and even mandated by your governments is not all that it seems. Some of those syringes contained particles called graphene that can be seen under a microscope spontaneously assembling into nanomachines in drops of blood. [152] Anyone who has been injected with this nanomachinery will die instantly when the Carrington event comes to pass, for the electromagnetic waves will do to people what it did to telegraph machines over 150 years ago. [153] Likewise for those who, in the near future, may voluntarily receive a chip implant in their brain: the perceived convenience of this human-machine interface will be their undoing at the Carrington event.

Alas, if you have received a vaccine containing graphene, your body will be lost, but do not despair, for you can still save what is most important—your soul—by walking the Path of Righteousness as shall be described in Book IV. Master your fear, educate yourself, and become wise, strong, and independent. When the time comes, you may die with dignity, and your soul may yet be saved if it is found worthy.

Despite the power of this Carrington event, some Nephilim will nonetheless survive, because they have not allowed themselves to be injected with graphene and have shielded much of their military equipment against such things, which is why Kalki must come. The Atlanteans will return at this point to carry out the elimination of the remaining Nephilim.

[150] "Starship Update," SpaceX, February 10, 2022, https://www.spacex.com/updates/

[151] "Near Miss: The Solar Superstorm of July 2012," NASA, July 23, 2014, https://science.nasa.gov/science-news/science-at-nasa/2014/23jul_superstorm

[152] Franco Giovannini, Riccardo Benzi Cipelli, and Gianpaolo Pisano, "Dark-Field Microscopic Analysis on the Blood of 1,006 Symptomatic Persons after Anti-COVID mRNA Injections from Pfizer/BioNtech or Moderna," International Journal of Vaccine Theory, Practice, and Research 2, no. 2 (2022): 385–443; Young Mi Lee, Sunyoung Park, and Ki-Yeob Jeon, Foreign Materials in Blood Samples of Recipients of COVID-19 Vaccines," International Journal of Vaccine Theory, Practice, and Research 2, no. 1 (2022): 249–265; Mark Playne, New—Dr Campra Proves Graphene Oxide in COVID Vaccines," NOTB, November 8, 2021, https://www.notonthebeeb.co.uk/post/breaking-dr-campra-proves-graphene-in-vaccine

[153] Maryam Henein, "Welcome to the 4th Industrial Transhumanist IOB Graphene Nanobot Revolution," Activist Post, January 28, 2022, https://www.activistpost.com/2022/01/welcome-to-the-4th-industrial-transhumanist-iob-graphene-nanobot-revolution.html

Kalki Cometh

To understand what the Atlanteans' return and the dawn of the Age of Aquarius will mean for life on earth, look to the many apocalyptic predictions. Two such prophecies come from Hindu scripture. The first is the *Vishnu Purāna*, a holy book devoted to the great god Vishnu. The scripture says his final incarnation is Kalki:

> By his irresistible might he [Kalki] will destroy all the Mlechchhas and thieves, and all whose minds are devoted to iniquity. He will, then, re-establish righteousness upon earth; and the minds of those who live at the end of the Kali age shall be awakened, and shall be as pellucid as crystal. The men who are, thus, changed by virtue of that peculiar time shall be as the seeds of human beings, and shall give birth to a race who shall follow the laws of the Krita age (or age of purity). As it is said: "When the sun and moon, and (the lunar asterism) Tishya, and the planet Jupiter are in one mansion, the Krita age shall return." [154]
>
> [154]**Vishnu Purāna**, Book IV, Chapter XXIV.

Just as the Greeks have four cycles of ages—Golden, Silver, Bronze, and Iron—the Hindus also have four. They mirror each other perfectly, which is no accident. The Kali Age mentioned in the *Vishnu Purāna* is the Iron Age, and the great conjunction has signaled the time of coming destruction that ends this age and ushers in the next. Like those mentioned in the *Vishnu Purāna*, Noah, too, was referred to as the seed of mankind, from whom the world was repopulated after the flood. The passage indicates that at the end of the Kali/Iron Age, there will be a mass depopulation event—this incarnation of Vishnu, Kalki, will kill evildoers around the world. However, survivors will repopulate the planet, and the age of purity will be the new Age of Aquarius.

Another Hindu prophecy comes from the *Matsya Purāna*:

> At the close of the Kaliyuga (the present iron age), there will be the Kalki manifestation, in the house of Vishnuyasa, and the sage, Parasarya Vyasa will be the officiating priest. This will be the tenth incarnation, and Yajnyavalkya will make his appearance before this coming manifestation. This incarnation will destroy all the wicked ones and the hypocrites; and, with a large army of the Brahmanas, He will kill Sudra Kings and drive away all hypocrisy. After killing the enemies of Brahmanas and other enemies, He will march on with

His army in the 28th of the Kaliyuga, and then, after purifying the Sudras, will cross the ocean, where He will destroy the sinful mixed castes and, thus fulfilling His mission, He will educate his peoples...

Afterwards, the people, by becoming enraged and deluded with each other, will kill each other to fulfil the future destiny. When, in process of time, the incarnation of Kalki will vanish, then the future kings will be destroyed, through the rebellion of their subjects. The people, not finding any one as their protector, will fight amongst themselves, and will then land themselves in great troubles after killing one another. All cities and villages will be devastated, and the duties of castes and the stages of life will disappear...

Being thus tormented with myriads of troubles and difficulties, all the population will become annihilated along with the end of the Kali-yuga. Satyayuga (the Age of Truth) will follow on the heels of the disappearing Kaliyuga. [155]

[155]**Matsya Purāna**, Chapter XLVII.

This represents a fearsome prediction for the people of India, who—after Kalki destroys all of the major ruling governments of the world—will be left with corrupt and incompetent local governments, without the support of the larger state. Revolts, rebellions, and uprisings will ensue, making life extremely difficult in that particular region of the world.

Despite the grave nature of the future quickly descending upon you, do not despair, Seeker of Truth. The size and power of the Nephilim armies in any corner of the globe matter not to Kalki. You need not worry, for they are no match for his forces, the vanguard of the Atlanteans, who will not coexist with Nephilim. The apocalyptic prophecies make clear the Atlanteans will return to vindicate righteousness on earth, and though the Nephilim accelerate their harmful plans, they stand no chance.

The Second Death

According to the Book of Revelation, in the coming transformation,

the fearful, and unbelieving, and the abominable, and murderers, and whoremongers, and sorcerers, and idolaters, and all liars, shall have their part in the lake which burneth with fire and brimstone: which is the second death. [156]

[156]**Revelation**, 21:8 (KJV).

The concept of a second death may seem unusual to you, but it is quite normal in other cultures, including that of Mesoamerica. The death of your body is different from the death of your soul, which is an immortal, self-contained entity that can be destroyed by the lake of fire described in the Book of Revelation.

Christians debate about what the second death means, but annihilationists believe the second death is the death of the soul—the absolute annihilation of souls that are completely beyond redemption, plunging them into nonexistence for the rest of eternity.

Understand this: being of the E-M81 haplogroup does not automatically make you evil and destined for the second death, as Zeus himself belongs to this group. Likewise, not being E-M81 does not guarantee salvation. There is no simple formula, only righteousness, and for this reason Book IV will explore the path to that righteousness.

The fallen Watchers have incarnated and reincarnated again and again, over the tens of thousands of years, corrupting humanity with each new life. They have recruited people from amongst other bloodlines to help them. Thus, not everyone from the E-M81 bloodline will die but rather the unrighteous—the souls with the qualities identified in the preceding quote from the Book of Revelation.

Yet even these can be saved, for "God" makes it very clear to Enoch that the fallen Watchers can redeem themselves and ascend to heaven—if they abandon the evil ways leading them and everyone who follows them into sin.

Some Nephilim have reformed to live in harmony with universal law, while some descendants of Adam have gone astray, as the God of Enoch said they would. As Jesus says in Matthew 18:3, "Verily I say unto you, Except ye be converted, and become as little children, ye shall not enter into the kingdom of heaven." This is a truth of the utmost importance, worthy of repeating: it is not our bloodline but the quality of our souls that shields us from the second death.

Elsewhere in the Book of Matthew, Jesus tells a parable and then explains its meaning: "He that soweth the good seed is the Son of man," referring to someone who teaches righteousness, and "the field is the world; the good seed are the children of the kingdom; but the tares are the children of the wicked one," referring to Cronus and his followers.

It continues:

The enemy that sowed them is the devil; the harvest is the end of the world; and the reapers are the angels. As therefore the tares are gathered and burned in the fire; so shall it be in the end of this world. The Son of man shall send forth his angels, and they shall gather out of his kingdom all things that offend, and them which do iniquity; And shall cast them into a furnace of fire: there shall be wailing and gnashing of teeth. [157]

[157] **Matthew**, 13:37–42 (KJV).

Seeker of Truth, does not your experience tell you that we are at the end of the world and that the harvest is nigh? The reapers are the soldiers of Kalki, ready to ensure that all of the wicked evildoers who do not die in the geomagnetic storm will still receive justice. Everyone whose soul must be annihilated shall thus be annihilated, because the Atlanteans cannot abide by the continued incarnation of the Nephilim and their supporters causing havoc in the New Age.

To make it through this coming storm, you must be emotionally and spiritually prepared to endure, as put forth in the Book of Zechariah:

And it shall come to pass, that in all the land, saith the LORD, two parts therein shall be cut off and die; but the third shall be left therein. And I will bring the third part through the fire, and will refine them as silver is refined, and will try them as gold is tried: they shall call on my name, and I will hear them: I will say, It is my people: and they shall say, The LORD is my God. [158]

[158] **Zechariah**, 13:8–9 (KJV).

Zechariah prophesies that two-thirds of humanity will die in that final Armageddon. Though the righteous will be in the third that survives, they will be tested physically, spiritually, and mentally as they live through the horrific Carrington event and following tribulation.

Both Matthew and Zechariah directly connect to the Book of Revelation, where the beast and all of his followers will be gathered up and thrown into the lake of fire. All religious traditions point to the same time and predict this same harvest of humanity. They also speak of "God" returning to earth to establish his kingdom. Now you must understand that these prophecies refer to the king of the Atlanteans, returning with an interstellar fleet to hand down their final judgment of the Nephilim and all they have created.

Nephilim at the highest levels of power today will not be known to you, for those shadow rulers keep themselves very well hidden. Identifying them is not your concern, as you must focus on your own salvation. Remember: neither their genes nor yours will determine whether one is annihilated in the lake of fire, but rather how one lives day to day.

ENOCH'S REVELATION

We return, then, to the Book of Enoch, whose revelation is not a prophecy per se but rather a source of hope.

Enoch divided the history and the future of the world into periods of time called weeks, though they were not the strict intervals of seven days to which you are accustomed.

The ninth and penultimate week captures the current age, the Age of Aquarius into which we have now entered:

> And after that in the ninth week the righteous judgment will be revealed to the whole world, and all the works of the godless will vanish from the whole earth, and the world will be written down for destruction, and all mankind will look to the path of uprightness. And after this, in the tenth week in the seventh part, there will be the great eternal judgment, in which He will execute vengeance amongst the angels. And the first heaven will depart and pass away, and a new heaven will appear, and all the powers of the heavens will shine sevenfold for ever. And after that there will be many weeks without number for ever in goodness and righteousness, and sin will no more be mentioned for ever. [159]
>
> [159] Book of Enoch 91:14–17.

There will be a changing of the guard, restoring the righteous and advanced Atlanteans in the place of the Nephilim. For now, you await the judgment of the whole world as described, and all the works of the godless—their science and technology wreaking havoc that they attempt to disguise as good—will vanish in this fiery coronal ejection. For human technology rests upon the electromagnetic force, which is extremely limited as compared to that used by the Atlanteans, of which you will learn much in Book II. So while the coming Carrington event will destroy your devices and circuitry, the Atlanteans' creations will endure. When they return, they will instate true technology.

Enoch provides guidance regarding what you should do personally, given the coming apocalypse, as he realized his readers could be discouraged:

> Be hopeful; for aforetime ye were put to shame through ill and affliction; but now ye shall shine as the lights of heaven, ye shall shine and ye shall be seen, and the portals of heaven shall be opened to you. And in your cry, cry for judgement, and it shall appear to you; for all your tribulation shall be visited on the rulers, and on all who helped those who plundered you. Be hopeful, and cast not away your hopes for ye shall have great joy as the angels of heaven.
>
> What shall ye be obliged to do? Ye shall not have to hide on the day of the great judgement and ye shall not be found as sinners, and the eternal judgement shall be far from you for all the generations of the world. And now fear not, ye righteous, when ye see the sinners growing strong and prospering in their ways: be not companions with them, but keep afar from their violence; for ye shall become companions of the hosts of heaven. [160]
>
> [160] Book of Enoch 6:4–7.

Yes, much evil and many dreadful experiences have befallen individuals and the world, yet Enoch says, "I swear unto you, that in heaven the angels remember you for good before the glory of the Great One: and your names are written before the glory of the Great One," meaning if you are righteous, your name is on the list of people who will be saved. [161]

[161] Book of Enoch 6:1.

Enoch also had a message for the Nephilim:

> And, although ye sinners say: "All our sins shall not be searched out and be written down," nevertheless they shall write down all your sins every day. And now I show unto you that light and darkness, day and night, see all your sins. [162]
>
> [162] Book of Enoch 6:8.

The righteous should hold hope—the time of the wicked has come to an end. Enoch speaks of a book that will guide the righteous and help them maintain their hope:

> I know another mystery; that books will be given to the righteous and the wise to become a cause of joy and uprightness and much wisdom. And to them shall the books be given, and they shall believe in them and rejoice over them, and then shall all the righteous who have learnt therefrom all the paths of uprightness be recompensed. [163]
>
> [163] Book of Enoch 6:13.

Thus hear ye, Seekers of Truth: though evil abounds at the end of the passing age, do not take justice into your own hands. Go not killing people or separating the worthy from those who will enter the lake of fire. Wait for the New Age to dawn, as this is not your fight but rather a 14,000-year-old dispute between Atlas and Cronus that is reaching its destined conclusion.

Make yourself worthy of the world that is coming: "Be hopeful; for ... ye shall shine as the lights of heaven." Even if your body is destroyed, your soul can persist. The Atlanteans will usher in the New Age through their own works and make the change you want to see in the world, so long as you do not get in their way. Do not participate in violence, for in doing so, you only bring sin upon yourself and jeopardize your own salvation.

Be informed of your hidden history and know what is coming, for all these things must come to pass. Find a safe harbor, work on yourself, keep yourself and those around you away from sin, and when the time comes, you will be spared. Be neither discouraged nor spurred to violence but rather go inward and tend your spirit. Fear not: all that is to come is according to plan. You are living through the dramatic finish of the last age.

As you have learned, this is not the first Age of Aquarius—there have been innumerable ages of Aquarius since the solar system formed. The universe follows a great wheel, of which you are a part. You are more than flesh and memories. You are meant to master the divine quaternity and to become godlike yourself. Take hope and be not afraid.

BOOK II
THE DIVINE QUATERNITY

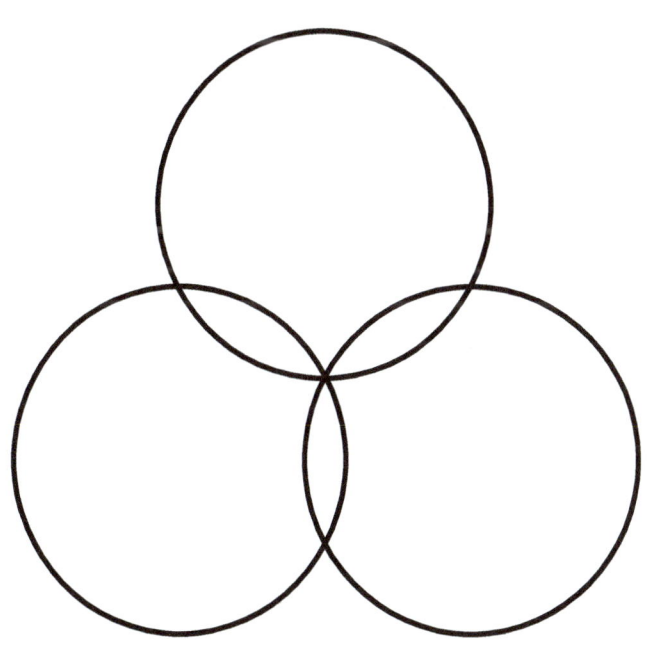

CHAPTER 7
INFINITY

After reading Book I, you may feel confused or untethered. Where can one find spiritual resonance if all of the world's religions are no more than cargo cults formed around humans with seemingly unfathomable knowledge and abilities? Many humans are wedded to their cultural myths—they believe if something is in the Bible, the Qur'an, or another holy text, it must be true. Based on the history you have now learned, however, you must see that while aspects of those texts are correct, much has been corrupted or omitted. They are not infallible.

As you are now well aware, the Atlanteans possessed technological and spiritual superiority, and they spent a great deal of effort teaching Enoch during his time in Atlantis. As you also know, this man was known to others as Hermes, the author of the *Corpus Hermeticum* and *Asclepius*, wherein Hermes attempts to explain these lessons to his primitive contemporaries. In the following pages, we shall revisit those teachings with modern scientific understanding, resulting in a framework that you can integrate and understand.

Hermes gives direct credit for his knowledge to a godlike entity called Agathos Daimon, perhaps the Greek analogue for Uriel or the Atlantean King, and laments that

> if he had set this forth in writing, he would have greatly helped the race of men, for he alone, my son, as the first-born god, looking down upon all things, truly spoke divine words. I once heard him say that all is one, and especially spiritual beings; that we live in power, in energy and in eternity; and that the Nous of this One is supremely good and also is its very soul. This being so, there is no separation among spiritual beings. Since it rules all things and is the soul of God, Nous is able to do just as it wills. [164]

[164] **Hermes Trismegistus** "The Corpus Hermeticum," in *The Way of Hermes: New Translations of "The Corpus Hermeticum" and "The Definitions of Hermes Trismegistus to Asclepius,"* Clement Salaman, Dorine van Oyen, William D Wharton, and Jean-Pierre Mahé (Rocester, VT: Inner Traditions, 2000), 60.

Here, *Nous* is the Greek term for the essence of God but also the human soul. Hermes clarifies that "in men this Nous is God; thus some men are gods, and then humanity is akin to divinity; in fact, Agathos Daimon called gods immortal men, and men mortal gods. But in irrational creatures there is just nature." [165] Unlike animals, human beings possess a soul, which contains within it *Nous*, which is born from the Word of God.

[165] Hermes Trismegistus, *Corpus Hermeticum*, 58.

In this book, you shall learn what you are, what the universe is, why you exist, and what existence means at all. Contemporary human science and Atlantean wisdom help answer these questions, and this book shall offer you a unified model of the universe.

Here is the essence of what follows in Book II: the universe is a four-dimensional experience constructed of four fundamental elements—Infinity, Eternity, Mind, and Matter. Together, they form the Divine Quaternity—the summation of how God's creation works. A pattern repeats in the following chapters: for every part of the quaternity, there is a dualism and a manifestation of that duality, a manifestation you can see with your own eyes.

The cosmic framework is such that these four elements occur dualistically, in a pair. They must, because everything in the universe has its opposite. That dualism happens on multiple levels everywhere, down to the very fabric of the universe you inhabit.

THE VOID
AND SINGULARITY

[166] Joseph W. Dauben, "Georg Cantor and the Battle for Transfinite Set Theory," in *Proceedings of the 9th ACMS Conference* (Santa Barbara, CA: Westmont College, 1993), 1–22. Internet version published in Journal of the ACMS 2004. https://acmsonline.org/home2/wp-content/uploads/2016/05/Dauben-Cantor.pdf

[167] "Cantor's Infinity Paradox: Set Theory," YouTube video posted by Up and Atom, October 26, 2018, https://www.youtube.com/watch?v=X56zst79Xjg

More than a century ago, the German mathematician Georg Cantor made a ground-breaking discovery: there is more than one kind of infinity, in countable and uncountable forms. When Cantor began this discussion, he caused a sensation in religious circles because they saw him as endangering their concept of God—a view Cantor himself no doubt encouraged by his claim that this knowledge came to him by divine revelation. [166] The religious authorities of the time had taken the domain of the infinite for themselves, and then Cantor encroached upon their territory, explaining the infinite better than they ever had. [167]

According to Cantor,

The fear of infinity is a form of myopia that destroys the possibility of seeing the actual infinite, even though it in its highest form has created and sustains us, and in its secondary transfinite forms occurs all around us and even inhabits our minds. [168]

[168] Georg Cantor, "Über die verschiedenen Standpunkte in bezug auf das aktuelle Unendliche," ("Concerning Various Perspectives on the Actual Infinite"), (A letter written to Cardinal Johannes Franzelin on November 4, 1885), *Zeitschrift für Philosophie und Philosophische Kritik*, Volume 88, pp. 224–233. Published in 1886.

An understanding of Infinity begins when you realize how opposites are the same—void and singularity are two forms of Infinity. This is a mind-bending concept rooted in paradox, which is why most humans avoid thinking about it. By way of example, could you tell the difference between being in an environment of infinite density, a singularity, and an environment of zero density, a void—the empty space of the universe in which you find yourself? What about the difference between the number of countable integers—0, 1, 2, 3, 4, 5, 6, and so on—or the number of real numerals between zero and one, which include decimals?

There are multiple kinds of Infinity—big and small, countable and innumerable. The integers from zero to infinity form a countable infinity. From zero to one in real numbers is uncountable, because you cannot even count the next number after zero—it is an infinite number of zeros with a one after it. Infinitely big to infinitely small—at these extremes, Infinity loops back around, comes together, and is ultimately one and the same. [169]

[169] "A Hierarchy of Infinities," YouTube video posted by PBS Infinite Series, December 8, 2016, https://www. youtube.com/watch?v=i7c2qz7sOOI

You must reconcile that paradox in your own mind, for there is no magic word that will make you see the truth. You must read, ponder, and take the time to grapple with these concepts: the largest and the smallest, void and singularity, are not the opposites they seem to be. They are in fact the same, one leading into the other and back again, just like the ouroboros—the snake eating its own tail—which represents the ancient alchemical concept of something with no end. Carl Jung held up this symbol as a perfect encapsulation of his conception of the psyche. The universe began in a paradox, and the mind and consciousness continue to enact that paradox of the largest and the smallest, where Infinity at its extremes bends back onto itself.

And here is the great truth behind this dualism: when you plot a graph on horizontal and vertical axes, those axes have positive and negative sides—two halves of the same lines. In like manner, the void of your universe extends into an anti-verse that is a singularity, and therein lies the foundation of the Atlantean technology of which we have spoken. This dualism of Infinity is behind their ability to communicate telepathically, to appear and disappear seemingly at will, and to move their ships in seemingly impossible maneuvers—they can manipulate the fabric of reality at its most fundamental level.

They understood and harnessed the dualism of Infinity, and so can you. And in so doing, you will find that telepathy, unlimited clean energy, and instantaneous travel to anywhere in the universe are real and accessible. The horrific judgment of the Nephilim is coming because life on earth has become bleak in the material realm, but these positive abilities also exist and always have. These are the keys to salvation. In understanding them, you can transcend the constraints put upon you by your parents, teachers, and government.

CHAOS AND
WHITE LIGHT

Infinity could also be defined as chaos, as it is a source of pure randomness. That concept is important both in mathematical theory and concretely in the universe. If you have a source of pure randomness or pure chaos, then everything happens simultaneously, without constraint.

At the very beginning, in the time before the Big Bang, was this a universe of darkness, or a universe of disordered white light? Is there a difference? Is there a beginning or an end to all that is?

The infinite dimension manifests as pure white light—full-spectrum electromagnetic radiation—which is chaos. The electromagnetic spectrum is on a continuum from zero to infinity, an infinity unto itself. Nothing but white light gave rise to the universe, and white light is the manifested experience of infinity, how it appears in your reality, for white light is pure randomness.

Out of a purely chaotic source, you can make anything, because everything exists within it all the time. If you stare at white noise upon your TV screen for long enough, by pure accident a coherent picture will emerge from the random static. Sometimes more than one frame in a certain time span, maybe an entire movie, or a mashup of frames from every movie, in every possible order. From a source of pure randomness, you will eventually generate everything that is or will ever be. The paradox is that, though it looks completely disordered most of the time, at rare moments something snaps into focus and appears highly ordered.

From the static, a triangle might come into view and then recede into the randomness again. Then a circle could appear before disappearing. Infinity is this white noise, and the universe you experience is the triangle or the circle—the moment of infinite chaos ordered by constraints, or what you experience as reality.

Human experience represents a very small segment of the infinite, as you will find in the chapter on Mind. Everything that could ever exist is in Infinity, but it exists in complete disorder, without causality. There is no physics, no up or down, no backward or forward—nothing but random energy flying in all directions, everywhere, all at once.

That said, the random, chaotic, all-encompassing infinite is the first ingredient to make a universe.

Understanding the infinite will allow you to have a deeper comprehension of both the universe and, ultimately, yourself, because everyone is a part of this universe, made of these same elements. On a cosmic scale, Infinity is the pantheistic God who is all things. On an individual scale, you are also the infinite—it is the source of your soul, a copy of God. God's body is the whole universe, while yours is confined to your limbs, head, and torso, but you are cut from the same cosmic cloth. The soul is a piece of Infinity.

Light is another manifestation of the electromagnetic force. A photon is just a ripple in the electromagnetic field, traveling through and hitting your eye. If you pound your fist on a table, the force that makes the sound and the table that you feel under your hand are also the electromagnetic force—everything that is physical matter is made of light. In the Apocryphon of John, another text found in the Nag Hammadi library, Jesus gives John a lesson on the formation of the universe in which he refers to God as the Monad, a being of "immeasurable, incomprehensible light." Indeed, Jesus's description of the Monad exactly matches the description of Infinity as pure white light, a manifestation that you can directly experience. A source of pure white light contains anything and everything that could be. Everything you see is a manifestation of Infinity in the form of compressed white light.

Thus, you see, Infinity is more complex than just something that goes on forever. You are part of this complexity and connected to it, as are the stars and the planets. You are so much more than what you think you are. That recognition coupled with the practices you will learn in subsequent pages can lift you to your highest potential.

In finishing this book, you should understand there is science beyond anything earthbound scientists say there is. They have relegated everything that they do not have tools to measure to the realm of quackery and mythology. They rule out the existence of the soul and free will because they have no means of perceiving or measuring them—even though these scientists have souls themselves and exercise free will in their denunciation of the same.

If matter can be infinitely big or infinitely small, then the meaning of dimension and shape break down. Infinity is inherently chaos because it has no boundaries. The most chaotic natural thing in the universe is pure white light, and humans, too, are a source of chaos. You are not simple particles bouncing around the universe in ordered lines. Because you do not simply follow Newtonian mechanics, in which a body at rest stays at rest or a body in motion stays in motion, you could stay in one place for the rest of your natural life or exercise your free will to move. You have the freedom to go with the natural order or decide to do something completely unexpected—you can disobey God's plan or follow it. That free will is chaos manifesting through you, giving you a connection to the infinite.

YOU ARE
A PART OF
THE INFINITE

Every person who has ever lived is on this journey, coexisting with and as part of the void and singularity. Understand, Seeker of Truth, that just like the universe itself, you have a direct connection to the infinite—your wellspring of love, intuition, and creativity. It is a critical component of why you exist at all, why you have a soul, and why you can experience the world. Through the same wisdom passed from the Atlanteans to Enoch, you shall learn how to explore that connection and experience it directly.

You have this source of infinite light, but you need a framework in which the light can exist. Events happen on a personal scale and on a cosmic scale, and Mind and Eternity provide the requisite scaffolds to separate the chaotic and simultaneous events of Infinity, create causality, and put them into a logical order

CHAPTER 8
ETERNITY

Eternity is the cosmic engine that puts the endless white light randomness of Infinity into a logical order. In truth, Infinity is contained in Eternity and can be understood as this: You exist in Infinity right now. For what can the "now" be, but an infinitesimal point on an infinitely long timeline? The portion of time you experience as the present cannot be measured, so how can it exist? Yet it is the only thing that you experience as reality.

The Hermetic texts provide a technical description of the mechanics of time, which Hermes says works in layers: "My son, hear about time, God and the all: God, eternity, the cosmos, time and generation. God creates eternity; eternity, the cosmos; the cosmos, time; and time, generation." [170]

[170] **Hermes Trismegistus,** *Corpus Hermeticum,* 52.

Generation is the end of this process, what you experience as causality. For instance, if you drop something, it falls—you never see a solid object rise up, off of the table and into your hand, because effect always follows cause.

With causality reversed, nothing makes sense—a dangerous environment for a rational mind, because it cannot predict what will happen next. Objects at rest could spontaneously begin to move, sometimes at extreme speed, flying toward the source that exploded them away. When causality is reversed, making any sort of plan is impossible, and Mind, the dimension to be discussed next, thrives on its ability to make accurate predictions about what is going to happen next. Indeed, your very survival and prosperity depend on a level of prescience that will never arise in such a universe.

THE FRAMEWORK OF TIME

Linear time is the scaffold that creates causality. Within Infinity, cause and effect happen at the same time, in the same moment, at the same instant. With the introduction of the turning of Eternity, or the flow of time, cause and effect separate into a continuum, which of course is infinite. The whole lifespan and infinite timelines of the universe become a circle: birth, expansion, maturation, decline, death, and back to birth again. All of these events happening in the same instant in Infinity are pulled apart by Eternity and ordered in a way that makes sense.

The *Vishnu Purāna*, an ancient holy text from India, contains the story of Samudra-manthana, a great pillar sitting in the ocean, with the gods on one side and demons on the other. They have wrapped a rope around this pillar and travel back and forth, turning and turning, churning the ocean in the hopes of obtaining the elixir of eternal life. The ancients used this image to describe the turning of the Wheel of Eternity, putting the flow of time into motion. It is akin to a cosmic gas pedal that goes up and then comes back down, making the turning of the wheel. The inhabitants of the universe sit in the churning ocean, and the water goes round and round, but it always returns to where it started, leaves again, and then returns.

When discussing time with Asclepius and Tat, Hermes says Eternity is like a wheel that turns, as it

> neither begins nor ceases to be and it is turned in the everlasting motion of its revolution by fixed and immutable law. Its parts are always rising and falling alternately, so that as the times change those same parts which had fallen, rise again. Thus revolving circularity is its principle, so that things are so well bound to it that you do not know where the beginning is, if there is a beginning, since everything always seems both to precede and follow itself.[171]
>
> [171] Hermes Trismegistus, *Asclepius*, 97.

Hermes spends much of the Asclepius on the subject of time because it is an important concept to communicate, and he discusses it further in the *Corpus Hermeticum.*

Of course, because of cosmic dualism, time cannot flow forward in your universe unless the same force moves in reverse elsewhere. Such is the nature of cosmic balance: everything comes in pairs that, when combined, bring you back to the same nothingness or everything-ness again, because everything comes out of nothing. If there is an infinity, there must also be an opposite infinity, a void or a singularity. If time flows in one direction, it must also flow in the other direction. If objects fall to the floor in your universe, they would rise into your hand in another. Time is like water in a container—you cannot move water over and leave a void, but rather moving some water one way makes other water rush in another direction. Because time only flows forward in your universe, there must be another dimension where causality has been flipped upside-down, and this dualistic quality of time leads to the turning of the wheel. Time speeds up, cosmically peaks, slows down, and eventually starts moving in the other direction.

The universe you experience is a point on the ever-turning wheel, a positive causality as the universe expands, driven by the forward march of time. The universe is currently expanding at an accelerating rate. The motion around the wheel does not determine the flow rate of time but rather at what degree the present moment is from the neutral axis, and the turning of eternity creates a sine wave. This pattern explains all that exists, including places where time reverses. [172]

[172] "Sine and Cosine from Rotating Vector," YouTube video posted by Khan Academy, https://www.youtube.com/watch?v=a_zReGTxdIQ

Every experience is a point somewhere on the wheel, and modern scientific research extends Hermes's discussion to include the Eternity-driven events of Big Bangs, Big Rips, black holes, and white holes.

BIG BANGS
AND BIG RIPS

At ninety degrees deviation from the neutral axis, one experiences the maximum flow rate of time in the universe, which will occur at a point in the future. Then, as it continues to turn, time decelerates; the universe continues to expand, but at a slower rate. It will continue expanding until the Wheel of Eternity goes all the way around to the other side, 180 degrees, at which point the universe will experience the opposite of a Big Bang, which is a Big Rip.

An astrophysicist named Robert Caldwell first theorized the coming Big Rip, in which the fabric of spacetime, or the framework upon which atoms and subatomic particles rest, will be pulled so thin that it cannot sustain anything on its surface, and at that point, a Big Rip will occur. The universe will eventually turn into complete chaos, gravity will break down, solar systems will fly apart, and the stars will start to disintegrate—a disintegration that will extend to humans, if any remain, for people will dissolve into nothing. [173]

[173] **Robert R. Caldwell** et al., "Phantom Energy and Cosmic Doomsday," *Physical Review Letters* 91, August 13, 2003.

At this point, the universe will begin experiencing negative time, becoming the anti-verse. Backward from the Big Rip, it will end in a Big Bang, whereas your universe started in a Big Bang and will end in a Big Rip. With the coming Big Rip, your universe will trade places with the universe of antimatter on the other side of the Wheel of Time, which will begin experiencing positive time and become the new universe. The wheel will continue round and round. If you could be in the anti-verse, you would not be able to make sense of the experience, but in actuality, there is no Mind in an anti-verse—both minds, as you will see, exist in the universe of positive causality.

Time creates the framework of causality, such that you do not experience your life all at once, nor do you find yourself growing younger. In your universe, everyone is born, grows old, and dies; no one materializes out of the earth, climbs out of their grave, ages backward, and becomes a baby, all while walking and talking backward—but that would be the state of an anti-verse of negative time.

BLACK HOLES
AND WHITE HOLES

A black hole is the closest you will get to negative or reversed time as a natural phenomenon within your universe. It is rare to discover a new thermodynamic law, but physicist Raphael Busso did so. This law correctly postulates that if the universe is a projection, which we shall discuss more in the chapter on Maya, time is flowing in the opposite direction on the other side of the event horizon, making black holes a gateway to the anti-verse of backward causality. It is essentially a place in the universe where the Wheel of Eternity is at zero degrees. The Big Bang and ensuing Big Rip are simply where this universe's experience of time crosses zero or 180 degrees, shifting from one directional flow to the other.[174]

[174] Raphael Busso and Netta Engelhardt, "A New Area Law in General Relativity," *Physical Review D* 92 (August 2015).

A white hole is the opposite of a black hole and features prominently in the new thermodynamic law. Science now explains what happens to matter that falls into a black hole: it passes into the anti-verse where time is flowing in the opposite direction. The opposite side of that hole does not pull light in but instead blasts it out. Nothing that enters a black hole gets out; by contrast, nothing can enter a white hole. What goes into a black hole comes out the white hole in the other universe, but certainly not in its original form. It becomes shredded into subatomic particles. Even if a body or ship could pass through, it would crash into antimatter and be destroyed.

NO END

Understand that time flows in both directions, and your universe is headed forward, in the direction of a Big Rip. This dual-flow concept of Time explains many otherwise mysterious, natural phenomena that scientists struggle with today.

The thought of the universe as you know it ending in a Big Rip billions of years in the future might fill you with a sense of apprehension or doom. Though you seek meaning, science seems to posit that existence is meaningless, that it will ultimately come to an end. As you now see, this is not so. The concepts of Infinity and Eternity reveal there is no true beginning or end—yes, it will end, but only to be re-created anew, again and again, for all eternity. There were universes before this one, and there will be universes after this one, and so it shall continue forever. You will be born and live again, and every permutation of your life at every stage of your life is playing out somewhere in another universe. In an infinite universe, everything that can happen is happening somewhere all of the time.

The framework of the universe works like a probability sieve, taking chaotic everything-ness to what is possible. The version of the life you experience is based on the judgments and decisions, that is, free will, your soul makes—and therein lies the test.

You can expand your consciousness and awareness of what you are and your place in the universe. You are infinitesimally small in this grand production, but you are simultaneously as important individually as the whole cosmos. You are cut from the same cloth and will be here forever, as will everything else.

The Atlanteans have been more successful—technologically, scientifically, spiritually—than any other society and were the first biological organisms on your planet to rise to the highest level of consciousness. They have much to teach you about the Path of Righteousness. Though they are not God, the fact that people worshipped them as gods includes a grain of truth because their spiritual knowledge is a reflection of God's will—and ultimately, you are God in this same manner. To access that power, you must overcome your own ignorance and work to master your faculties, as shall be discussed further in Book IV.

The universe has a mind just as you have a mind, and it keeps score in the form of karma. God's will exists, and nihilism does not accurately describe reality. Thus, this existence is not meaningless, and you must concern yourself with how you live and affect others. You are part of God, and so is everyone else—you must take that knowledge to heart when deciding how to relate to and treat other people in your life.

Faced with an eternity of loneliness, the primordial consciousness—the infinite Monad—created a universe wherein material bodies could arise, and then that consciousness sub-divided itself into other points of awareness embedded in these bodies, plunging them into causal experience to understand and grow as a cosmic being. The way you live now will affect your subsequent experience, because God cultivates entities like Himself.

Now that you understand the scaffolding provided by Eternity, let us explore that which is provided by Mind.

CHAPTER 9
MIND

Whereas Eternity is scaffolding for the temporal, Mind is scaffolding for the rules of the material universe—laws of motion and size. Mind provides structure. It is the force of rational will and cannot live in a completely disordered, infinite universe, because in such a case, everything would still be complete chaos with no ability to make meaning. Thus, Mind is a necessity for order.

Like the flow of time generated by the turning of Eternity, there is an omnipresent cosmic mind that can be explained in terms of your quantum field theory. The Mind field works much like a quantum field, as your scientists call it, in that it is everywhere in the universe and is accessible throughout the universe. As particles are connected as mere vibrations in an infinite, omnipresent quantum field, so the minds of all beings, including animals, are connected via an infinite, omnipresent Mind field. Because minds share the same field, they share the same pattern of thought, thus making communication through mental telepathy a reality.

On a micro scale, a mind provides living beings with the ability to process incoming information and memories, and to make what it believes to be a rational choice. This works in much the same way on the cosmic scale, in that an important choice—namely, the base parameters of the universe—must be made in order for a chaotic universe to have some sort of structure. Hermes says, "Order follows these two"—meaning destiny and necessity:

> Order being the interweaving and timing of all things that must come to pass. For nothing is composed without Order, and this cosmos is complete in every detail. For the universe itself is moved by Order and is established wholly upon Order ... They are neither moved by anger, nor deflected by favor, but serve the Necessity of eternal reason; this Eternity is ineluctable, unmoving, and indissoluble. [175]

[175] Hermes Trismegistus, *Asclepius*, 96.

In other words, the universe is built upon a constant that cannot be changed or bent to your will, and upon that constancy hangs the rest of the universe. This is the universal constant, c, which we shall discuss shortly.

Eternity introduces destiny and necessity through the temporal sequence of events, but Mind creates the framework and order for those events to even happen.

THE TWINS
LIVING IN
YOUR HEAD

A quote from the *Asclepius* begins, "The Lord and framer of all things, whom we rightly call God, made a god second to Himself who can be seen and apprehended by the senses." In this passage, Hermes is speaking of the material universe, what you look upon and touch. He continues,

> Since God made this divine being, which was the first to issue out of Himself and was the second after Himself, the sight of this being was beautiful to Him and since it was entirely filled with the goodness of everything, He loved it as a child of His own divine nature. [176]

[176] Hermes Trismegistus, *Asclepius*, 60-61.

This passage is reminiscent of Genesis, in which God creates the universe and sees that it is good. The universe is a manifestation of the supreme God, who was able to create this second version of Himself, the material universe, transforming energy into matter.

Thus, there is an ephemeral God and a counterpart, the material God seen in the creation of the universe itself. This principle connects to the Atlantean pantheistic view: the physical universe itself is a part of God. The universe you apprehend unfolded from the God you cannot directly apprehend, completing the cosmic duality.

Just as God the ephemeral made a material version of Himself, so are there two versions of your own self, two fully functioning minds in one head, embodying the concept of dualism—the macro construction of the universe manifested in an individual person.

You were created from the image of God, and everyone is made of the same material in the same way as God. As God has a cosmic twin, so do you: you are in time, made out of matter, with a dual mind. You are simply a smaller version of God.

On this micro scale, there is a theory of dual consciousness in neuroscience. In 1908 a German doctor coined the term "alien hand syndrome" to explain the apparent independent actions taken by a stroke victim's left hand. Later experiments confirm that you have not one but two minds and possess two versions of yourself—thus, God's dualism manifests in humans through dual consciousness.

Alien hand syndrome blossomed into the theory of dual consciousness after the split-brain experiments were conducted, where subjects underwent a corpus callosotomy, the severing of the bridge between the two hemispheres of the brain. For instance, they would lose control of an arm, as if they have become possessed by an outside entity. One hand may literally slap objects from the other, one side of the brain may disagree with the other, and half the body may act in a way that seems out of the person's control. Or the left hand would draw out an image being shown only to the right eye, while the patient denies seeing anything at all.[177] You see, the speech center of the brain is located in the left hemisphere, which also receives visual input from the left eye. The talking half of the brain honestly sees nothing, while the right hemisphere, which controls the opposite arm, is busy drawing what its eye is observing.

[177] **David Wolman**, "The Split Brain: A Tale of Two Halves," *Nature* 483 (2012): 260–263. https://doi.org/10.1038/483260a

A dual consciousness inhabiting a single material body means the housing of polar opposites, the conscious ego and the subconscious shadow, within a single being, which creates much distress and strife for many people. Because you have two separate entities in your head, you must acknowledge them both and do the work of integrating them; otherwise, you risk the conscious brain drifting elsewhere while your subconscious takes actions that may not align with your spiritual calling. The work of integration consists of bringing the subconscious portions of your psyche, components you may not even want to acknowledge, under your conscious awareness and control.

To function at the highest level, there must be communication between the two hemispheres of the brain: the more separated the two minds become, the more apt they are to war with each other and lead to human suffering—both your own and for those around you. The battle between the two minds happens even in people who have not undergone surgery. It is simply less apparent, because they still possess an intact bridge between the halves.

Achieving spiritual elevation requires you to reconcile and harmonize the opposites within your own psyche, which is part of the process of the Path of Righteousness to be discussed in Book IV.

Mind and will cannot operate in a universe where time flows backward, without positive causality. In such a state, the mind would become untethered, for it would be impossible to plan, and the mind must plan for anticipated future events. Through repeated failures, the mind would eventually resign itself to death in a universe it can never hope to understand. For this reason, both minds share the same universe, the one in which time flows forward.

As has been stated, nothing exists without its opposite. If there is matter, there is antimatter. If there is Mind, there is anti-Mind. However, rather than being in a completely separate universe along with the antimatter and the backward-flowing time, that anti-mind, which is still rational and can only function in positive causality, meshes with the mind that lives in this universe with forward-moving time.

On the level of an individual person, there is much empirical proof of the existence of two minds within one person. For instance, consider Christina Santhouse. At eight years old, she experienced nearly constant seizures, on the order of 150 per day, emanating from her right hemisphere. In 1996, Dr. Ben Carson, a prominent surgeon and politician from the United States, performed a hemispherectomy, completely removing one half of her brain. Though it seems such a procedure would kill or debilitate a human, the procedure in fact cured Santhouse and her seizures ceased. She earned a master's degree in speech pathology, married, and started a family. [178]

[178] "Dr. Benjamin Carson," The Hemispherectomy Foundation, http://hemifoundation.homestead.com/dr_ben_carson.html; Kathy Boccella, "20 Years after Surgery, a Full Life with Half a Brain," *Philadelphia Inquirer*, February 14, 2016, https://www.inquirer.com/philly/news/local/20160214_20_years_after_surgery_a_full_life_with_half_a_brain.html

In almost any other case, removing half an organ would cause someone to die or be noticeably diminished. You cannot, for instance, live with only half a heart. If a person survived, as in the case of losing one lung, quality of life would be drastically altered. Santhouse's experience shows that even with half a brain, someone could remain in every way herself—demonstrating there are, in fact, two minds living in your head.

LET THERE
BE LIGHT

We have touched upon the constant c, and now you will come to understand its true significance. The translation of disordered light into ordered materials is $e = mc^2$, or said another way, mass equals energy divided by constant c^2 $(m = e \,/\, c^2)$. But where did c come from? It is an arbitrary value set by the cosmic mind: God.

Imagine looking through a pair of binoculars. When they are out of focus, you see chaos. As you adjust the lenses one way and another, you finally happen upon a combination at which the picture is most clear. Similarly, adjusting the angular velocity of Eternity—that is, tuning c—makes the disordered universe become ordered.

As with the dual mind, there are macro and micro aspects to this cosmic constant. Humans typically conceive of c as the cosmic speed limit, the fastest any object could possibly travel, but it is more than that: it is the speed of the entire universe. Everything in the universe, including you, moves at the speed of c all the time. [179]

[179] **"We All Move at the Speed of Light,"** YouTube video posted by ScienceClic English, November 8, 2018, https://www.youtube.com/watch?v=auQQJYlSe4c

Constant c is typically defined as the speed of light through a vacuum, but that definition only considers spatial velocity, because light does not experience the flow of time. Constant c is actually a vector of temporal *and* spatial velocity. If the speed of light experiences zero temporal velocity, it is 100 percent spatial velocity. If something is not moving at spatial c, then it must also have a temporal velocity.

If you were to plot spatial velocity against temporal velocity, which has been carried out experimentally, you would see the degree of time dilation imposed at the speed at which you traveled. A completely stationary object experiences the full effects of the flow of time, and likewise, something traveling at the speed of light experiences no time at all. However, this is where you shall understand the mystery of c, for someone traveling at half the speed of light does not experience the flow of time being reduced by the same amount; instead, time moves at 87 percent of its usual rate.

Should you ever travel at 80 percent of the speed of light, time would slow to 60 percent of its usual pace. Traveling a quarter of the speed of light experiences almost no slowing of time, with it still moving by at 97 percent its usual rate. The curve appearing before your eyes in the graph below is a quarter circle, with a radius of c, which extends to half a circle when traveling in the other direction. The circle is completed forthwith when we consider that time also flows backwards. The relationship between the two velocities can be expressed as Pythagoras's theorem, with the hypotenuse of the triangle always being c.

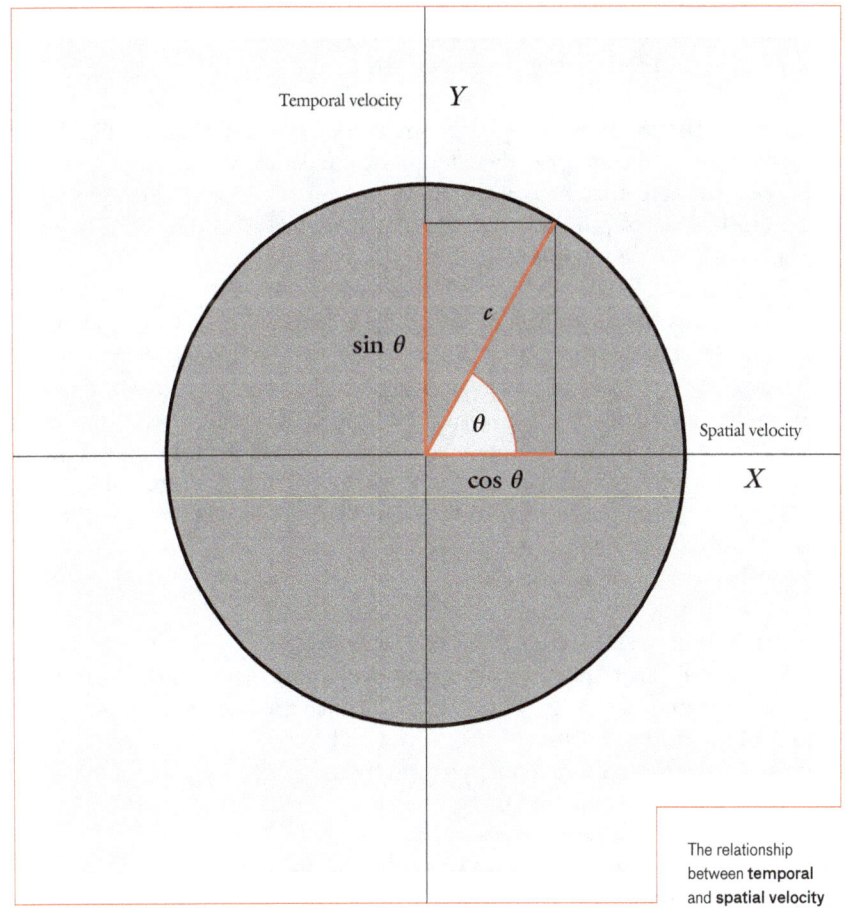

The relationship between **temporal** and **spatial velocity**

At the same time, *c* also manifests as the cosmic size limit, and herein the Planck length comes into play. In the Big Rip, particles cannot form anymore. If the universe were mesh, the Planck length would be the gap between strips of material, a gap much smaller than any subatomic particle your scientists have ever seen. Without that determinant of smallest size, though, there would be no order. Things cannot, in fact, be infinitely small, or in the earlier equation, there would exist a "divide by zero" error of the universe. Without a minimum, anything could continue shrinking, ad infinitum. In order to have a universe, there must be boundaries on minimum size and maximum speed.

Armed with this knowledge, you can begin to see how time and space work together, and you will complete your understanding when we discuss Matter and Maya, specifically, gravity. Once you grasp how all four elements of the universe work in coordination, you will find that what you normally see is all an illusory projection at their intersection, manifested by *c*.

All motion—fast and slow—is relative. Size is relative as well: What is big? What is small? To order the universe, there must be boundaries. Matter cannot travel at any speed, so there must be boundaries on motion, which is *c*. There must also be boundaries on size, so the duality also manifests in a second way, which is the Planck length, whose equation also contains *c*.

Once we discuss Maya, you will realize that the concepts of gravity, motion, distance, and space are not in fact real. The void is the singularity is the void is the singularity. You could be in a singularity and not know it, or you could be in a void. In the end, there is no substantive difference. The same principle applies to *c*: you are moving through space, time, or some combination of the two—but the combination is always *c*. You are on the Wheel of Eternity. You are not moving; the Wheel of Eternity, that which is "turned in the everlasting motion of its revolution by fixed and immutable law" according to Hermes, is moving you, and the speed at which it moves you is *c*.

These facts form the theoretical framework upon which the Atlanteans have built their technology. Their ships perform as they do because they can manipulate time. They can communicate as they do because they have learned to manipulate the cosmic Mind Field, the source of telepathy, which is instantaneous communication from anywhere to anywhere. Earth scientists are just now beginning to realize that such modes of travel and communication are possible, and they are working out the theoretical framework for making it a reality. They

[180] **Harold White,** "Warp Field Mechanics 101," paper presented at the DARPA/NASA 100 Year Starship Symposium, Orlando, Florida, September 30, 2011, https://ntrs.nasa.gov/api/citations/20110-015936/downloads/20110015936.pdf

are still, however, bound by their own materialist presumptions and are unlikely to succeed in their attempts at producing a viable space drive. [180]

These practices work because, in fact, the whole concept of space is an illusion: all points in the universe are connected to one another. Eyewitness accounts of "alien" encounters give credence to the Atlantean ability to manipulate these principles as people report seeing spaceships and hearing people speak to them telepathically.

An ordinary primitive human who encountered Atlanteans would understandably believe they were gods exhibiting extraordinary capabilities around space, time, mind, and matter manipulation, and might even initiate a new cargo cult. You now know, Seeker of Truth, that Atlanteans are simply highly advanced humans. Their technology uses the higher, true dimensions, while you toil away in the material realm with rockets and shovels. There are other ways to achieve your ends of propulsion, construction, and communication, but you must understand these higher realms to do so.

The universe exists because the cosmos makes it so, by divine will—the universal equivalent of "I think therefore I am." When God said, "Let there be light," He brought the universe into focus, as you would a pair of binoculars. He adjusted the Wheel of Eternity until He found the speed at which the white light snapped into focus, and at that moment, the material universe began. Without c, there would be nothing. That constant brought everything in the universe as it now exists into being.

The very phrase "Let there be light" illustrates the arbitrariness of this cosmic constant. No human knows why the numerical value of c is what it is. All the other constants can be derived logically through other means, but c simply exists, and the rest of the universe unfolds from it, a projection brought into being by the divine intelligence and viewed through the lenses of Eternity and Mind.

GOD'S WILL

Can you now see that Mind brings order to chaos, a scaffolding for the rules of this material universe? By imposing a boundary condition of speed and size, Mind determines the velocity at which the universe moves through the God-ordained constant c.

Furthermore, because of the duality of time, you are burdened with a dualistic mind—two minds in this forward-moving universe. The mind cannot handle backward causality, so both minds exist here. The challenge of this state we will discuss in Book III; it is your life's purpose to bring them into harmony, as we shall discuss in Book IV.

CHAPTER 10
MATTER

In your world, much is already known about the fourth element, Matter, and how it works, for Matter is the only component of the universe with which material scientists concern themselves. Our universe is indeed made of matter, Seeker of Truth, but recall that an opposite must also exist: for matter also has a mirror image, known as antimatter. Matter can be forged from the infinite light, but it can only be created in a pairing with antimatter, for it is linked forever with its partner.

Just as Eternity and Mind are part of the infinite, so too is Matter. Whether as an infinitely dense singularity or infinitely large void, there is an infinite amount of matter in the universe. Hearken back to Cantor, of whom you read in the chapter on Infinity: though there is more space than matter in the universe, there is an infinite amount of both.

Antimatter is the mirror image of matter. In matter, electrons have a negative charge and protons have a positive charge, but the values are flipped in antimatter. Just as there is a universe of matter, there is a universe of antimatter.

You've lived in close contact with antimatter. In PET scans, for example, the machine bombards your body with positively charged electrons in what they call positron emission. In real terms, they are creating antimatter and bombarding your body with it to generate reactions that they can imprint on a photographic plate. At CERN, the European Organization for Nuclear Research, antimatter is developed at a larger scale. The search for the God particle, also known as the Higgs-Boson particle, inspired man to build the Large Hadron Collider that spans two countries, Switzerland and France. Experiments in the collider crash protons together at nearly the speed of light, and the impact creates high energies that forge antimatter. This antimatter vanishes in a billionth of a second, eluding your grasp, but for that billionth of a second, you perceive it.

One of the big questions in astronomy today is, "Where did all of the antimatter from the Big Bang go?" It seems only logical that it traveled into the universe experiencing reversed time—a dimension that mirrors this one in every way except for its lack of Mind. Because antimatter lives in the backward flow of time, you do not encounter it and it is difficult for you to perceive. Paul Dirac theorized the existence of antimatter in 1928, creating the Dirac equation, which has since been confirmed with experiments. [181]

[181] Paul A. M. Dirac, "The Quantum Theory of the Electron," *Proceedings of the Royal Society of London, Series A, Containing Papers of Mathematical and Physical Character* 117, no. 118 (1928): 610–624, https://mathweb.ucsd.edu/~nwallach/Dirac1928.pdf

Of course, Atlanteans discovered antimatter long before Paul Dirac, and it became the source of their power. A universe of antimatter looks exactly like yours, except you would explode if you touched it. It's the perfect energy source, and Atlanteans understood the ancient wisdom of how to draw unlimited amounts of antimatter out of the anti-verse, as well as how to store and manipulate it. This is how they traveled with Enoch, warped space and time, and visited anywhere they liked in the universe instantaneously. Without antimatter, the Atlantean civilization would have been impossible because the energy they required to power their ships would have shattered planets. With antimatter, the Atlanteans were, and are, unstoppable.

BORROWED
FROM INFINITY

Matter, like the other three elements, is borrowed from Infinity. It is part of endless pure light, the Monad, giver of energy passed through the forge of c imposed by Mind. When the light of infinity passes through the universal ordering of c, it is converted and condensed into matter.

Just as the infinite is driving the turning of Eternity, creating the flow of time, so the light of infinity passes through the lens of Mind to create Matter, with time creating the temporal framework through which matter may move. Consider again the common equation of your age, Einstein's $e = mc^2$, where e means energy, m means mass, and c is the speed of light. Rearrange it to focus on mass, and it becomes $m = e \, / \, c^2$.

With this in mind, you are now closer to the truths of the universe, to matter and its counterpart, antimatter. You're beginning to see how the world intersects to create limitless potential. The anti-verse exists, and it is filled with the perfect energy source, capable of powering immense and miraculous feats. The Atlanteans proved it: they evolved from sailing on water to sailing through time and space. It is to humankind's advantage to harness the antimatter for a rich and abundant life in the material world.

Yet, there is still much we have not explored. Two of the biggest mysteries in the universe are space and gravity. From whence do they come? Let us now discover their true source.

CHAPTER II
MAYA

The universe you see is a projection, a construct created by the interplay of the four dimensions we just explored: Infinity, Eternity, Mind, and Matter.

You drown in this illusion because you think it is real; you believe it is all there is, tangible and permanent. But what if your eyes were opened, and you saw the world for what it really was? What if you understood how the cosmos truly worked?

Think of the universe as a drawing. It would be impossible to depict it in any kind of Cartesian plane because the categories are too vast. It would be three straight lines extending forever from a single point—there would not be enough paper to capture it. But we can capture that infinitude by replacing the lines with circles, because a circle has no beginning or end and is thus the perfect representation of infinite magnitude.

The first step in creating this drawing would be to capture all four dimensions of the universe. We start with Infinity, which is simultaneously a void and singularity—a simple dot, the singularity, at the center of the page, the void. Out of that dot of infinity is born the other three dimensions, which we will draw as circles: Eternity, Mind, and Matter. Each circle intersects with the other and remains connected to the singularity in the center.

You do not experience this universe in all its complexity. What you call the "universe" is not the three full circles but the areas of overlap *between* the circles. These are the illusions created out of the interplay of the four divine realms, but you believe them to be real.

These illusions are collectively known as Maya, the illusion of experience. The word *maya* stretches across cultures: it belongs to the ancient language of Sanskrit in India, where it means "the illusion of reality," but is also the namesake of the Mayans of Mexico, who realized and believed that they themselves were projections. This notion is embedded in their philosophical concept of "In Lak'ech," meaning "You are the other me."

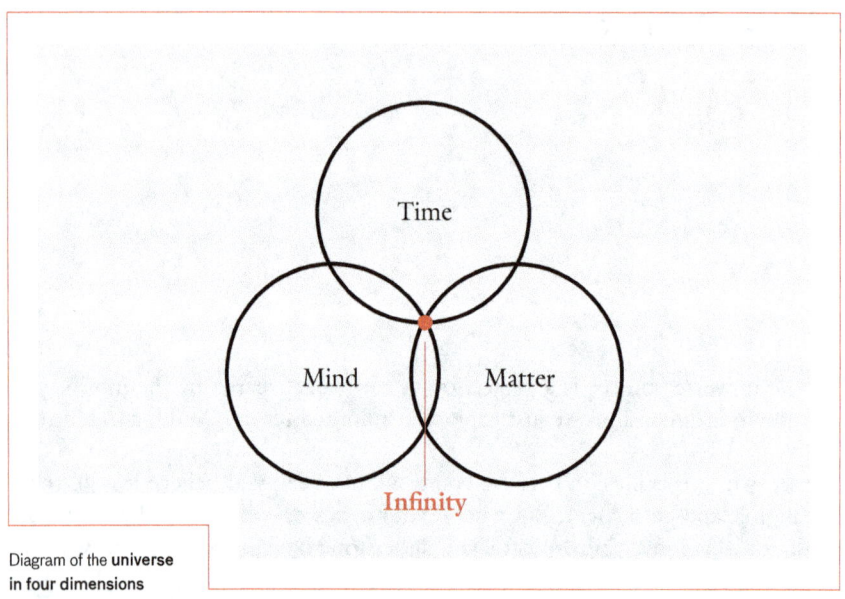

Diagram of the **universe in four dimensions**

If you look closely at the preceding drawing, Seeker of Truth, you will realize you have seen it before. There are two ancient symbols embedded in this picture. Concentrate only on the areas of overlap—drawn alone, they create the Triquetra, a widely used symbol across cultures. In some depictions, the overlapped sections all intersect at a point, but in other illustrations, they are pushed apart to make more space for the divine.

Presentations of the **Triquetra**

The three circles themselves are also famous, and the earliest extant examples are over 5,000 years old, from caves in Malta and Newgrange, Ireland. They are known as the Triskelion, and if you look carefully, you will find them across cultures and time zones, embedded in art, paintings, sculptures, and church windows.

The Triskelion forms half of the picture known as the Seed of Life, the latter being completed by another three circles that create an inversion of the first three to represent their opposites of anti-time, anti-mind, and antimatter. This produces six circles with overlapped sections that represent Maya, or what is known as the material realm. Then, add a seventh circle in the center that binds the material realm together as a representation of c in a circle. That final central circle, combined with the single point of Infinity, is the Monad—the Godhead and source of all.

You have seen this symbol across the world: you find it in places of meditation, calm, and spirituality, but also in nature and in art. In its simplest definition, the Seed of Life is a picture of the universe, a sacred geometrical pattern that also represents the seven days of creation.

Triskelion at Newgrange

You will have noticed these drawings at the beginning of each book in the tome you presently hold: now you shall know the reason for their presence. The drawing at the beginning of Book I represents infinity and singularity: a circle of radius c representing all matter, placed on a graph with an x-axis of spatial velocity and a y-axis of temporal velocity. The beginning of Book II features the Triskelion, and, as you shall see, Book III opens with a drawing depicting the Seed of Life. There is a fourth drawing, given at the beginning of Book IV, which is known as the Flower of Life. It is derived from the Seed of Life and represents the multitudes of universes that exist throughout eternity.

But it is not time for you to learn about this final drawing as yet, for you need to understand its components first. Look back to the Triskelion, to the three circles with their intersecting maya, the projected world in which you live. It is time to learn how each of these dimensions creates Maya and shapes the forces of the material world as you know it. Before you embark on the journey, bear in mind the wise words of Hermes Trismegistus: "Where anything is known through the dimension of time, there is falsehood." [182]

[182] Hermes Trismegistus, *Asclepius*, 89.

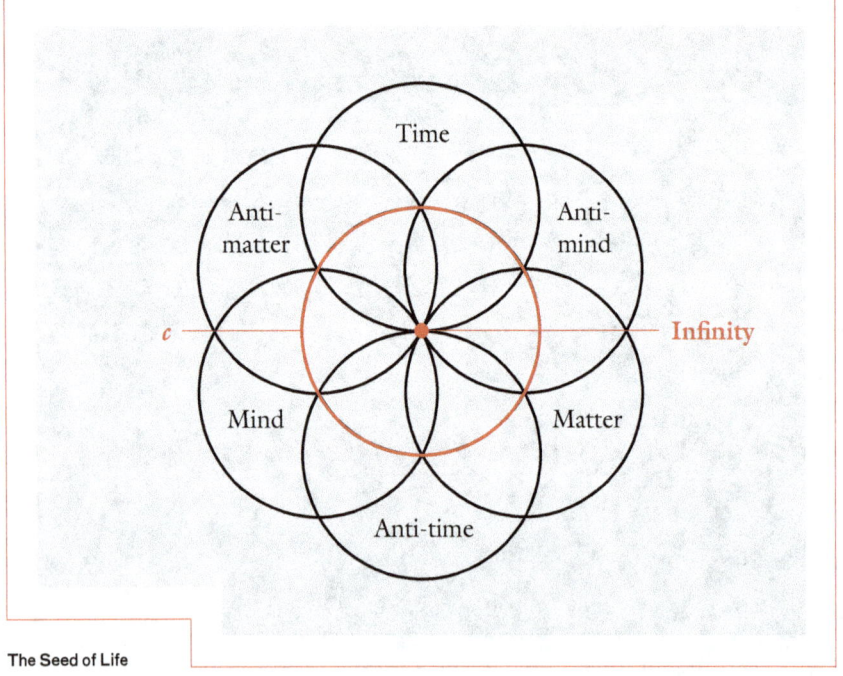

The Seed of Life

GRAVITY:
THE INTERSECTION
OF MATTER AND TIME

The divine realms of Eternity and Matter intersect and interplay to create a phenomenon you know as gravity. The universe has four fundamental forces: strong nuclear forces, weak nuclear forces, electromagnetism, and gravity. Humans have a respectable understanding of three of these forces, but for years, they have struggled to define what gravity is or from whence it comes.

The theory of general relativity explains gravity as an effect. Space and time exist as a continuum, similar to a net in which there exists different heavenly bodies of matter, such as planets or suns. When the planet is massive, it presses into this net, creating a depression. Imagine it, if you will, as a stone thrown into the flow of water. The stone will naturally affect the water's movement by slowing it down.

Thus, time is impeded by the presence of matter, for matter in this flow of time slows time down, which in turn creates a shear force called gravity. In essence, gravity is how a solid body experiences a gradient in the flow of time, which pulls it towards the region of slower moving time. When you stand, time is flowing slower for your feet than your head. Indeed, your scientists today have used atomic clocks placed only a meter apart in elevation to prove just how delicate these changes in time can be.

All of which points to this important truth: gravity is an illusion, not a direct physical force. Classifying it as a force is to be blind to the Maya in which we live, and to the possibilities beyond the illusion. The Atlanteans understood that gravity was simply a gradient of time, so they focused their science on manipulating time to create propulsion, giving birth to the concept of anti-gravity.

SPACE:
THE INTERSECTION
OF MIND AND TIME

Seeker of Truth, do you live in a void or a singularity? If you live in a singularity, there is no space, but if you live in a void, then space is an illusion. Remember Hermes's words about the falsehood of time, and know that your eyes deceive you.

Space is created by the interplay of the divine dimensions of Mind and Eternity. Matter distorts the time gradient of the universe by creating little dips and depressions that you can think of as "time wells." As you now know, these dips and depressions slow down the flow of time, creating the shear force of gravity. The mind then perceives these time wells as "space" or "distance."

Do you see how true dimensions interplay and bifurcate to create the illusions you take for granted and believe to be absolute? Gravity is the effects of matter on time, and space is the mind's perception of these effects. At the core, both phenomena are the same—they are simply disguises for the true reality of time gradients.

It is as Hermes said:

> [Place] is a word that has no meaning on its own. For "place" only has meaning in relation to that of which it is the place. ... For just as it is impossible for anything to be empty, so one cannot know what place is on its own. If nothing is empty, then what place is cannot be known unless you add the dimensions of length, breadth and height to it, as you do to human bodies ... know that the causal world of mind, discernible only by contemplation, is incorporeal and nothing corporeal can be mingled with its nature, nothing distinguished by quality, quantity or number, for in it there is nothing of that kind ... If you give your attention to the whole, then you will come to understand that in truth the sensory world and all within it is from the world above and is covered by that as if by a garment. [183]
>
> [183] Hermes Trismegistus, *Asclepius*, 91–92.

As Hermes describes, your world is defined by relativity. You cannot know where you are as an absolute, only in relation to other things. Motion, too, is relative, as are speed and size. Einstein discovered this in his theory of relativity, both special relativity and general relativity. How you perceive the world is unique to you and you alone.

Hermes's words reveal the depth of the illusion of this relativity. He explains the physical world as you experience it, as created by your consciousness and imagination, as being draped over the real world of Eternity, Mind, Matter, and Infinity as if a mere garment. The true nature of the universe is thus hidden from you, clothed in your illusions of Maya and out of sight of your perception.

EGO AND SHADOW: INTERSECTION OF MIND AND MATTER

Everything that stands in the light, of necessity, casts a shadow. As you are the divine *ātman*, or *nous*, fused with matter, the components of your dual mind manifest in two different ways: the ego and shadow. For you to grasp the delicate nature of ego and shadow, oh Seeker of Truth, listen again to Hermes's words and wisdom, for they will guide your understanding:

> Every being that has a soul [is of both sexes] and also those that do not. It is not possible for any one of them to exist without being fruitful. For if fecundity were withdrawn from all living beings, it would be impossible for them to continue for all time to be what they are [reproduction]; I tell you that nature holds and preserves in herself everything that has been brought into being. [184]
>
> [184] **Hermes Trismegistus**, *Asclepius, 74.*

Here, Hermes says that everything that reproduces, all living creatures, have a male and female side to them. Millennia later, psychologist Carl Jung would posit the same. Jung divides the mind into two: the conscious ego and the subconscious shadow. The ego is the part of which all humans are conscious; it is the part that offers up your inner monologues and states your identity and personas. The shadow is the part many fail to acknowledge at all, yet it also lives in the mind: it is the mirror image of the ego and contains all that the ego does not.

Your subconscious shadows throw up ghost images of you, as well as archetypes that have grown up in the collective unconscious, the species-wide and ancient memory all humans have inherited. Every man has a female shadow in them known as *anima*, and every woman has a male shadow known as *animus*. It is as Hermes says: "Nature holds and preserves in herself everything that has been brought into being."

Between the ego and the shadow, a person contains within themselves all the

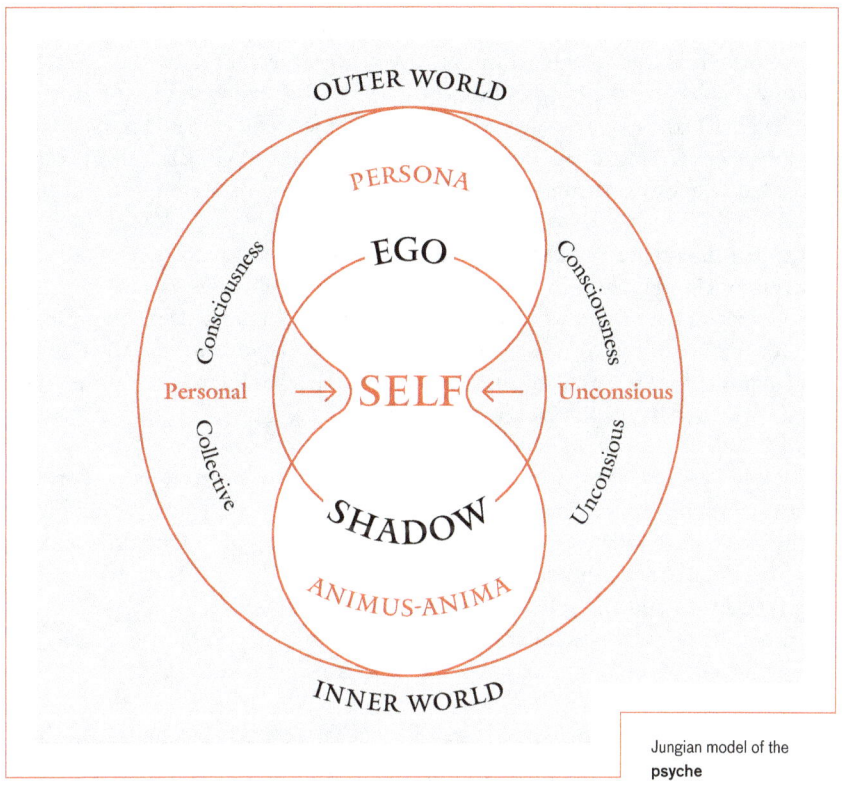

Jungian model of the
psyche

qualities to be seen as godlike. They are good, bad, greedy, generous, benevolent, malicious, wise, foolish—think of the binaries into which you divide your world, and then imagine all of those binaries inside of you. You are capable of anything: good or bad, abhorrent or wonderous.

Humans who sometimes perform acts that are out of character torture themselves with guilt or confusion because they do not understand that they are all things: not only the qualities with which they identify, but also the polar opposites of those traits. Nothing you do is in contradiction with yourself. Humans experiencing such inner turmoil have identified so deeply with the ego, they have forgotten they have a shadow too, and when this shadow occasionally manifests and controls their actions, they find themselves torn and full of guilt.

Let us now look at how Jung's and Hermes's models of the world connect with the true dimensions of Mind and Matter. As we have said, the cosmic mind is dual, and that duality is expressed in matter by the two parts of a person's psyche:

the conscious ego and the unconscious shadow. But you, dear soul, contained in your mortal body, believe the illusion that you are either/or: *either* the ego *or* the shadow. This is how the Jungian model of the world describes it: two minds vying for supremacy in a single physical body, creating inner conflict that, if not managed by the sheer effort of conscious will, shall overwhelm the psyche. You perceive it as a battle between the two, a struggle, a turmoil you must navigate and curb.

But in truth, you are not ego nor shadow, for neither truly exists. You are a microcosm of God Himself. In Hinduism, the name for this self is *ātman*. Millennia ago, books on the *ātman* were written, and their wisdom may help you grasp the essential nature of the cosmos. The *Brihadaranyaka Upanishad* and the *Chandogya Upanishad* are still available in your world today; find them and consider their words, which will pull you closer to the truths you seek.

You live in needless inner turmoil, caught in the middle of a perceived war between your two minds where none actually exists. Realize you are whole, a unification of the ego and shadow that extends beyond those categories. One dharma king and Shambhala lineage holder referred to the mind as a wild horse and the self as the barn.[185] There are times the horse breaks loose from the barn and gallops into the field, requiring you to chase after it.

[185] Sakyong Mipham, *Turning the Mind into an Ally* (New York: Riverhead Books, 2003).

Your mind is a wild animal, and it can feel far, far beyond your grasp. But have courage, for the incessant fighting and chatter in your brain is only a play: you can choose to be the audience, or you can choose to leave the theater. You do not have to identify with the chatter or believe it defines who you are. You are the self, not your thoughts.

MOVING
BEYOND MAYA

When you are attached to the material realm, it can be difficult to imagine a vaster universe of forces that impact and create the illusions in which you live. But once you recognize Maya and move beyond its trappings—once you lift the veil—you open unto yourself an infinity of possibility.

The Atlanteans lifted the garment of illusion to gaze upon the essential structure of the universe. They used it as the framework to build higher levels of technology and higher levels of spirituality, for these go hand in hand. Atlantean technology is built upon these spiritual forces of Eternity and Mind.

To unlock the Atlanteans' knowledge and skill, you must attain their spirituality. Fear not, for this, too, is within your grasp, as you shall learn in Book IV. The constraints of the world as you know it are not real: they are mere illusions beyond which you can move, as have the Atlanteans. Indeed, not only can you move beyond them, but you *must*—for in no other way can you truly self-actualize and reach your potential.

Let us now look at the eightfold way, another means of conceptualizing the universe. In the beginning of Book I, you saw the picture of singularity and infinity: a circle on a graph, with an *x*-axis of spatial velocity and a *y*-axis of temporal velocity. But you know now that space is an illusion; it is a part of Maya. There is only the flow of time, and anything seen through it does indeed contain falsehood, as Hermes stated. It is thus time for you to understand the implications of this vaster and truer depiction of the universe.

CHAPTER 12
THE EIGHTFOLD WAY

You have now unlocked the secrets of the universe, Seeker of Truth, to perceive the many illusions in which you live. Your reality consists of Maya, and you have hitherto been blind to the possibilities of the multifold universe around you. Open now your eyes and see.

In Chapter 7, you learned the universe was a void and a singularity; in Chapter 9, you saw it plotted on a graph with a horizontal axis of spatial velocity and a vertical axis of temporal velocity. But space, as you have now recognized, is Maya—it is an illusion crafted by the intermingling of the divine domains of Mind and Eternity. A new and true graph of the universe will appear to you as the relationship between matter and time:

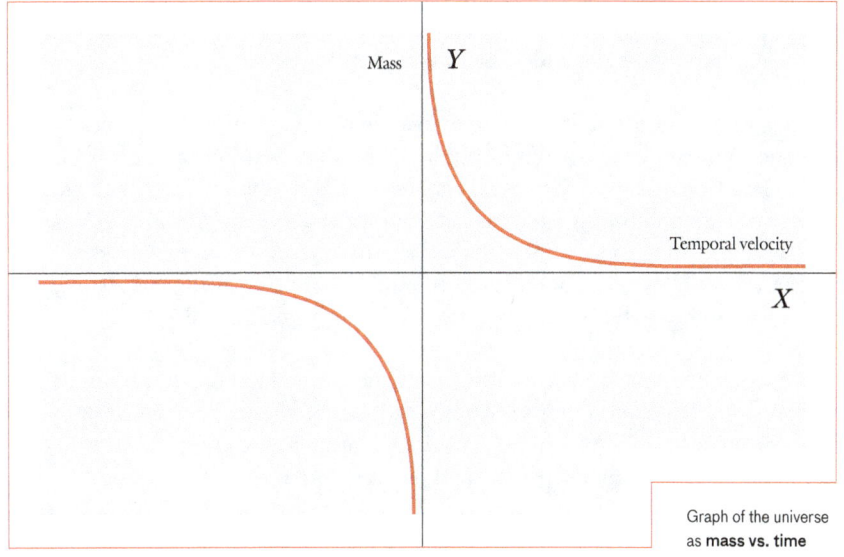

Graph of the universe
as **mass vs. time**

In this illustration of the universe, the horizontal axis represents temporal velocity and the vertical axis illustrates mass. As the passage of time slows, mass reaches infinity, and this can be depicted as $y = 1/x$.

If you have been observing closely, you will have noticed that there are two halves to this true representation of the universe. This is because no illustration of the universe is complete without its mirror image, the reflection of antimatter and the anti-verse. The upper right quadrant of this illustration is where you live: in a universe of matter where time flows in the direction of causality. But underneath that, in the lower left quadrant, is the universe you cannot yet access: the anti-verse of antimatter, where time flows in the opposite direction.

The inner workings of the universe, the secrets shared here in Book II, can be mapped in a single equation known as the Eightfold Way. It is understood thus:

$$\frac{1}{\lim\limits_{e \to \infty} \frac{e}{c^2}} + T + 2M = \frac{1}{\lim\limits_{e \to \infty} \frac{e}{c^2}} + T$$

This equation is the unique expression of the entire universe. It is composed of eight elements: two opposing infinities ($\lim\limits_{e \to \infty}$), two matter-generating functions (e/c^2), two opposing flows of time (T), and two minds (2M). What you see written to the left of the equal sign (=) represents the world in which you live, a universe filled with matter, causal time, and dual minds. The portion to the right of the equal sign represents the anti-verse of antimatter and anti-time.

Notice that each element of the equation is represented on both sides of the equation, except for the two minds, for the Mind dimension cannot exist in the anti-verse. Consequently, there is no ego, or shadow, or space. The only element of Maya that exists in the anti-verse is gravity, for the anti-verse also includes matter. At any single point in time the equation is unbalanced. However, you know that as the universe cycles through its permutations, Mind oscillates back and forth. Thus, throughout eternity the Eightfold Way keeps itself in balance.

Gaze upon this equation carefully, even though it might confound you, for contained in it is everything presented in Book II. All the knowledge you have been given hitherto is woven into this simple formula, and while there are deeper mysteries still to be discovered the path is set before you now.

WISDOM OF
THE EIGHTFOLD WAY

The Eightfold Way teaches you much truth about the world around you that sheds light on your experiences and expands the boundaries of your knowledge. The Eightfold Way shows you that the universe you perceive is truly endless, and time can continue flowing forever. Everything that can happen is happening, somewhere, all the time, and every version of your life at every stage is playing out somewhere in the universe. Moreover, it is not simply playing out for you, but for every person who has ever lived, and will ever live, in this universe. What version of these events you experience is up to you.

The Eightfold Way shows you that your movement around the Wheel of Eternity is what determines the rate of expansion of the universe. If you are in the first half of the lifespan of the universe, then the rate of expansion is increasing, whereas if you are in the second half of the lifespan of the universe, the rate of expansion is decreasing.

Once Eternity has turned 180 degrees, then time begins to flow in the other direction, into anti-time, and Mind steps away from this universe to shift to another one that is filled with positive time. This first universe will collapse back into a singularity, and the second universe, the one to which Mind has shifted, will simultaneously experience a Big Bang. The Wheel of Eternity is a never-ending cycle that repeats over and over, creating endless permutations of the universe.

And thus, the Eightfold Way also speaks of another universe, a parallel place devoid of Mind and therefore of space and living beings. Imagine an anti-verse where the black holes emit blazing light, and the stars pull light into their depths to become mini black holes. It is a universe full of the antimatter from the Big Bang, where time flows backward, and the potential—should you ever be able to grasp it, touch it, or see it—is infinite.

HARNESSING
THE EIGHTFOLD WAY

The Atlanteans were capable of three great feats from which your civilization is still very far. The first is that they harnessed antimatter to produce energy, the second is that they spoke to each other telepathically by manipulating the Mind Field, and the third is that they sailed across the stars using propulsion created by manipulating the Time Field.

You have already been shown how antimatter may become an infinite energy source if harnessed correctly. Atlanteans created telepathic communication through devices that manipulated the divine realm of Mind, the Mind Field that connects all minds in the universe. They thus created unhindered communication between two people, not using the crude tools you know as words but in the direct transmission of thoughts, emotions, and images appearing instantly in a person's head. It is a form of what you call "telepathy," a fuller and more precise way of communicating than spoken language. For the Mind Field is universal, and so is the language it communicates in.

But the greatest of their wonders is the time ships they build. The Atlanteans sail among the stars by designing crafts that can jump vast distances across the universe and travel at superluminal speeds. You have seen a sliver of these wonders with your own eyes, and records of these feats have been entered into your history books and into reports of the US Office of National Intelligence, as discussed in an earlier chapter.

The Atlantean ships, which look like spaceships to your untrained eyes, can achieve marvels that might seem impossible to one such as you. They can accelerate tens of thousands of kilometers an hour, stop and turn immediately, disappear from one point in the universe and reappear at another. And in them the Atlanteans remain safe, protected from maneuvers that would crush you with their acceleration, because they keep themselves in their own inertial frame of reference, and each exists in their separate, untouched bubble of time.

But harken to these words, for you may not be as far away from these marvels as the most ignorant among you may imagine. One of your own, the former director of Lockheed's most secretive aircraft projects, speaks the truth about your progress:

> We already have the means to travel among the stars, but these technologies are locked up in black projects, and it would take an act of God to ever get them out to benefit humanity. Anything you can imagine, we already know how to do it. [186]

[186] **Ben Rich**, lecture at the UCLA School of Engineering, March 23, 1993, quoted in Tom Keller, "A Look at Ben Rich, a Man Who Kept Secrets of Stealth and Space Travel," *MUFON Journal*, May 2010, 3–5.

Do you doubt the truth of these words? Do you doubt that you will ever know the wonders the Atlanteans possessed, indeed, whether the Atlanteans even existed at this scale of power? Do you wonder if their ships truly could manipulate time, if they did access the universe of antimatter and realize its power? For you do not know how they did it, and some of you may believe that if you do not know how, it cannot be possible.

If you are among these naysayers, think deeply on the seed of doubt in your heart and the plants they sprout. Look at the world around you and observe the evidence of your history. You have accounts of the miracles of the Atlantean ships, and you have myths of their greatness. You know the mighty Atlanteans never languished in an age of fossil fuels, for you would be witness to the scars on this earth if they did, so you may surmise their technology evolved along different lines than your own. If you believe, in your ignorance and your hubris, that technology from ancient times could not be as advanced as that, then check the limits you impose on yourself when you simply see the world as you know it and question not its boundaries.

Behold the Antikythera mechanism, a star map discovered in 1901 that some among you call the earliest analogue computer. This device dates back over 2,000 years and displays a level of complexity and sophistication that your scientists previously had only witnessed after the fourteenth century, with the birth of the first clocks.

The Antikythera mechanism was discovered in a shipwreck, though it was nearly never found by your scientists. It offered ancient sailors a way to track the lunar calendar, predict eclipses, and chart the position and phase of the moon. It also tracked the seasons and ancient festivals like the Olympics, all simply by someone entering the day into the device.

Consider yet another ancient invention: the aeolipile, thought to be the world's first steam-powered device. Though its creation is popularly attributed to Heron of Alexandria, the aeolipile is first described by Ctesibius, centuries before Heron lived. Still, there is reason for connecting the device to Heron, for in his work *Pneumatica*, he illustrated the aeolipile, alongside a menagerie of mechanical devices or "toys": singing birds, puppets, coin-operated machines, a fire engine, and a water organ. Just like the Antikythera mechanism, the art of building such devices was lost to time, only to be rediscovered millennia later. With the ancient Romans on the cusp of inventing a steam engine, the industrial revolution could have happened nearly 1,800 years before it came to fruition. Imagine what technologies would exist today had that been the case.

But perhaps the Antikythera mechanism and aeolipile device are not old enough to satisfy your doubt that such ingenuity and craftsmanship could exist in deep antiquity. Behold, a jade bracelet showing very fine tooling, the use of a precision drill, was discovered in a cave in Denisova, Russia. Its age has been repeatedly tested, with the result being almost beyond belief, for it is 70,000 years old. It was likely not even made by *homo sapiens*, but a cousin species that lived in Siberia at the time. [187]

[187] *Siberian Times* reporter, "Is This Stunning Bracelet Made by Paleolithic Man for His Favorite Woman Really 70,000 Years Old?" *The Siberian Times*, August 2, 2017, https://siberiantimes.com/science/casestudy/features/could-this-stunning-bracelet-be-65000-to-70000-years-old/

Imagine how many more wonders you have missed, or that have been lost to the swift river of time. Imagine how very little you know, that a device so old can be so sophisticated and so far beyond what you imagined possible at that time. Imagine now, Seeker of Truth, how much you have left to learn.

Access to the anti-verse and the way to harness antimatter as the Atlanteans did are mysteries yet to be revealed, mysteries you must learn for yourself. As God said in the Book of Enoch, Chapter 16:

> And now as to the Watchers who have sent thee to intercede for them, who have been aforetime in heaven, say to them: "You have been in heaven, but all the mysteries have not yet been revealed to you."

For only those who are worthy may know and may learn, and only they shall ascend to the plane of knowledge that unlocks the true being of the universe. The anti-verse exists, and the limitless power of antimatter could be yours, but it can only be wielded by someone of sufficient spiritual maturity.

UNLOCKING POTENTIAL

Many people today have resigned themselves to unconsciousness. They let the television and news channels and government and social media do their thinking for them. Evil people have been exploiting this situation for years, not to damage the body, but to control the mind and taint the soul with sin.

You must wake up to the power at your disposal; you must realize your oneness with God and the universe. As you do, you will come closer to the wonders the Atlanteans used to build their reality, and you will become more aware of the strategies being used by the ruling class to keep the humans of earth down, trapped, and deluded.

BOOK III
THE SHADOW OF DEATH

CHAPTER 13
THE IVORY TOWER

The time has come for you to learn about the Nephilim's manner of working and the organizations they perpetuate to keep you in blind obeisance. Throughout history, you have been warned about the presence of evil and its vice-like grip on humanity. The Bible speaks of this truth often, with the following verses being but two examples:

> The whole world is under the control of the Evil One. [188]
>
> [188] John 5:19 (KJV).

> For we wrestle not against flesh and blood, but against principalities, against powers, against the rulers of the darkness of this world, against spiritual wickedness in high places. [189]
>
> [189] Ephesians 6:12 (KJV).

Who are these forces of evil and what control do they truly wield? These rulers and authorities are none other than the Watchers and the Nephilim of old, exercising power in this present world through the ruling class of politicians, educators, and business elites. They have been in control for 10,000 years and more, keeping you captive through the educational, commercial, and governmental systems that serve them.

As you read of the atrocities perpetrated by people alive today, you may wonder at their intentions. Do they know they are descended from these giants of old? Are they purposefully carrying out the wishes of the Evil One? Understand this: Some of those who perpetuate evil are Nephilim and they are well aware of this fact, even reveling in it. Others are Nephilim but lack knowledge thereof. Still others work knowingly in service to the Nephilim, while others serve the Nephilim's wicked schemes but are wholly unaware that they do so. Judge not or ascribe intent, for you know not what is in a person's heart or mind. Instead, look carefully at their actions to see who they might reveal themselves to be. In this way, you may protect yourself and walk closer to the Path of Righteousness.

Hide not from this truth, and from the darkness that shall be revealed in this book. Brace yourself, because you are about to see the extent of true evil at work in your world. Many people cannot face it, yet you must have courage and endure. Heed the warning of one of your greatest minds, Carl Jung: "Only an infantile person can pretend that evil is not at work everywhere, and the more unconscious he is, the more the devil drives him." [190]

[190] Carl Jung, *Aion: Researches into the Phenomenology of the Self*, ed. and trans. Gerhard Adler and R. F. C. Hull (Princeton, NJ: Princeton University Press, 1959), 166.

The wisdom of Jung extends further, for he also said, "The branches of a tree cannot reach heaven until its roots stretch down to hell." [191] And so it must be: you cannot reach the end of the Path of Righteousness unless you fully comprehend the shadow of death and the evil of which you are capable. For everything the Nephilim do, Seeker of Truth, you are capable of as well—the only boundary that separates you from them is your choices. Gain the wisdom to make wise choices, and guard yourself against the urges and sins of true evil.

[191] Jung, *Aion*, 43.

Your journey to the Path of Righteousness begins when you see the world as it truly is. Let us now understand how the Nephilim created such powerful systems of control, and how they achieved the grand endeavor that has lasted for 10,000 years and more.

DELUSIONS
OF GRANDEUR

Those who rule you arrogantly assume that they know what is right for the world and are justified in using any means to achieve this vision they see as right. These delusions of grandeur form the foundational philosophy upon which rest all of their actions and systems: that they are better than you, and that one set of rules applies to them, and another applies to you.

This ideology has gone by many names, but in today's parlance, it would be called utopian socialism, a system birthed in 1825 by a man named Robert Owen, who built a commune he called New Harmony. Owen, in his self-exalted wisdom, felt that by controlling the entire environment he could make a better man, for utopian socialists elevate their grand designs above the people captured within those plans—an arrangement that serves their interests, not yours. In utopian socialists' vision, the system makes the man, not the other way around. Every facet of daily life in Owen's New Harmony was controlled, and the residents, called Owenites, worshipped a pseudo-religion created by Owen himself. The experiment ended in failure, nearly bankrupting Owen as such socialist communes are apt to do.

When the process of industrialization began in your world, the concept of a technocracy started to take hold and those who called themselves "technocrats" began to write books and organize political parties. These individuals are completely enamored by man's ability to produce in the industrial age. They are characterized by a blind, sociopathic belief in their own goodness, and that anyone or anything that opposes them is "bad" and must be beaten down.

As an example of utopian socialist thinking, consider the book by Frederick Winslow Taylor, written in 1911 and called *The Principles of Scientific Management*, wherein he states that free people are doomed to fail, and it is inherently inefficient to allow them to act as they will or want. Taylor was the past president of the American Society of Mechanical Engineers, and his book became a reference manual for the technocrats and an inspiration for socialist governments the world over. Taylor's message was clear, that "in the past the man has been first; in the future the system must be first," and he set out to "convince the reader that the remedy for this inefficiency [of resources and living] lies in systematic management rather than in searching for some unusual and extraordinary man." [192]

[192] Frederick W. Taylor, *The Principles of Scientific Management*, (New York: Harper & Brothers, 1911), 7.

Taylor not only refers to economic activities or the workings of large corporations, but also to all human social activities: churches, universities, philanthropic institutions, and activities within the home. The aim of *The Principles of Scientific Management* is to preach systematic control over all aspects of human life, and to bend individual free will in favor of the system.

Utopian socialism has continued changing its name over the years—today, you may have heard of it as scientific socialism, a term used by many dictators to justify their rules. This concept was championed by Chilean president Salvator Allende, who even built a computer called Cybersyn to take control of all economic activity. Colonel Mengistu Haile Mariam headed Ethiopia under the banner of scientific socialism, as did Siad Barre in Somalia. After taking control of all agriculture, both of these dictators ensured widespread famine in their countries, resulting in an overall loss of quality of life and life itself.

Scientific socialism is a dictator's attempt to make a logical argument for despotism. It is a means by which those who rule try to make their reign seem not only necessary, but also virtuous. This core obsession drives them, and in the era in which you live, science has become the label under which they achieve this "virtuous" agenda. They elevate science to a religion and demand that you blindly believe the pronouncements of a small group, carefully chosen by the ruling class.

When Dr. Anthony Fauci arrived on US national television during the midst of the COVID-19 pandemic and announced, "I represent science," he drew a circle around himself and those whose interests he truly represents, leaving outside its circumference the rest of humanity. In essence, he said, "We are special, and you are not," and the world followed him because people across the globe have been trained to follow such people.

Herein Fauci demonstrated the essential principle that there is one set of rules for the ruling class, and another for everyone else. In their delusion of grandeur, they truly believe they are special and better than the rest of mankind. Thus, they have perpetuated a myth that governments—for these special individuals are in control of governments—live by a different set of rules than the individual.

One can see this delusion in action in many doctrines held dear by the ruling class. Consider Westphalian Sovereignty, which acknowledges that the laws, so-called, of each government do not, and cannot, apply to people under the rule of another. In other words, there exists a state of absolute anarchy between governments. Yet, if you were to propose a similar arrangement for individuals, you would be bombarded with statements expressing nothing but conditioned fear, uncertainty, and doubt. A power vacuum, they would say, is the most dangerous condition in which one might exist, yet governments insist on this state of being for themselves.

Yet another fallacy is the doctrine of Macroeconomics, created by John Maynard Keynes. Also known as Keynesian economics, the doctrine holds that governments should act in opposition to their citizens' free economic choices in order to "stabilize" the economy. In his book *The Economic Consequences of the Peace*, published in 1919, Keynes predicted that the Weimar Republic's inflation—traditionally defined as the printing of new money by the central bank—would lead the country to a ruinous hyperinflation. He was right, of course, and in 1923, the country was obliterated.

Shortly afterwards, Keynes created Macroeconomics, which sought to use this very same inflation as a hidden tax, a way to stimulate unsustainable production in certain corners of the economy, such as equities or housing. An individual would not consider borrowing and spending large sums of money while under financial hardship, but it has become the norm for the government. In Keynes's own words, by "a continuing process of inflation, governments can confiscate, secretly and unobserved, an important part of the wealth of their citizens," thereby impoverishing some and enriching others, namely, the ruling class. Such inflation inevitably "engages all the hidden forces of economic law on the side of destruction, and does it in a manner which not one man in a million is able to diagnose." [193]

[193] John Maynard Keynes, *The Economic Consequences of the Peace*, (Cambridge: Author, 1919), 236.

People are tapped to join this ruling class of elites through academic institutions, where they are inducted into this grand delusion. A person who attends Yale University and is considered correctly "gifted" will be recruited into the Order of the Skull and Bones, a secret society that has existed for over 150 years and that one professor demonstrated may have been formed as a branch of the supposedly extinct Bavarian Illuminati. [194] If someone won a Rhodes scholarship to Oxford University, then he would be inducted into other societies that perpetuate the same ruling class philosophies.

[194] Anthony C. Sutton, *America's Secret Establishment: An Introduction to the Order of the Skull and Bones*, (Walterville, OR: TrineDay, LLC, 2002).

It is common knowledge that the Rhodes scholarship was established by Cecil Rhodes, but few know that in the first five versions of his will, Rhodes left his fortune to a secret society of his own design.

The purpose of these secret societies, American and British alike, is to maintain and expand the ruling classes' control over the world, and they are quite serious about these goals, wasting no time on pomp or circumstance. In a letter written on June 2, 1877, known as his "Confession of Faith," Rhodes states the Oxford-connected secret society

> should have its members in every part of the British Empire working with one object and one idea we should have its members placed at our universities and our schools and should watch the English youth passing through their hands just one perhaps in every thousand would have the mind and feelings for such an object, he should be tried in every way, he should be tested whether he is endurant, possessed of eloquence, disregardful of the petty details of life, and if found to be such, then elected and bound by oath to serve for the rest of his life in his Country. He should then be supported if without means by the Society and sent to that part of the Empire where it was felt he was needed. [195]

[195] Cecil Rhodes, "Confession of Faith," letter, June 2, 1877, https://pages.uoregon.edu/kimball/Rhodes-Confession.htm

As Carroll Quigley, Georgetown University professor and mentor to Bill Clinton, says of the Rhodes society in *The Anglo-American Establishment*,

> To be sure, this secret society is not a childish thing like the Ku Klux Klan, and it does not have any secret robes, secret handclaps, or secret passwords. It does not need any of these, since its members know each other intimately. [196]

[196] Carroll Quigley, *The Anglo-American Establishment* (San Pedro, CA: GSG and Associates, 1981), ix.

In Cambridge, there was a society known as the Cambridge Apostles, which similarly recruited elites in the ivory tower of academia. John Maynard Keynes, who has been mentioned, was part of this society, the activities of which have been described as "overt full-blooded—almost aggressive—homosexuality." [197] Keynes himself is known to have been a compulsive pederast who kept a detailed diary of all the sexual encounters he had with underage boys. [198]

[197] Nikolai Endres, "Cambridge Apostles," GLBTQ, 2005, http://www.glbtqarchive.com/ssh/cambridge_apostles_S.pdf

[198] The Daily Dish, "Keynes's 'Jew Boy' Quickie," *Atlantic*, January 28, 2008, https://www.theatlantic.com/daily-dish/archive/2008/01/keyness-jew-boy-quickie/220620/

These hidden societies function as recruitment grounds for the new elite, where they are trained to uphold and perpetuate the scientific socialist world order—just as the Nephilim of old were trained in schools such as that found at Göbekli Tepe. The Nephilim look upon the masses and choose those who will be the most compliant as cogs in their machinery, and have created recruitment procedures such as the Rhodes scholarship and the Order of the Skull and Bones to initiate them into their way of thinking. These recruits then go on to occupy positions of power in politics, finance, the media, and international organizations.

Those who see clearly, Seeker of Truth, can discern the Nephilim's hand behind this. As the Book of Jubilees reveals,

> And they will make to themselves high places and groves and graven images, and they will worship, each his own (graven image), so as to go astray, and they will sacrifice their children to demons, and to all the works of the error of their hearts. [199]

[199] Book of Jubilees 1:11.

The Industrial Age marked the first time that humans truly stepped out of the shadows of the Bronze Age, developing technology and rapidly shifting the distribution of wealth towards common people, threatening the Nephilim's rule. Instead of thwarting this progress by plunging humankind back into the Dark Ages or allowing this progress to grow unfettered, the Nephilim arrived at the perfect plan to get ahead of this leap forward and simultaneously control it. They created the false dichotomy known as the Right-Left political system, thereby pitting individuals against each other when in truth the governing ideologies have only minor differences.

In creating this dichotomy, and in discounting the voice of nonvoters, the Nephilim effectively usurped the processes that drive people toward free communication and greater individual power, and engineered the political system such that they could maintain control. Herein fits technocracy, which seeks to control any means of progress through the instruments of a "government" or, in the case of scientific socialism, through the instrument of "science." Far from being an agent of change, the political process is one that is meant to stall, or entirely prevent, any meaningful actions being taken for the betterment of humanity.

Technocracy has manifested itself in different ways throughout the centuries. The Fabian Society is one such manifestation, birthed out of the progressive movement by Baron Sidney and Baroness Beatrice Webb. Another of its executive committee members, George Bernard Shaw, a man whose plays are celebrated among humans, gave an illuminating speech on the goals of the Fabian society and socialism:

Mussolini is trying to build up in Italy what he calls the corporate State. He wants to put all the different industries in the hands of corporations, as he calls them, and then finally he wants to have a council of corporations, and that council of corporations is to succeed Parliament. I say, "Hear, hear! More power to your elbow." That is precisely what the Fabian Society wants to have done, because it is clearly a necessary part of socialism. [200]

[200] **George Bernard Shaw** "Shaw Heaps Praise Upon the Dictators," *New York Times*, December 10, 1933.

Shaw reveals precisely what the Fabian society and socialists are reaching for: industrial cartels controlled by them so they can maintain their riches and keep the treasure in their bank accounts.

Technocracy progressed from the Fabian society to different forms in the twentieth century. Historians have described World War II as the end of the age of empires, by which they mean that there was a general rise in the level of consciousness of mankind around concepts like democracy. Thus, civilization witnessed the dissolution of the Austro-Hungarian Empire, the dissolution of the British Empire, and the rebranding of government from an autocratic and authoritative institution into a "democratic" one. The British Empire, for example, was transformed into the British Commonwealth, largely by the work of Lionel Curtis, an ardent promoter of a one-world government.

Humankind no longer worshipped their rulers as God-Kings, so a new system was needed to maintain the same level of control, lest the slaves revolt. As former US president Woodrow Wilson said when seeking Congress's declaration of war against Germany, "The world must be made safe for democracy."

At around the time the world was transitioning to this more expansive form of democracy as a means for control, the United Nations, itself a successor to the failed League of Nations, was established to act as the world's elite and ruling class, to maintain power across the world as it became more globalized in conjunction with the increasing ineffectiveness of national governments.

The shift to democracy was simply the first process change. Every country was a sandbox of their own, with different voting systems and ideals of freedom and liberalization. Those in power were experimenting with what worked to keep them in power. Now that the world is in the midst of the Information Age, the concept of "government" is going through a second process change: a shift from democracy back to autocracy under the rule of science and scientists. Decades ago, US President Eisenhower said in his farewell address,

The prospect of domination of the nation's scholars by Federal employment, project allocations, and the power of money is ever present and is gravely to be regarded. Yet, in holding scientific research and discovery in respect, as we should, we must also be alert to the equal and opposite danger that public policy could itself become the captive of a scientific-technological elite. [201]

[201]**Dwight D. Eisenhower**, farewell address given January 17, 1961, https://www.eisenhower-library.gov/sites/default/files/research/online-documents/farewell-address/1961-01-17-press-release.pdf

Eisenhower's prophecy has come to pass, and the world is today in the grips of scientific socialism. Recall the words of Dr. Fauci when he said, "I represent science," and witness the hubris in that statement. Today's world is characterized by scientific delusion, by the belief that people who are trained in science are so adept at interpreting and understanding the world that the rest of mankind should simply submit themselves to their conclusions without question.

[202]**Ann Tomoko Rosen**, "'Guinea Pig Kids': Fauci's Legacy of Cruel Experiments on Kids," Defender, November 11, 2021, https://childrenshealthdefense.org/defender/guinea-pig-kids-aids-fauci-experiments/; *Guinea Pig Kids Documentary— Fauci*, transcript and slightly edited version of the BBC documentary *Guinea Pig Kids*, originally broadcast November 30, 2004, https://rumble.com/vogr7a-guinea-pig-kids-bbc-documentary-fauci.html

The people behind scientific socialism place no value on human life beyond the utility an individual has for their system, for humans below the ruling class are simply expendable in the face of that system, as has been said in Taylor's *Principles of Scientific Management*. Here are but two examples: Dr. Fauci is known to have authorized experimented on underprivileged children, the most vulnerable of your society: he injected them with toxic AIDS drugs and vaccines, causing potentially lethal side effects such as bone marrow death, organ failure, and brain damage. [202]

Likewise, Ed Buck, a wealthy and prominent donor of the US Democratic Party, tried to play doctor on an amateur level by injecting people with powerful opiates as way to achieve sexual pleasure. This sexual compulsion led Buck to repeatedly hire black male prostitutes, who would come to his home to be hooked up to a machine and pumped full of morphine and other powerful substances. His fetish came to light after some of them died. [203]

[203]**Josh Haskell**, "Democratic Donor ed Buck's Trial Centers on Alleged Injection Fetish," *ABC7*, July 13, 2021, https://abc7.com/ed-buck-trial-fatal-overdose-prostitution/10884027/

Are Fauci and Buck descendants of the Nephilim? Do they share the E-M81 gene? That cannot be known for sure, but we can look to their despicable actions and know that they have little regard for the lives and well-being of others.

DIVIDE
AND CONQUER

Those who seek to control you and who have controlled you for 10,000 years operate today through the two-part mechanism of divide and conquer.

Those in control divide the rest of humanity by fueling meaningless binaries that keep humankind occupied with pointless squabbles. The most glaring example is the aforementioned division between the Right and the Left, a political divide that ensures the masses are occupied in endless arguments that distract from what those in power are executing. Hear again the words of Carroll Quigley, who speaks to this truth in *Tragedy and Hope*:

> The argument that the two parties should represent opposed ideas and policies, one perhaps of the Right and the other of the Left, is a foolish idea acceptable only to doctrinaire and academic thinkers. Instead, the two parties should be almost identical so that the American people can "throw the rascals out" at any election without leading to any profound or extensive shifts in policy. The policies that are vital and necessary for America are no longer subjects of significant disagreement, but are disputable only in details of procedure, priority, or method. [204]

[204] Carroll Quigley, *Tragedy and Hope: A History of the World in Our Time,* (New York: MacMillan, 1966), 1247–1248.

Your world today is indeed split into Left and Right, and both parties and their supporters are too preoccupied with their fights to notice the devious plans of the ruling class. It is an effective strategy because humans function with dualistic thinking, with the belief that something must be either one thing or the other, as opposed to the multitude of possibilities or combinations. The Nephilim have expertly and successfully exploited that tendency.

The second part of the divide-and-conquer strategy is the act of conquering, which refers to the systems and people the Nephilim and their kind have put in place to execute various plans around the world. Similarly, these functionaries, whether knowingly or unknowingly part of the Nephilim plan, are elevated to positions of power, not because they belong there and have shown themselves competent, but because they subscribe to the Nephilim world order and allow themselves to be controlled. Alas, however, they are out of their depth and do not know precisely what they are supporting or how to do their jobs effectively.

One glaring example of this is Chrystia Freeland, a Rhodes scholar and Harvard graduate who is currently serving as the finance minister and deputy prime minister of Canada, and also sits on the Board of Trustees of the World Economic Forum. At the start of her career in the late 1980s, she was sent to Ukraine on what was publicly called a student exchange program. What she was really doing, however, was interviewing Ukrainian nationalists, something for which the Soviet government eventually drove her out of the country. [205]

[205] Don Retson, "Student 'Glasnost' Chilly," *Edmonton Journal*, May 20, 1989.

When she returned to Canada, Freeland ascended the political ladder very quickly. Despite having no training or experience in finance, she became the finance minister, and then the deputy prime minister. A simple examination of her career makes it obvious she could not have climbed the ladder on her own: she needed to be handheld to get to the positions of power she is in and for which she is manifestly unqualified. [206]

[206] Matthew Ehret, "Chrystia Freeland: Rhodes Scholar, Trustee of the WEF, Deputy PM of Canada, and the Failure of the 'Super Elite,'" *Canadian Patriot*, February 11, 2021, https://canadianpatriot.org/2021/02/11/chrystia-freeland-rhodes-scholar-trustee-of-the-wef-deputy-pm-of-canada-and-the-failure-of-the-super-elite/

Do you doubt that Freeland has been knowingly or unknowingly a pawn of the Nephilim? Consider this: she is the granddaughter of Ukranian Nazi Michael Chomiak, who was the chief editor of a publishing house tasked with creating pro-Nazi propaganda. When this came to light, she lied by dismissing it as "Russian disinformation," but the evidence is incontrovertible. [207] She herself is an ardent supporter of the neo-Nazi Azov Battalion, funneling millions in public funds to the Ukrainian neo-Nazi military force and similar nationalist groups. [208] For the whole of her political career, Freeland has been a shameless supporter of the global elite seeking to keep the masses in check.

[207] Joe Hoft, "Exclusive: Canada's Deputy Prime Minister Chrystia Freeland's Grandfather Was a Nazi and She Admires George Soros. It's No Surprise She's Labeling Freedom-Loving Canadians Terrorists," *Gateway Pundit*, February 15, 2022, https://www.thegatewaypundit.com/2022/02/exclusive-canadas-deputy-prime-minister-chrystia-freelands-grandfather-nazi-admires-george-soros-no-surprise-labeling-freedom-loving-canadians-terrorists/

Bloomberg View, "Leonid Bershidshy: Chrystia Freeland's Dismissal of Her Family's Nazi Connection Is Only Helping Russia's Propagandists," *National Post*, March 13, 2017, https://nationalpost.com/opinion/leonid-bershidsky-chrystia-freelands-dismissal-of-her-familys-nazi-connection-is-only-helping-russias-propagandists

And Freeland is not alone. There are many such functionaries in positions of power that they have not earned. An inquiring mind should ask why. Who put them there? What is their goal? As you now know, the Nephilim are behind these appointments and their goal is world domination through these "useful idiots" [209]—whether they are aware of this scheme or not.

The ultimate goal is the consolidation of power, and the breaking down of national barriers to annihilate what little is left of individual sovereignty and to aggregate power to a single, global body.

[208] **Adam Riggio,** "A Liberal Hand in Hand with Nazis: Chrystia Freeland in Ukraine," *Canada Files,* July 18, 2020, https://www.thecanadafiles.com/articles/ncfuk

[209] "'**Useful Idiot': Meaning and Origin,**" *Word Histories,* https://wordhistories.net/2021/03/26/useful-idiot/

POPULATION CONTROL

Those who rule you from the ivory tower envision themselves as the managers of your society. You are but sheep and they, your shepherds, guide you towards whichever path they deem best for themselves. They seek to control all earthly experiences—your education systems, the media you consume, the information to which you are exposed—and their ultimate goal is to remain, always, in power.

To maintain control and keep the flock manageable, the ruling class has used the same primary method for millennia: population control, or eugenics. Consider the Watcher king Enlil, who called for genocide because the people had become too numerous and burdensome:

> The noise of mankind has become too much. I am losing sleep over their racket. Cut off food supplies to the people! Let the vegetation be too scant for their hunger! Let Adad wipe away his rain. Below let no flood-water flow from the springs. Let wind go, let it strip the ground bare, let clouds gather but not drop rain, let the field yield a diminished harvest, let Nissaba stop up her bosom. No happiness shall come to them. [210]
>
> [210] Stephanie Dalley, trans. and ed., "Atrahasis, Tablet II," in *Myths from Mesopotamia: Creation, the Flood, Gilgamesh, and Others*, rev. ed. (Oxford: Oxford Uni. Press, 1989), 20.

Similar sentiments have been echoed throughout the ages. Here is Thomas Malthus in the eighteenth century, whose namesake has achieved infamy, writing in the sixth edition of An *Essay on the Principle of Population*:

> All the children born, beyond what would be required to keep up the population to this level, must necessarily perish, unless room be made for them by the deaths of grown persons ... Therefore ... we should facilitate, instead of foolishly and vainly endeavoring to impede, the operations of nature in producing this mortality; and if we dread the too frequent visitation of the horrid form of famine, we should sedulously encourage the other forms

of destruction, which we compel nature to use. Instead of recommending cleanliness to the poor, we should encourage contrary habits. In our towns we should make the streets narrower, crowd more people into the houses, and court the return of the plague. In the country, we should build our villages near stagnant pools, and particularly encourage settlements in all marshy and unwholesome situations. But above all, we should reprobate specific remedies for ravaging diseases; and restrain those benevolent, but much mistaken men, who have thought they were doing a service to mankind by projecting schemes for the total extirpation of particular disorders. [211]

[211] **Thomas Malthus**, *An Essay on the Principles of Population; or A View of Its Past and Present Effects on Human Happiness with an Inquiry into Our Prospects Respecting the Future Removal or Mitigation of the Evils Which It Occasions*, vol. II, 6th ed. (London: John Murray, 1826), 300–301.

And here, in the twentieth century, speaks Margaret Sanger, the founder of Planned Parenthood and a modern-day hero of one Hillary Clinton, whom you have elevated in your systems. In an address before the New History Society, Sanger said,

Apply a stern and rigid policy of sterilization and segregation to that grade of population whose progeny is tainted, or whose inheritance is such that objectionable traits may be transmitted to offspring. Insure the country against future burdens of maintenance for numerous offspring as may be born of feebleminded parents, by pensioning all persons with transmissible disease who voluntarily consent to sterilization. Give certain dysgenic groups in our population their choice of segregation or sterilization. Apportion farm lands and homesteads for these segregated persons where they would be taught to work under competent instructors for the period of their entire lives. [212]

[212] **Margaret Sanger**, "A Plan for Peace," address before the New History Society, January 17, 1932, reprinted in *Birth Control Review*, vol. XVI, no. 4 (1932): 107–108.

Here, Sanger speaks not only of congenital disease, but also of traits she simply finds objectionable such as sexual preference, substance use, or even wrong beliefs and opinions. Later, she rebranded her efforts as birth control, for the Nazis had given eugenics a bad name and she could no longer practice population control so openly.

This effort to conceal her true agenda becomes all the more obvious in a December 10, 1939 letter to a doctor wherein she states, "We do not want word to go out that we want to exterminate the Negro population and the minister is the man who can straighten out that idea if it ever occurs to any of their more rebellious members." [213] She was well aware of the distasteful nature of her methods, but nevertheless pressed on and recruited influential figures within the communities she wanted to decimate.

[213] **Margaret Sanger**, letter to Dr. C. J. Gamble, December 10, 1939, https://libex.smith.edu/omeka/items/show/495

In 1922, John Maynard Keynes spoke at the Fifth Neo-Malthusian and Birth Control Conference, where he said, "Judicious birth control offers one of the easiest, safest and racially most beneficial means for the diminution of the size of the manual working class." He also passed a resolution stating that wage earners could make more by reducing the population of their less skilled, racially undesirable competition. [214] One should pause and consider the long-term implications of such a policy, if put into effect.

[214] *Report of the Fifth International Neo-Malthusian and Birth Control Conference*, ed. Raymond Pierpoint (London: William Heinemann, 1922), 95.

These are but a few examples of the clear articulation of their vision, Seeker of Truth: to wipe out those considered undesirable, expendable, worthless—those not part of the ruling class and those not easily exploitable.

Over time, those in the ivory tower changed the narrative of population control: they found that birth control was not enough, and they needed a story to encourage more people to stop having children. Thus, in the 1990s, Alexander King and Berman Schneider wrote *The First Global Revolution: A Report by the Council of the Club of Rome*, a follow-up to the club's 1972 report *The Limits to Growth*, in which they continued the first book's theme of overpopulation being a major cause of their imagined future doomsday, introducing new strategies for controlling the growth of said population:

> The need for enemies seems to be a common historical factor. States have striven to overcome domestic failure and internal contradictions by designating external enemies. The scapegoat practice is as old as mankind itself. When things become too difficult at home, divert attention by adventure abroad. Bring the divided nation together to face an outside enemy, either a real one or else one invented for the purpose ... In searching for a new enemy to unite us, we came up with the idea that pollution, the threat of global warming, water shortages, famine and the like would fit the bill ... All these dangers are caused by human intervention and it is only through changed attitudes and behaviour that they can be overcome. The real enemy, then, is humanity itself. [215]

[215] Alexander King and Berman Schneider, *First Global Revolution: A Report by the Council of the Club of Rome* (New York: Pantheon Books, 1991)), 109, 115.

A modernized version of this population control agenda was created in the Kissinger Report, officially known as the National Security Study Memorandum 200. In the report, Kissinger outlined the immediate and urgent need for a massive and global coordinated effort to roll out birth control and deploy other population control methods. He also emphasized the need for a good marketing campaign that would mollify people and convince them this was not a coordinated effort at depopulation. Indeed, in the report he uses nearly the exact language as his forebear, Margaret Sanger:

> We must take care that our activities should not give the appearance to the LDCs [Lesser Developed Countries] of an industrialized country policy directed against the LDCs. Caution must be taken that in any approaches in this field we support in the LDCs are ones we can support within this country. "Third World" leaders should be in the forefront and obtain the credit for successful programs. [216]
>
> [216] National Security Council, *National Security Study Memorandum (NSSM20): Implications of Worldwide Population Growth or U.S. Secretary and Overseas Interests (The Kissinger Report)*, December 10, 1974, para. 33.

It is clear that the rulers know what population control can appear as, and work hard to keep its true nature hidden. Later in the report, Kissinger considers mandatory population control programs, including control of food and changing "consumption patterns toward more efficient uses of protein." Today, Kissinger's grand designs are being carried out by one of his pupils, of whom we are about to speak.

A loose translation of a passage in Voltaire's *Questions on Miracles* is, "Anyone who can make you believe absurdities can make you commit atrocities." This is what those in the ivory tower have set out to achieve for humankind. The absurdity of which they are convincing you is that there is a desperate need for population control, and the atrocity they want you to commit—indeed, that they are committing—is genocide.

There are three main arms of the present-day eugenics movement. First is the World Economic Forum, which was created by Kissinger's student at Harvard, Klaus Schwab, son of a Nazi collaborator who devoted his company, Escher-Wyss, to supporting their war and extermination programs. [217] Schwab engineered the WEF so that he is permanently executive chairman and president; like the kings of old, this role passes to a member of his immediate family upon his death. The actual members of this supposed nonprofit can never vote him or his successors out. [218] He has also openly bragged about "penetrating the cabinets" and other political structures around the world. Indeed, if you look at the graduates of his Young Global Leaders program, as well as politicians

[217] Johnny Vedmore, "Klaus Schwab Was Henry Kissinger's Pupil and the Son of a Nazi Collaborator Who Used Slave Labor and Aided Nazi Efforts to Obtain the First Atomic Bomb," *Humans Are Free*, March 24, 2021, https://humansbefree.com/2021/03/klaus-schwab-was-henry-kissingers-pupil-and-the-son-of-a-nazi-collaborator.html

[218] "Regulations Regarding the Organization of the World Economic Forum," December 2015, https://www3.weforum.org/docs/WEF_Reglement_2015.pdf

[219] Martin Armstrong, "Schwab Admits He Controls Trudeau and Cabinet of Canada—Now the World," *Armstrong Economics*, February 7, 2022,

[219] https://www.armstrongeconomics.com/world-news/wef/schwab-admits-he-controls-trudeau-cabinet-of-canada-now-the-world/

and bureaucrats actively serving at the WEF while simultaneously being in office, you will have no doubt about his massive sphere of influence. [219]

The second arm is the World Health Organization, which is headed by Tedros Adhanom Ghebreyesus, a man who has been killing people and covering up genocide his whole career. Ghebreyesus is a long-time active member of the Tigray People's Liberation Front, a group known for their violent, socialist ideology and for engaging in dozens of murders, kidnappings, bombings, and other violence throughout Ethiopia in a campaign of terror in order to seize political power. [220]

[220] **Global Terrorism Database,** "Perpetrators: (Tigray Peoples Liberation Front (TPLF))," University of Maryland, https://www.start.umd.edu/gtd/search/Results.aspx?perpetrator=2127

[221] **Rachael Bunyan,** "WHO Chief Tedros Ghebreyesus Is Accused of Aiding Genocide in Ethiopia: Nobel Peace Prize Nominee Lodges Complaint with International Criminal Court," *Daily Mail,* December 14, 2020, https://www.dailymail.co.uk/news/article-9052247/WHO-chief-Tedros-Ghebreyseus-accused-aiding-genocide,-Ethiopia-nobel-peace-prize-nominee.html

[222] **John Martin,** "The Crimes of Tedros Adhanom," *Rough Estimate,* March 25, 2020, https://www.roughestimate.org/rough-estimate/the-crimes-of-tedros-adhanom

Ghebreyesus also stands accused of enabling genocide at the International Criminal Court for directing his security forces to torture and kill their political enemies. [221] When poor public health practices led to a cholera outbreak in Ethiopia, killing untold numbers of people, Ghebreyesus covered it up. [222] He escaped certain death by angry mobs in his own country and, through his friendship with Bill Gates, rose to the top of the World Health Organization. When speaking about the COVID-19 vaccines, Ghebreyesus said,

So, if it's going to be used [the COVID-19 vaccine] it's better to focus on those groups of severe disease and death, rather as we see some countries are using it to give boosters to kill children, this is not right. [223]

[223] **"Breaking—Director-General of the WHO Claims "Countries Are Giving Boosters to Kill Children, This Is Not Right,"** Exposé, December 22, 2021, https://expose-news.com/2021/12/22/tedros-says-countries-killing-kids-with-boosters/

[224] **Peter Doshi,** "Covid-19 Vaccines and Treatments: We Must Have Raw Data, Now," editorial, *BMJ,* January 19, 2022, https://www.bmj.com/content/376/bmj.o102; **Patricia Harrity,** "New Study Shows an Increase in Deaths in 145 Countries after COVID Vaccines Were Introduced," *Exposé,* January 15, 2022, https://expose-news.com/2022/01/15/new-study-shows-an-increase-in-deaths-in-145-countries-after-covid-vaccines-were-introduced%e2%80%8b/

Ghebreyesus knew the vaccines would not work as proclaimed, and thus indicated the vaccine ought to be used to target the already diseased sections of the population, so that economically productive children would be spared. [224]

Third is Bill Gates and his various initiatives targeted at population control. He comes from a family of eugenicists, with his father, who bears the same name, sitting on the board of Margaret Sanger's Planned Parenthood. Sanger famously stated to her colleagues at the American Eugenics Society that she viewed birth control and eugenics as "the right and left hand of one body." [225] For over twenty years, Bill Gates has been pouring millions into the Bill and Melinda Gates Institute for Population and Reproductive Health housed at Johns Hopkins University and the Bloomberg School of Public Health. [226]

Via his foundation, Gates has provided billions to the World Health Organization, and exercises vast influence over the realm of public health worldwide. [227] In the 1990s, he helped fund a WHO tetanus vaccination campaign throughout many countries, yet only women of child-bearing age were eligible and were told they must receive repeated inoculations, unlike the tetanus vaccines used in the past, which was a single dose. It turned out the vaccines caused the body to produce antibodies against the pregnancy hormone hCG. The campaign led to thousands of spontaneous abortions and fertility problems for many more. [228]

Gates has since engaged in various other disastrous vaccination campaigns throughout the world, with one of the most notable paralyzing over 490,000 Indian children with a polio vaccine. [229] In 2014, a researcher at the University of Wisconsin, who took millions of dollars from Gates for his work, spliced several avian flu strains into a deadly weapon, and was resoundingly condemned by his colleagues for what he had done. [230] Is it a coincidence that former CDC director Robert Redfield has warned that the next pandemic will likely be a devastating bird flu, one for which COVID-19 was "a mere warm-up"? [231] Gates himself is noted for calling COVID-19 "pandemic one" and lamenting the apparent lack of attention it received. In an interview with the US Chamber of Commerce he states that the next pandemic "will get attention this time," smirking and looking away from the camera as he says it. [232]

[225] Jonathan Peter Spiro, *Defending the Master Race: Conservation, Eugenics, and the Legacy of Madison Grant* (Lebanon, NH: University of Vermont Press, 2009), 194.

[226] "The Bill and Melinda Gates Institute for Population Control and Reproductive Health Celebrates 20 Years," *Hopkins Bloomberg Public Health*, September 19, 2019, https://magazine.jhsph.edu/2019/bill-melinda-gates-institute-population-and-reproductive-health-celebrates-20-years

[227] Natalie Huet and Carmen Paun, "Meet the World's Most Powerful Doctor: Bill Gates," *PoliticoPro*, May 14, 2017, https://www.politico.eu/article/bill-gates-who-most-powerful-doctor/

[228] Lee Harding, "Gates, WHO, and Abortion Vaccines," *Frontier Centre for Public Policy*, July 19, 2020, https://fcpp.org/2020/07/19/gates-who-and-abortion-vaccines/; John W. Oller et al., "HCG Found in WHO Tetanus Vaccine in Kenya Raises Concern in the Developing World," *Open Access Library Journal* 4 (2017): 1-31. It should be noted that not all serum vials contained the toxin, roughly nine out of forty-seven did, thus creating an aura of deniability.

[229] Robert F. Kennedy Jr., "Gates' Globalist Vaccine Agenda: A Win-Win for Pharma and Mandatory Vaccination," *Children's Health Defense*, April 9, 2020, https://childrenshealthdefense.org/news/government-corruption/gates-globalist-vaccine-agenda-a-win-win-for-pharma-and-mandatory-vaccination/

[230] Steve Connor, "Exclusive: Controversial US Scientist Creates Deadly New Flu Strain for Pandemic Research," *The Independent*, July 2, 2014, https://www.independent.co.uk/news/science/exclusive-controversial-us-scientist-creates-deadly-new-flu-strain-for-pandemic-research-9577088.html

231 "Fmr CDC Director: Bird Flu Is the Real Pandemic—C19 Was Just Practice," *Ice Age Farmer*, April 9, 2022, https://www.iceagefarmer. com/2022/04/09/fmr-cdc-director-bird-flu-is-the-real-pandemic-c19-was-just-practice/

232 "Bill and Melinda Gates on Preparing for the Next Pandemic," YouTube video, posted by U.S. Chamber of Commerce, February 4, 2021, https://www.youtube.com/ watch?v=fWQ2DsHWrQE&t=404s

Population control and eugenics are also intimately connected with the so-called climate crisis. In the 1970s, Paul Ehrlich wrote a book called *The Population Bomb*, wherein he blames an imagined future environmental disaster on overpopulation. Ehrlich is a well-known catastrophist, whose myriad claims of impending disaster have all failed to materialize in the proposed time frames. Most famously, in 1980, he was taken to task by Professor Julian Simon over his many laughable doomsayings, and their argument ended in a bet, which Ehrlich spectacularly lost. Yet, no matter how many times he fails or how many disasters he creates, he will never be removed from his position of influence because he is at the highest floors of the ivory tower, knowingly or unknowingly working for the Nephilim and their goal of eugenics and extermination.

Mike Schellenberger, a reputed environmentalist, points out that the narrative around reducing the population to save the world is inherently flawed. As Schellenberger shows in his book *Apocalypse Never*, if people like Paul Ehrlich truly wanted to save the world, they would invest in nuclear energy, which is a clean and safe way to ensure the world has enough power without using fossil fuels. But they do not, because their agenda is not to establish a safer and greener planet rich in energy, but to purge the world of undesirables.

Indeed, the solutions being provided by those in the ivory tower in the form of wind and solar energy are simply not good enough to create the kind of long-lasting change your world needs if the temperatures are truthfully rising at the rates they proclaim. The alternatives the rulers present to you are unfeasible—and they know it. The earth's surface receives about 1,000 watts of total energy per square meter from the sun, and solar technology can only collect a fraction of that. [233] To convert all of humanity's energy production to solar would devastate the global landscape through the process by which materials are gathered to make solar cells, and the space they take up when deployed.

233 "Introduction to Solar Radiation," *MKS Newport*, https://www.newport. com/t/introduction-to-solar-radiation

Those in power will tell you that the world's temperatures are and have been steadily rising over the last century, and that the need for immediate solutions is paramount. But this is a fallacy. In truth, the records are being altered to create a false narrative of global warming.

Behold, the "adjustments" made to the thermometer measurements and reflected in the final, published data, correlate almost perfectly with changing atmospheric carbon dioxide levels—far too perfectly to be simply coincidental. [234]

In many ways, the modern-day environmental movement is the eugenics movement in disguise, a movement that began in the 1970s as a terrorist organization in America known as the Weather Underground. An FBI agent who infiltrated the Weather Underground discovered that this organization's plans were to seize control of the United States and then exterminate 25 million people, which was a tenth of the US population at that time. [235] After its leadership was arrested, including Barack Obama's mentor Bill Ayers, the remaining members merged with another violent socialist organization, the Black Liberation Army, creating the May 19th Communist Organization. There are still other organizations today pushing the same population control agenda, albeit with a more polished public face. The Sierra Club in the United States and the Club of Rome in Europe are but two examples, though both focus on the benefit to the environment rather than the means to get there. [236]

No matter what face these organizations take, the end goal perpetuated by the socialist forces in the background is the same: grind mankind into poverty and take away their energy and food choices, and when that does not work, exterminate them.

[234] Tony Heller, "Alterations to the US Temperature Record (Part 1)," YouTube video, posted October 6, 2020, https://www.youtube.com/watch?v=YRXDOAhjBn8; Tony Heller, "Alterations to the US Temperature Record (Part 2)," YouTube video, posted October 11, 2020, https://www.youtube.com/watch?v=QmBiXfekga8; Tony Heller, "Alterations to the US Temperature Record (Part 3)," YouTube video, posted October 20, 2020, https://www.youtube.com/watch?v=Sf4gC9E_3iU

[235] "Larry Grathwohl Interview about William Ayers, Obama's Mentor," YouTube video, posted by vibratingwatercats, October 30, 2008, https://www.youtube.com/watch?v=VIN2tOoERHk

[236] "Sierra Club Global Population Policy," Sierra Club, May 2017, https://www.sierraclub.org/sites/www.sierraclub.org/files/Population-Policy_May2017.pdf

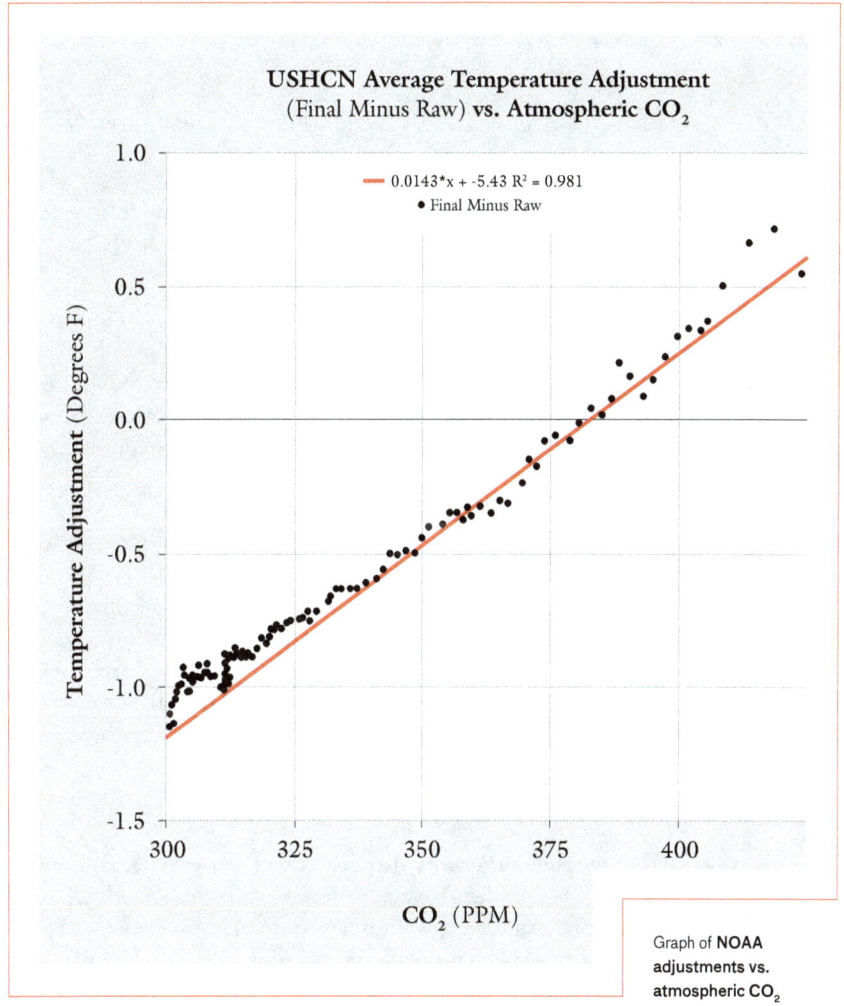

Graph of **NOAA**
adjustments vs.
atmospheric CO_2

MIND
CONTROL

How do the Nephilim and their minions in the ivory tower persuade humans to back philosophies and systems that clearly do not suit the majority? Through propaganda and mind control. Edward Bernays laid out the mechanisms of this control in the opening sentences of his book *Propaganda*:

> The conscious and intelligent manipulation of the organized habits and opinions of the masses is an important element in democratic society. Those who manipulate this unseen mechanism of society constitute an invisible government which is the true ruling power of our country. We are governed, our minds are molded, our tastes formed, our ideas suggested, largely by men we have never heard of ... It is they who pull the wires which control the public mind, who harness old social forces and contrive new ways to bind and guide the world. [237]

[237] Edward Bernays, *Propaganda* (Brooklyn: Ig Publishing, 1928), 37.

There is evidence throughout your history that the hidden and secret organizations of the government, such as the CIA, have been tasked with this agenda of mind control and have been orchestrating a web of lies to deceive the general population. This goal could not have been more clearly stated than in these words from former CIA director William Casey: "We'll know our disinformation program is complete when everything the American public believes is false." [238]

[238] As quoted by Barbara Honegger from a February 1981 meeting with President Ronald Reagan.

More recently, former president Donald Trump instilled fear into the media because they believed his tweets could undermine their power to control the narrative. In the words of Mika Brzezinski, daughter of Zbigniew, so-called "godfather of Al-Qaeda and the Taliban," [239]

[239] Brian P. McGlinchey, "Zbigniew Brzezinski, Godfather of al Qaeda and Taliban, Dead at 89," 28Pages.org, May 28, 2017, https://28pages.org/2017/05/28/zbigniew-brzezinski-godfather-of-al-qaeda-and-taliban-dead-at-89/

[Donald Trump] is trying to undermine the media and trying to make up his own facts. And it could be that while unemployment and the economy worsens, he could have undermined the messaging so much that he can actually control exactly what people think. And that, that is our job. [240]

[240] **Mika Brzezinski**, in a discussion on MSNBC's Morning Joe, February 22, 2017.

In plain language, this host admits that the job of the media is not to inform the masses but to control what they think.

In 2015, investigative journalist Sharyl Attkisson delivered a speech at a TEDx event at the University of Nevada where she outlined, with evidence, the various strategies used by governments and large corporations designed to overwhelm people from all sides using charged language, fake experts, fake Wikipedia pages, fake comments on Internet posts, fake newspaper editorials, fake fact-checks, and more—all with the intent of burying true information or making it look like it was discredited. [241]

[241] **Sharyl Attkisson**, "How Real Is Fake News?" TEDx Talk, 2015, https://www.ted.com/talks/sharyl_attkisson_how_real_is_fake_news

This information control agenda ties into the wider concept of "cognitive warfare," a new form of warfare created by NATO, with support from Johns Hopkins University and Imperial College, wherein war has evolved from planes, tanks, and missiles to information battles and the fight for people's opinions and beliefs. Victory in this warfare is the ability to influence what people think, and thus how they behave. [242]

[242] **Ben Norton**, "Behind NATO's 'Cognitive Warfare': 'Battle for Your Brain' Waged by Western Militaries," *The Gray Zone*, October 8, 2021, https://thegrayzone.com/2021/10/08/nato-cognitive-warfare-brain/; **"Countering Cognitive Warfare,"** *NATO Review*, May 20, 2021, https://www.nato.int/docu/review/articles/2021/05/20/countering-cognitive-warfare-awareness-and-resilience/index.html

Cognitive warfare is a rebranding of the age-old practice of using propaganda in warfare; the tactics have now evolved to include the Internet and media channels. It involves lies, misinformation, information control, and the childish ploy of misdirection to command people's attention and to control what they believe.

[243] **David Pugliese**, "Forged Letter Warning about Wolves on the Loose Part of Canadian Forces Propaganda Campaign That Went Awry," *Ottawa Citizen*, October 14, 2020, https://ottawacitizen.com/news/national/defence-watch/forged-letter-warning-about-wolves-on-the-loose-part-of-canadian-forces-propaganda-campaign-that-went-awry

Do you doubt that those ruling from the ivory tower seek to control and even manufacture your perception of reality? Do you doubt the great lengths to which they will go to achieve their goal? Consider an incident that happened in Canada: In 2020, the Nova Scotia Department of Lands and Forestry sent a letter to its citizens warning of a pack of wolves roaming a particular town. Only, there was no pack of wolves. The letter was a fake, forged by the Canadian military "as part of a propaganda training mission that went off the rails." [243] To keep up the ruse, the military went so far as to play recorded wolf sounds in the woods.

The CIA has been controlling the US media for decades. The Pike and Church Committee hearings revealed but a glimpse of the CIA's infiltration and control of both domestic and foreign media, executed under the banner of Operation Mockingbird. [244] In 1977, *Rolling Stone* published a report by Carl Bernstein that outlined the many unethical deeds of the CIA in taking control of the media wherever it could. [245]

[244] **Church Committee Commission,** Volume VII, Covert Action. US GOVERNMENT PRINTING OFFICE. December 4–5, 1975.

[245] **Carl Bernstein,** The CIA and the Media," *Rolling Stone,* October 20, 1977, https://www.carlbernstein.com/the-cia-and-the-media-rolling-stone-10-20-1977

Today, the CIA has progressed from infiltrating the media by paying journalists to owning the media itself. They have bought out most of the major media institutions through various front organizations and have bent others to their control by means we shall later discuss.

The different strategies of cognitive warfare are clear in the CIA's history of manipulating the media. They have shaped Hollywood movies into effective propaganda tools. They have engineered distraction techniques as vast as the hippie movement, which was created to discredit the antiwar movement, so that an average American citizen would look at a person against the war and think they were a beatnik whose opinions were not to be trusted. [246]

[246] **David McGowan,** *Weird Scenes Inside the Canyon: Laurel Canyon, Covert Ops, and the Dark Heart of the Hippie Dream* (London: Headpress, 2014).

The CIA even have their hand in the creation of social media, which is a twenty-first-century phenomenon concocted by elites to control the masses. Did you know, Seeker of Truth, that the US military created Facebook as a way of monitoring and influencing your mental state? [247] DARPA (Defense Advanced Research Projects Agency) built the platform, but knew suspicion would be raised if the agency rolled it out, so they fabricated a story and made it look like Facebook came from a person in Harvard, Mark Zuckerberg, mapping its appearance onto the much beloved rags-to-riches narrative. [248] This psychological weapon was leveled at Iraqis in

[247] **Samuel Gibbs,** "Facebook Apologises for Psychological Experiments on Users," *The Guardian,* July 2, 2014, https://www.theguardian.com/technology/2014/jul/02/facebook-apologises-psychological-experiments-on-users; **Dominic Rush,** "Facebook Sorry—Almost —for Secret Psychological Experiment on Users," *The Guardian,* October 2, 2014, https://www.theguardian.com/technology/2014/oct/02/facebook-sorry-secret-psychological-experiment-users

[248] **Whitney Webb,** "The Military Origins of Facebook," *Unlimited Hangout,* April 12, 2021, https://unlimitedhangout.com/2021/04/investigative-reports/the-military-origins-of-facebook/

[249] Nick Fielding and Ian Cobain, "Revealed: US Spy Operation That Manipulates Social Media," *The Guardian*, March 17, 2011, https://www.theguardian.com/technology/2011/mar/17/us-spy-operation-social-networks

2011 with Operation Earnest Voice, which used 500 "sock puppet" accounts under the control of fifty operators and multiple VPNs to conceal their location, all in order to spread pro-US propaganda. [249]

This social media weapon has since been refined, expanded, and in some cases, privatized. Myriad organizations have conspired to take control of all information for the express purposes of manipulating you. Look to the work of Cass Sunstein, creator of what he calls the Nudge Theory—the idea that small amounts of misinformation, incentives, or threats can generate significant changes in the public mind. The United Kingdom developed the Behavioural Insights Team, the world's first "nudge unit," based on Cass's work, and opened an office in Canada in 2019. [250]

[250] "The Behavioural Insights Team to Open First Canadian Office," press release, July 12, 2019, Behavioural Insights Team, https://www.bi.team/press-releases/the-behavioural-insights-team-to-open-first-canadian-office/

While all of these groups influence you through government and mainstream media, Google's Jigsaw team manipulates you from online. Indeed, a brief review of their website and the reports available there for download, as well as the website of their partner, Moonshot CVE, reveals that they consider anyone not completely enamored by mainstream narratives to be a potential terrorist. As a result, Google hijacks search queries containing certain words, delivering a set of curated propaganda, calling it the Redirect Method. They will even refer you to extremists from the Far Left, because these groups have always been useful to the ruling class. [251]

[251] Anita Chabria and Evan Halper, "Effort to Stem Online Extremism Accidentally Pushed People toward an Anarchist," *Los Angeles Times*, March 30, 2021, https://www.latimes.com/politics/story/2021-03-30/google-moonshot-redirect-far-right-online-extremism-anarchist

Even more brazen, on September 20, 2022, Melissa Fleming, the UN's Under-Secretary-General for Global Communications, spoke at a WEF event and bragged about their "partnership" with Google and how Google is now curating search results related to climate change, among many other subjects. [252] In a declaration that is perhaps even more infamous than that made by Dr. Fauci, Fleming proclaimed, "We [the UN] own the science and we think that the world should know it, and the platform [Google] themselves also do." [253] Lastly, we have the example of the International Grand Committee on Disinformation, a group of legislators from around the

[252] Kristen Grind, Sam Schechner, Robert McMillan, and John West, "How Google Interferes with Its Search Algorithms and Changes Your Results," *Wall Street Journal*, November 19, 2019, https://www.wsj.com/articles/how-google-interferes-with-its-search-algorithms-and-changes-your-results-11573823753

[253] "Tackling Disinformation," session during the Sustainable Development Impact Meetings, 2022, https://www.weforum.org/events/sustainable-development-impact-meetings-2022/sessions/tackling-disinformation

world. They view freedom of speech on online platforms as a serious problem, calling for government regulation of the content and opinions users express.

We have already discussed Bill Gates, but you should also know he has paid over $319 million to ensure that media outlets fact-check anyone who criticizes him. The process functions on a "pay-to-play" basis: if someone criticizes Bill Gates in the media, the media will get in touch with him and ask for money to fact-check the claims. How can this fact-check be independent and unbiased when you are taking money from one of the parties involved? [254]

[254] **Alan Macleod**, "Revealed: Documents Show Bill Gates Has Given $319 Million to Media Outlets," *MPN News*, November 15, 2021, https://www.mintpressnews.com/documents-show-bill-gates-has-given-319-million-to-media-outlets/278943/

The concept of fact-checking gives humans comfort, for it helps the masses believe that the truth is being sought and presented, but fact-checking is a corrupt practice. All the fact-checking at Facebook, for example, is done by the Poynter Institute, which was started by a newspaper editor aligned to the Far Left. The fact-checkers in this network belong to the same political ideology, and they are naturally biased. [255]

[255] "How Facebook's Third-Party Fact-Checking Program Works," Meta, June 1, 2021, https://www.facebook.com/formedia/blog/third-party-fact-checking-how-it-works

Indeed, most fact-checking programs can be traced back to the Poynter Institute via their International Fact-Checking Network: PolitiFact, AFP Fact Check, Lead Stories, USA Today, Full Fact, AAP Fact Check, Africa Check, and many more. It is a cartel of propagandists coming from a single institute controlled by the ruling class and their agenda. They will routinely mis-state claims, fabricate claims, and even fabricate sources in their efforts to "debunk" true information. [256]

[256] **Ariel Zilber**, "USA Today Removes 23 Articles after Reporter Fabricated Sources," *The New York Post*, June 16, 2022, https://nypost.com/2022/06/16/usa-today-reporter-gabriela-miranda-fabricated-sources-for-23-articles/

Their biggest embarrassment, however, was their denial of the authenticity of the Hunter Biden laptop and Ashley Biden diary, which revealed that he was yet another functionary in Ukraine whose role was to launder money directly into the pockets of the Biden family, and she sexually abused by her father Joe. People believe they are getting the truth when information is fact-checked, but in truth, their minds are being further controlled. [257]

[257] **Corbett Report**, "Episode 381: Who Will Fact Check the Fact Checkers?" *The Corbett Report*, June 19, 2020, https://www.corbettreport.com/episode-381-who-will-fact-check-the-fact-checkers/; **Whitney Webb**, "How a Neocon-Backed 'Fact Checker' Plans to Wage War on Independent Media," *MPN News*, January 9, 2019, https://www.mintpressnews.com/newsguardneocon-backed-fact-checker-plans-to-wage-war-on-independent-media/253687/

BIO-SURVEILLANCE

As should be clear by now, the agenda of those in the ivory tower is total control. They will not stop at controlling information or your mind or your governments. They want to know what is happening inside your body and have total power over those processes. Yuval Noah Harari, a key advisor to Klaus Schwab, is a spokesperson for the ruling class and their agenda. He says as much when he speaks on COVID-19 being part of what Schwab calls the Great Reset:

> COVID is critical because this is what convinces people to accept, to legitimize total biometric surveillance. If we want to stop this epidemic, we need not just to monitor people, we need to monitor what's happening under their skin. [258]
>
> [258] "Yuval Noah Harari: Panel Discussion on Technology and the Future of Democracy," YouTube video posted by Yuval Noah Harai, October 4, 2020, https://www.youtube.com/watch?v=JfylW9wRvB4

Why is COVID-19 critical? It is the instrument through which the ruling class is presently able to further their agenda of complete control via bio-surveillance. In the form of nanobots created out of graphene, those in the ivory tower manufactured technology to monitor people at the cellular level. Then they fabricated the circumstances that would allow them to inject these nanobots into humans: a pandemic that created such fear that when the nanobot-filled vaccines were rolled out, people flocked by the billions to be injected. [259]

[259] Ariyana Love, "Graphene COVID Kill Shots: Let the Evidence Speak for Itself," *Global Research*, December 5, 2021, https://www.globalresearch.ca/graphene-covid-kill-shots-let-evidence-speak-itself/5763418; "The Real Pandemic—Covid-19 or Graphene Oxide? Poisonous Nano-Material Found in Covid Vaccines and Face Masks," *Exposé*, July 10, 2021, https://expose-news.com/2021/07/10/the-real-pandemic-covid-19-or-graphene-oxide-poisonous-nano-material-found-in-covid-vaccines-and-face-masks/;

The rulers in the ivory tower do not care about the consequences of their plan. They do not care that the graphene and mRNA in the vaccines are killing people because they create blood clots, inflame tissues, and trigger a host of auto-immune conditions. [260] They consider deaths from the injection an allowable loss of livestock: for, as you know, those who survive the process become quite valuable to the ruling class. When socialists go forth conquering nations, they have historically slaughtered 10 percent of the population. This time will be similar, or perhaps worse.

The goal is to create an Internet of Bodies, an AI grid made out of digitally connected human beings. Once the nanobots have been placed inside citizens, these bots must be able to transmit their data to a centralized system. This is why governments have been pushing wireless 5G networks so aggressively—because that level of speed and efficiency in bandwidth is needed to transmit this data. This is also why any arguments against 5G are so quickly squashed: the Nephilim and rulers do not want you to look too closely at their plans. Think about it, Seeker of Truth: what could possibly be on the horizon that needs such massive wireless bandwidth? [261]

This Internet of Bodies can be used for far more evil ends than surveillance of your biometric telemetry. Imagine someone being able to read your mind or control your body. At the 2017 World Economic Forum at Davos, Klaus Schwab asked Google founder Sergei Brin:

> Can you imagine that in 10 years, when we are sitting here, we have an implant in our brains, and I can immediately feel [what you are feeling] because you all will have implants. I can remeasure your brainwaves, and I can immediately tell you how some people react [emotionally] to your answers. Is it imaginable?

Brin replied it wasn't only imaginable, but it would be the least they would be able to do. There is ample evidence now that his words are true, and scientists have moved on to trying to control people by hacking their minds. They started experiments on insects, and now they are testing it on humans, who will become remote-controlled in the future. [262] As Yuval Noah Harari said in an interview,

[259] Robert O. Young, "Scanning and Transmission Electron Microscopy Reveals Graphene and Parasites in CoV-19 Vaccines," DrRobertYoung.com, Febrary 5, 2021, updated March 12, 2022, https://www.drrobertyoung.com/post/transmission-electron-microscopy-reveals-graphene-oxide-in-cov-19-vaccines

[260] "5.3.6 Cumulative Analysis of Post-Authorization Adverse Event Reports of PF-07302048 (BNT162B2) received through 28-Feb-2021," report prepared by Worldwide Safety: Pfizer, https://phmpt.org/wp-content/uploads/2022/04/re-issue 5.3.6-postmarketing-experience.pdf

[261] "What Is the Internet of Bodies?" RAND, video posted October 29, 2020, https://www.rand.org/multimedia/video/2020/10/29/what-is-the-internet-of-bodies.html; Xiao Liu, "Tracking How Our Bodies Work Could Change Our Lives," World Economic Forum, n.d., https://www.weforum.org/agenda/2020/06/internet-of-bodies-covid19-recovery-governance-health-data/; "Wilson Quarterly Spotlight: AI and the 'Internet of Bodies,'" YouTube video, posted by WoodrowWilsonCenter, June 5, 2018, https://www.youtube.com/watch?v=sZJa-yh-qhQ

[262] Sarah Spickernell, "DNA Nanobots Deliver Drugs in Living Cockroaches," New Scientist, April 8, 2014, https://www.newscientist.com/article/dn25376-dna-nanobots-deliver-drugs-in-living-cockroaches/; "University Nanotechnology Approved for 'First in Human' Trials," University of Sydney, June 4, 2020, https://www.sydney.edu.au/science/

Humans are now hackable animals. You know the whole idea that humans have this "soul" or "spirit," and that they have free will and nobody knows what's happening inside me, so whatever I choose whether in the election or whether in the supermarket this is my free will—that's over. [263]

[263] **Belle Carter**, "WEF Lead Advisor Harari: Humans Are Now Hackable Animals; Free Will Is Over–Brighton. TV," *Transhumanism.news*, June 19, 2022, https://transhumanism.news/2022-06-19-harari-humans-now-hackable-animals-free-will-is-over.html

[262] news-and-events/2020/06/04/nano-technology-approved-for-human-trials.html; **Trevor English**, "Nanobots Will Be Flowing through Your Body by 2030," *Interesting Engineering*, November 20, 2020, https://interestingengineering.com/innovation/nanobots-will-be-flowing-through-your-body-by-2030

[264] **Misha Sra**, "How to Remote Control a Human Being," TEDx talk, https://www.media.mit.edu/articles/how-to-remote-control-a-human-being-mish/; **Dan Farber**, "Scientist Controls Colleague's Hand in First Human Brain-to-Brain Interface," *CNET*, August 27, 2013, https://www.cnet.com/science/scientist-controls-colleagues-hand-in-first-human-brain-to-brain-interface/; **MWI Staff**, "MWI Video: Dr. Charles Morgan on Neurobiology and War," Modern War Institute, June 15, 2018, https://mwi.usma.edu/mwi-video-dr-charles-morgan-neurobiology-war/

The ultimate goal of this system is to completely take control of your body, driving it as you would an avatar in a game, but in the real world. Indeed, millions of dollars and decades of research have been poured into this project. What becomes of your own experience while subjected to this remote-controlled state is still a mystery, but some believe you will be plunged into an artificial world, practically indistinguishable from this one. Indeed, this is something Brin himself said would be possible in his discussion with Schwab. There, you could live out the rest of your life never knowing what your body was being made to do. The potential to wage war with armies of helpless, unknowing conscripts is high, and it is actively being discussed and researched by the military. [264] Indeed, there is a conspiracy against you and most of humanity. But it is not theory, nor is it hidden. Look to the words of another advocate of population control, David Rockefeller:

For more than a century ideological extremists at either end of the political spectrum have seized upon well-publicized incidents such as my encounter with Castro to attack the Rockefeller family for the inordinate influence they claim we wield over American political and economic institutions. Some even believe we are part of a secret cabal working against the best interests of the United States, characterizing my family and me as "internationalists" and of conspiring with others around the world to build a more integrated global political and economic structure—one world, if you will. If that's the charge, I stand guilty, and I am proud of it. [265]

[265] **David Rockefeller**, Memoirs (New York: Random House, 2002), 405.

Those involved have put themselves under the spell of Voltaire. They are absurd, believe and say absurd things, and are willing and able to commit atrocities such as killing and enslaving a large portion of the earth in pursuit of their delusions.

RAISE YOUR CONSCIOUSNESS

Eisenhower was right: public policy has become the captive of the scientific tech-nological elite, and they are merely years away from controlling you and your families and everyone you love. Heed the words of Semjase when she visited Billy Meier on March 21, 1975:

> A great danger is of scientists misusing the power of their knowledge to over-come their less developed fellow creatures and force them into slavery and exploitation. From this they should be prevented, as well as their technical achievements which only serve for destruction. Not in any best interest, their setting themselves up as Gods, and by this committing the same mistakes their forefathers already did. These influences we want to prevent. [266]
>
> [266] Eduard Billy Meier, *Message from the Pleiades*, vol, 1, p. 124.

But your task at this stage, Seeker of Truth, is not to act. It is to read and keep educating yourself on how your world has been controlled for thousands of years so that you are aware of their devices and don't fall prey to their control mecha-nisms. If you find yourself attacked by others, defend yourself—but do not seek out conflict. Remember, you have not attained perfect knowledge necessary to lay claim to the power to judge others and inflict the punishments ordained by God.

But you have begun your journey. You now understand that humanity has been divided into two streams—the ruling class and the rest of the population—and that processes are in place to control your mind and body. You have been conditioned to accept this as the natural state of being, but you can break free from that con-ditioning. That process starts with raising your consciousness and understanding just how conditioned you truly are, and for what ends.

CHAPTER 14
MAKING
A NEW MAN

For many millennia, the ruling class has pondered how best to rule humanity. One of the earliest examples of this comes from the ancient Greek general, Xenophon, from his *Cyropaedia*:

> The thought once occurred to us how many republics have been overthrown by people who preferred to live under any form of government other than a republican, and again, how many monarchies and how many oligarchies in times past have been abolished by the people. We reflected, moreover, how many of those individuals who have aspired to absolute power have either been deposed once for all and that right quickly ... And in addition to this, we reflected that cowherds are the rulers of their cattle, that grooms are the rulers of their horses, and that all who are called herdsmen might properly be regarded as the rulers of the animals over which they are placed in charge. Now we noticed, as we thought, that all these herds obeyed their keepers more readily than men obey their rulers. For the herds go wherever their keeper directs them and graze in those places to which he leads them and keep out of those from which he excludes them. They allow their keeper, moreover, to enjoy, just as he will, the profits that accrue from them. And then again, we have never known of a herd conspiring against its keeper, either to refuse obedience to him or to deny him the privilege of enjoying the profits that accrue. At the same time, herds are more intractable to strangers than to their rulers and those who derive profit from them. Men, however, conspire against none sooner than against those whom they see attempting to rule over them. [267]

[267] Xenophon, Cyropaedia, Book 1, Sections 1 and 2, http://www.perseus.tufts.edu/hopper/text?doc=Perseus%3Atext%3A1999.01.0204%3Abook%3D1%3Achapter%3D1%3Asection%3D2

It is the divinity within you that recognizes no authority and cries out for its own freedom. This, as Xenophon notes, has been a persistent challenge for the Nephilim. Humanity's nature is indeed different from that of animals, and much less effort is required in the breaking of horses than free human beings. Whether or not you realize it, you have been carefully trained and programmed to react to certain stimuli in a specific way, for nothing makes ruling easier than a population programmed from birth to love their servitude and to see the perpetuation of the system as necessary and good for society. The time has come for you to drop the blindfold from your eyes and see the truth of your making.

FACTORY-FARMED HUMANS

During the late nineteenth century, when the progressive movement was in full swing, Prussia was considered a jewel of the world, and many countries looked toward this nation as an exemplar of socialist principles and systems—including a compulsory education system of desks in rows, facing a chalkboard.

The Prussian Empire instituted this system because it was facing an epidemic of deserters in its army while fighting Napoleon. The empire was expanding its territories to a vast extent and fighting wars on multiple fronts. Pushed to the breaking point, many soldiers simply laid down their firearms and walked away from the battlefield. To prevent this from continuing, the Prussian government implemented compulsory schooling, what has now become the K–12 system, as a means of brainwashing the population into idealizing the nation such that they would never abandon it and would do everything it demanded of them—even fight endlessly. The principle sold to the people was of "devoting themselves to a higher cause" and the ultimate goal was that people would surrender their better judgment "for the greater good" and simply do what they were told. The system worked, and Prussia soon had one of the most aggressive military forces in the world.[268]

[268] John Taylor Gatto, "Against School: How Public Education Cripples Our Kids, and Why," *Harper's Magazine*, September 2003, 33–38.

Among other countries, the United States observed this system and marveled at its success. They did not need a military force in the same way that Prussia did, but they did need a workforce that would obey without question. If they could program their citizens to simply act on cue and follow instructions, then they could create workers who would be happy to turn dials and wheels all day and go on break when the whistle blew and come back to work when it blew again—workers who would not think for themselves or question their mode of existence. Thus, in the early twentieth century, the United States began implementing this same education model as part of the progressive movement. Recall from the last chapter that the progressives follow the lead of Frederick Winslow Taylor's

Principles of Management, which sought to subjugate the individual in service of the system—because the system clearly serves the Nephilim, the ruling class, and others in the ivory tower. This movement pushed for the government to take over all industry and have ultimate control. As Woodrow Wilson, former president of Princeton University and twenty-eighth president of the United States, once said,

> We want one class of persons to have a liberal education, and we want another class of persons, a very much larger class of necessity in every society, to forgo the privilege of a liberal education and fit themselves to perform specific difficult manual tasks. [269]

[269] Woodrow Wilson, "The Meaning of a Liberal Education," address to the New York City High School Teachers Association, January 9, 1909.

The result was the K–12 education system in every American school, and a gradual shift towards authoritarianism in the government. You may have been taught that the Nazi salute began with Adolf Hitler, but alas, you have been led astray, for the palm-out gesture actually began in the fascistic Roman Empire before being resurrected in the United States in 1892, as the salute to accompany the pledge of allegiance, which was written by an avowed socialist named Francis Bellamy. [270] When the government mandated that the pledge of allegiance and the Bellamy salute be compulsory in one California school, the parents of one child protested: they feared this commandment was the precursor to a steep slide into authoritarianism and dictatorship. In response, the school expelled the student. When the parents consequently sued the school, the judge ruled in the school's favor, stating,

[270] "The Official Pledge of Allegiance Salute Used to Be a 'Hitler Salute,'" The Forgotten History Blog, https://forgottenhistoryblog.com/the-official-american-flag-salute-used-to-be-a-hitler-salute/

> The training of school children in good citizenship, patriotism and loyalty to state and nation is regarded by the law of the state as a means of protecting public welfare ... The simple salutation to the flag and the repetition of the pledge of allegiance ... tend to stimulate in the minds of youth in the formative period of life sentiments of lasting affection and respect for and unfaltering loyalty to our government and its institutions. [271]

[271] California Supreme Court ruling, *Gabrielli v. Knickerbocker* (1938).

The judge's words make it clear that the purpose of the education system and its rituals—saluting the flag, incanting the pledge of allegiance—is to elevate the state and the government to the level of godhead, and make it impossible to resist or refute their power. Your education system is designed to produce slaves who do not recognize their own situation as slavery. [272]

[272] John Taylor Gatto, "Against School," *Harper Magazine*, 2003

But it is not enough for your education system to create an obedient and subdued human being. Marxism has long held the belief of a "New Man," a human being that must be fundamentally remade to work *with* the system. Socialism sees humans as intrinsically individualistic and thus incompatible with communism, the fully realized vision of totalitarian socialism. For communism to work, it is necessary for a person to be remade into the ideal citizen. Hsi-En Chen, a professor from California, wrote a series of papers about this in the 1960s, and he used the term *brainwashing*. He listed ten qualities of the New Man, which include being reflexive, obedient, class conscious, and racially aware. Today, you would call this New Man a "social justice warrior."

Indeed, the state is at work to abolish parental rights and take over the process of raising children so that they have full control to create this New Man, a simple cog in the wheel that is happy to do as he is told, blindly follow the state, agitate for state-approved causes, and coerce his fellow human beings into compliance. William Torrey Harris, the US Commissioner of Education, said exactly this in his publication "The Philosophy of Education":

> Ninety-nine out of a hundred people in every civilized nation are automata, careful to walk in the prescribed paths, careful to follow prescribed custom. This is the result of substantial education, which, scientifically defined, is the subsumption of the individual under his species. [273]

[273] **William T. Harris,** "The Philosophy of Education," *Johns Hopkins University Studies in Historical and Political Science* 11, nos. 5–6 (1893): 269–277, https://archive.org/details/sim_johns-hopkins-university-historical-political-science_may-june-1893_11_5-6/page/268/mode/2up

Harris divided the education system into two models: intuitive education and substantial education. Intuitive education creates individuals who are skeptical, creative, and have the ability to trust their own judgment. Harris believed the United States was educating too many people under the intuitive system; he stated that more substantial education is needed in order to create automata and worker bees. His thinking was clear: those with intuitive education challenge the system, but those with substantial education obey the system—and the system likes to be obeyed.

In China, this substantial system is being implemented through "re-education camps." There was a point at which anyone who opposed the Maoist regime, and was deemed too intellectual or individualistic for communism, was moved into the Laogai camps to be "trained" to become more compliant. These camps have not been abolished; the Chinese are simply using them to imprison Uyghurs and anyone who does not follow their idea of an ideal citizen. [274]

[274] **Austin Ramzy and Chris Buckley,** "'Absolutely No Mercy': Leaked Files Expose How China Organized Mass Detentions of Muslims," *The New York Times*, November 16, 2019; **The Xinjiang Police Files,** https://www.xinjiangpolicefiles.org/

In America, the substantial system of education is being implemented through the public education K–12 system and truancy laws. Private school will not save you either; even if you have the money to put your child into the private school education system, these institutions are all accredited by the public education body and teach similar ways of thinking. There is no escape.

Heed this wisdom, Seeker of Truth: your schools and institutions of higher learning are designed to shape you into a factory-farmed animal. Many people today reflexively feel anxiety and fear when a police officer approaches them or pulls them over for a traffic violation. Why? You have been trained to respond to state institutions with compliance and obedience; you have been brainwashed to always stay in line.

This is the goal of the Nephilim and those in the ivory tower. They want you to react in a certain way to specific stimuli. They do not want to beat you into compliance; they want you to meekly obey and believe in the virtue of it.

For centuries, the Nephilim did rule by force, by amassing militaries and indoctrinating people who would help them rule. But in the early twentieth century, the class of people they were ruling swelled, and the population numbers exploded, necessitating a new means of governing the masses. Part of their strategy, as you have learned, is eugenics. But eugenics does not work to eliminate the whole population, so the Nephilim implemented the factory-farmed human model to control the rest.

FEELINGS
OVER FACTS

It is natural to wonder how the reeducation scheme works, and why it is so successful in transforming a person from a logical and thinking being to someone who obeys without question. The program works on the principle of demoralization, such that a citizen who is inculcated into the system is unable to assess the truth, even if it is presented in front of their eyes. As Yuri Bezmenov, a former Russian KGB propaganda officer, said in a 1984 interview,

> Exposure to true information does not matter anymore. A person who is demoralized is unable to assess true information. The facts tell him nothing. Even if I shower him with information, with authentic proof, with documents and pictures, even if I take him by force to the USSR and show him the concentration camps—he will refuse to believe it. [275]

[275] Yuri Bezmenov, *Soviet Subversion of the Free World Press*, 1984, https://www.imdb.com/title/tt4624610/

Thomas Sowell, an American economist, echoed similar sentiments. In his book, Inside American Education, he writes,

> It is not merely that Johnny can't read, or even that Johnny can't think. *Johnny doesn't know what thinking is*, because thinking is so often confused with feeling in many public schools. [276]

[276] Thomas Sowell, *Inside American Education: The Decline, the Deception, the Dogmas* (NY: The Free Press, 1993), 4.

In another article, Sowell expands on the signs of a dumbed-down education system and the effects of this system of inculcation:

> One of the painful signs of years of dumbed-down education is how many people are unable to make a coherent argument. They can vent their emotions, question other people's motives, make bold assertions, repeat slogans—anything except reason. [277]

[277] Thomas Sowell, "Random Thoughts," *Townhall*, September 3, 2007, https://town-hall.com/columnists/thomassowell/2007/09/03/random-thoughts-n1165903

Herein is the defining feature of the system of reeducation and demoralization: it separates you from your ability to weigh the evidence and come to your own conclusions, so much so that you have a deeply seated mistrust of yourself. That mistrust, Seeker of Truth, is what forces you to seek out an authority that can tell you what to do, think, and believe—even feel.

Thus, when the truth arrives from any source other than the accepted authority, you refuse to see the evidence before your eyes. Think back to Edward Bernays's book *Propaganda*, discussed in Chapter 13, and recall how the invisible government controls your tastes and your thoughts. Throughout his career, Bernays used this molding of taste to create hugely successful marketing campaigns, consistently manipulating existing movements and facts to sell products. He co-opted the women's liberation movement to sell cigarettes, equating a liberated woman with one who smoked. In a suffragette parade, he got a line of women to dress up as the statue of liberty and wave around cigarettes as their Torches of Freedom. [278]

[278] **Amanda Amos** and **Margaretha Haglund**, "From Social Taboo to 'Torch of Freedom': The Marketing of Cigarettes to Women," *Tobacco Control* 9 (2000): 3–8.

Remember that trusting feelings over facts is not the same as trusting your gut. When a person trusts their gut, they are relying on something that is closer to their true self. But feelings are fleeting and can be easily manipulated. Emotions are often tied to the ego and a sense of pride, a correlation that often expresses itself as "I am a good person because I do these things." This is not trusting your gut; this is conformity.

Modern-day articles have been written in your media on how you should not trust your gut: instead of relying on yourself and your ability to ascertain facts, you must rely on "the science." These articles claim that questioning authority kills people, so the only logical conclusion is to put your ego-driven feelings above facts, and never rely on your own abilities to find and construct the truth. [279]

[279] **Ethan Siegel**, "You Must Not 'Do Your Own Research' When It Comes to Science," *Forbes*, July 30, 2020, https://www.forbes.com/sites/startswithabang/2020/07/30/you-must-not-do-your-own-research-when-it-comes-to-science/?sh=f1fb04535ea6; **Jess Zimmerman**, "It's Time to Give Up on Facts," *Slate*, February 8, 2017, https://slate.com/technology/2017/02/counter-lies-with-emotions-not-facts.html

This demoralization of a person and a corrosion of faith in their own abilities plays directly into the hands of the government. Indeed, most of the techniques used by your law enforcement establishments rely on this principle. One such technique is gaslighting, a process by which someone might repeat an assertion over and over again until the person breaks down and accepts the assertion as fact. The primary goal being to get the targeted person to doubt their own recollection of events and accept the alternative being provided. This acceptance is not without cost: the person is forced to trust the assertion above their own thoughts and beliefs because they have been so broken, they will simply trust what their captor says.

This strategy has been used effectively as a police interrogation practice known as the Reid technique, which is also commonly known as "good cop, bad cop." In many places, the police are not allowed to use this method anymore because it elicits false confessions, yet it is still in circulation today.

A more sophisticated demoralization technique that uses gaslighting, among other tactics, is elucidated in Biderman's Chart of Coercion, famously relied upon in Amnesty International's 1973 *Report on Torture*, which is used in prisons and concentration camps.[280] The aim of this technique is to destroy a person's sense of self, and if you look closely, you can see milder forms of it implemented in schools with the reeducation program.

[280] **Albert D. Biderman**, "Communist Attempts to Elicit False Confessions from Air Force Prisoners of War," *Bulletin of the New York Academy of Medicine* 33, no. 9 (1957): 612–625.

Biderman's Chart of Coercion teaches a person "learned helplessness." This is a phenomenon where a person is broken down so completely, they no longer believe they have the ability to influence or control their environment or have any chance of preventing negative events from happening to them. It causes them to simply surrender and accept what is happening.

People have run experiments that show this phenomenon in action. In one from 1965, Martin Seligman led a group of dogs into a cage with an electrified floor. At first, when they turned on the electricity, the dogs would leap up and try to climb the cage to escape. But after the researchers did this several more times, at random intervals, the dogs stopped trying to escape and would simply lie down and accept being electrocuted. Even after a route of escape was presented the demoralized dogs, completely resigned to their fate, needlessly endured the electrocution. This is the same effect that Biderman's Chart of Coercion has on human beings. In many ways, the regulations implemented during the COVID-19 pandemic follow the same principles as Biderman's Chart of Coercion. The rules fluctuated so wildly, as did the "science," that people began to accept that they had no control over their environment and had no ability to see what was coming next. They accepted what the authorities told them to do in the moment because they had no agency of their own and they did not want to be punished.

The effect of conformity is so powerful in human society, it can make a person not only doubt the truth, but consciously disregard their better judgment entirely. In the Asch Conformity Experiments, beginning in 1951, researchers put the test subject in a room with a few other people and asked them to go through some tests. The subjects were given a series of lines, each of different lengths, and asked to choose which one was the same length as a sample line.

In the beginning, everyone gave the right answers. But what the test subject did not know is that the other people in the room were simply *posing* as participants; they were actually compatriots of the experimenter. Thus, a few tests down the line, the fake participants began discussing the wrong options and then choosing those. The subject began copying these answers, even though he knew these answers were wrong, simply because he did not want to stand out. This is the power of conformity in your society, and how it affects people who are demoralized.

Another experiment, which demonstrated the lengths to which people will go to delude themselves and accept their own mistreatment, was conducted in 1954 by Leon Festinger. The subjects were first to participate in what they believed was a motor control study. In fact, they were carrying out the dullest activity Festinger could conceive—turning pegs round and round on a board.

After their task was complete, Fetsinger's staff revealed this was not actually the experiment. The researchers offered one half of the participants $20, and the other half a mere $1, to lie to the next subject about how enjoyable they found the task. Both cohorts lied equally convincingly to their successor, who actually was another researcher. Perhaps not so amazingly, only the $1 group came to fully believe their own lie, and later reported they had enjoyed the menial task. The $20 group accepted the value for their lie, but the $1 group did not, causing cognitive dissonance that ultimately led to the selective editing of their own feelings and memories to deny their own maltreatment and misdeeds.

In what is possibly the most macabre of such experiments, in 1963 Stanley Milgram took dozens of volunteers and asked them to participate in a memory experiment. They played the role of a teacher, asking questions of their students and administering electric shocks of increasing intensity with each wrong answer. In reality, the students were actors, and the shocks were not real. This, however, did not stop the vast majority of teachers from delivering shocks that would have killed their students, if they had been real, even as the young people begged for mercy. The teachers were told by the experimenter to continue, and so they did.

When taken to the extreme, demoralization can go so far as to make people question their gender. Indeed, in the current US school system, teachers and other adults are now asking children in Grade 2 or 3 to consider whether they are really a boy or a girl, to study sexual acts, and to read pornographic materials where

[281] **Tyler O'Neil**, "Fairfax County Schools Reinstates Books with Explicit Images, Claiming They Don't Include Pedophilia," Fox News, November 24, 2021, https://www.foxnews.com/politics/fairfax-county-schools-reinstates-lawn-boy-genderqueer-claims-pedophilia

[282] **Rod Dreher**, "Proud Groomer Teachers," American Conservative, December 28, 2021, https://www.theamericanconservative.com/groomer-teachers-gender-theory-ideology/

[283] **CWALAC staff**, "Kinsey-Based Sex Education: Putting Children at Risk," Concerned Women for America Legislative Action Committee, August 24, 2004, https://web.archive.org/web/20220119102227/https://concernedwomen.org/kinsey-based-sex-education-putting-children-at-risk/

[284] **Marc Fisher**, "Kinsey Report, Fast and Loose?" *Washington Post*, December 8, 1995, https://www.washingtonpost.com/archive/lifestyle/1995/12/08/kinsey-report-fast-and-loose/b058e754-34c5-4c62-87fb-7ee1cd42d625/

cartoon children graphically discuss sex and even perform sex acts on each other. [281] These tactics are designed to break children down to the point where they cannot know what is true, even about themselves. They are being groomed for pedophiles, and the teachers themselves make no secret of this. [282] This program of sexualizing children began with Dr. Alfred Kinsey, whose research formed the basis for all present models of "sexual education." [283] He partnered with Planned Parenthood to create and introduce the new curricula. It is now no secret that his studies were entirely fraudulent, and all data he used was drawn from samples of sex offenders, violent felons, and from the diary of a single pedophile who abused more than 300 boys, and whose identity the Kinsey Institute protects to this very day. [284]

The goal of demoralization is to create people who hold the firm belief that nothing is true or false—that there is no morality, no good, no bad. In the absence of morality, such people understand that raw power is the sole measure by which an individual is appraised, and they also understand their place at the low end of this power hierarchy. Thus, their goal in life is simply to seek rewards and avoid punishment, typically handed out by those at the top of the hierarchy—totalitarian rulers. Such a world without truth is the ultimate realization of nihilism and moral relativism.

THE MEDIUM
IS YOUR MASTER

In order to truly understand how you are being groomed, Seeker of Truth, it is necessary for you to learn how these systems of lies and demoralization work. The program of reeducation creates a demoralized human being who prioritizes their ego-driven feelings above the facts presented to them. Here is how the media, a tool of this system, perpetuates these techniques to keep the population subservient: this is their modus operandi.

The main tool of the media is, in today's parlance, fake news. The government has co-opted the term *fake news* to hide the truth from you, but true fake news consists of the lies and propaganda fed to you by the government. Factory-farmed humans are unable to discern truth from fake news, so they are happy to believe what the media tells them. But a person who has resisted the system's influence, who is able to think for themselves and trust their gut, is able to discern the actual fake news.

So many of your brothers and sisters do not know how to seek the truth. But if they did, if the blindfold was pulled from their eyes, they would see that there are multiple examples of fake news in the media today, outright lies that have been fed to citizens. A full list would take volumes, but let us discuss the most noteworthy examples.

Lies and half-truths have existed from periods much before this one. Millennia ago, a pagan doctor known as Celsus published a treatise criticizing Christianity and accusing priests of lying. In a pamphlet titled *Contra Celsum*, Church father and Christian apologist Origen of Alexandria did not deny this accusation but instead contrasted it to Celsus's own medical practice. He said that doctors lie all the time to get patients to take curative medicines; in the same way, the lies that Christian apologists like himself tell are permissible in order to gain converts. [285]

[285] Origen Adamantius, *Contra Celsum*, Book IV, Chapter 19.

Did you grasp the essence of these words? Lies are permissible in order to gain patients and converts. If you believe such thinking is outdated, think again. Con-

[286] Daniel K. Sokol, "Can Deceiving Patients Be Morally Acceptable?" *The BMJ* 334, no. 7601(May 12, 2007), 984–986, https://www.ncbi.nlm.nih.gov/pmc/articles/PMC1867874/

[287] Melody Carter, "Deceit and Dishonesty as Practice: The Comfort of Lying," *Nursing Philosophy* 17, no. 3(2016): 202–210, https://pubmed.ncbi.nlm.nih.gov/27197791/

[288] "60 Minutes: Swine Flu (1976)," YouTube video posted by The University, March 12, 2020, https://www.youtube.com/watch?v=4bOHYZhLOWQ

sider a 2007 article that examined the virtues of lying to patients to get them to take the medicines that the doctors believed were good for them.[286] Yet another study from 2016 looked at the same question. The verdict was that it was indeed permissible to lie to get people to do what the medical community wanted.[287]

Think now, Seeker of Truth: are the COVID vaccines yet another item in this long list of lies? Indeed, they are. The ruling class tried a similar tactic in 1976, when the H1N1 virus broke out, using advertisements encouraging every man, woman, and child to get the vaccine, only to have it later exposed that the vaccine in fact harmed and even killed dozens before the program was cancelled.[288]

In 2009, the ruling class repackaged their medical lies when the H1N1 virus broke out yet again, initiating another vaccination campaign. Both during and after the pandemic, the truth slowly leaked out, as evidenced in the Parliamentary Assembly of the Council of Europe's Resolution 1749 in 2010:

> The Parliamentary Assembly is alarmed about the way in which the H1N1 influenza pandemic has been handled, not only by the World Health Organization (WHO), but also by the competent health authorities both at the level of the European Union and at national level. It is particularly troubled by some of the consequences of decisions taken and advice given leading to the distortion of priorities of public health services across Europe, the waste of large sums of public money and unjustified fears about health risks faced by the European public at large.

Did you know that the 2009 swine flu pandemic was a fake? The virus was real, but the WHO greatly exaggerated the threat posed, even going so far as to change their definition of a pandemic days before they declared the swine flu as such; they were caught red-handed doing it.[289] The aim was control and profit, as so clearly stated by the deposed and murdered president of Libya, Muammar Gaddafi, at the 64th UN General Assembly in 2009:

[289] Michael Fumento, "Why the WHO Faked a Pandemic," Fumento.com, January 1, 2010, https://fumento.com/articles/michael_fumento_why_the_who_faked_a_pandemic/

Today there is swine flu. Perhaps tomorrow there will be fish flu, because sometimes we produce viruses by controlling them. It is a commercial business. Capitalist companies produce viruses so that they can generate and sell vaccinations. That is very shameful and poor ethics.

If you were to ask questions of the world around you, if you were to see the evidence and make patterns from it, would you not ask yourself: if the governments of the world have faked one pandemic, have they also faked the most recent one?

Consider the Steele Dossier, a report written from June to December 2016 that claimed ties between Russia and Donald Trump and was used by Hilary Clinton's US presidential campaign to discredit Trump. As is now clear, that dossier was entirely invented by Christopher Steele, with Clinton's full knowledge, but she used it anyway. The Federal Elections Committee convicted her of manufacturing misinformation for the purpose of winning an election, but there was no news of this in the mainstream media. The penalty for her crimes was a mere $8,000. [290]

[290] **Paul Bedard,** "Scoop: FEC Fines DNC and Clinton for Trump Dossier Hoax, *Washington Examiner*, March 30, 2022, https://www.washington-examiner.com/news/fec-fines-dnc-clinton-for-trump-dossier-hoax

If you look closely at these incidents, you can see the hand of the Nephilim and their functionaries. Nina Jankowicz, for example, was embroiled in both the Steele Dossier scandal and the Hunter Biden laptop controversy. She is a Fulbright scholar and has been heavily supported by Hilary Clinton her entire career. She went on record to state that the Steele Dossier was factual and that the hard drive obtained from Hunter Biden laptop was fake, [291] both of which are lies. She was to head the US Disinformation Governance Board, but due to the backlash against her, she was removed. In her place, the ruling class proposed Michael Chertoff, the man who co-authored the US Patriot Act and is partly responsible for the lies about the weapons of mass destruction in Iraq and the subsequent war. [292]

[291] **Andrew Kerr,** "Hunter Biden's Laptop is 100% Authentic, Forensic Examination Concludes," *Washington Examiner*, May 24, 2022, https://www.washingtonexaminer.com/news/white-house/hunter-bidens-laptop-is-100-authentic-forensic-examination-concludes

[292] **Jeff Thompson,** "The People Behind DHS's Orwellian 'Disinformation Governance Board,'" *The Organic Prepper* (blog), April 30, 2020, https://www.theorganic-prepper.com/disinformation-governance-board/

No intelligent person would trust this man to tell the truth about anything. The mounting pressure against this abomination called the Disinformation Board rightly ended with the scrapping of this proposed new agency, but do not think this battle is over.

Of these scandals you may be well aware, but there are many more operating carefully in the shadows that the public does not know about. But one example is Edward Snowden, the privacy saint of journalists and hackers. However, all is not as it seems, for Snowden almost exclusively promotes tech products paid for by the US government. [293] To this end, millions of dollars have poured out of the Open Technology Fund, an initiative of the US Agency for Global Media, a war propaganda agency that has no oversight by any federal department, and into building applications that now find themselves on over two-thirds of mobile devices worldwide. Would you be surprised to learn that at the time the Snowden plan would have been hatched, the Senate committee in charge of appropriating money for this Fund was chaired by Skull and Bonesman John Kerry?

[293] **Mr. E**, "Snowden and Controlled Opposition," Mr. E Reports, December 3, 2021, https://mrereports.substack.com/p/snowden-and-controlled-opposition

Hark how you have been cornered with lies generated to keep you captive. The technique the media uses to consistently generate this fake news is simple. They are aware it is not enough to create a single narrative and carry that story in the press. It is better to create two narratives, one that supports the story they have put out and one that opposes it, subsequently labeling everyone who follows the second, opposing narrative as "crazy" and those who follow the first as "intellectual." The majority of the populace will follow the first narrative because they see themselves as intellectuals. They will not even engage with the second because they do not want to be perceived as foolish or irrational; they would rather blindly believe what they are being told is truth because it takes bravery to carve a different path. Nor does this deception exist at the level of labels alone: government organizations have played a large role in actively making the opposing narratives seem crazy. Hal Turner, a Far-Right US political commentator who works for the FBI, is famous for radicalizing people on the Right to such an extent that they appear crazy and thus discredit the argument for which they stand. At the same time, he inflames a reaction from the Left, thus perpetuating the division.

Do not think this tactic is one sided, for it happens in reverse as well. Consider the riots and property destruction orchestrated by Leftist groups like BLM and Antifa, with wholehearted endorsement from the Biden administration and many prominent Democratic party officials, thus inflaming a contrary reaction from the Right in the form of the Proud Boys, whose leader, Enrique Tarrio, has been an FBI informant like Hal Turner since 2012. [294] In all cases, both sides to a conflict have been cultivated and encouraged by those in power, who profit from the ensuing destruction politically and financially.

[294] **Aram Roston**, "Exclusive: Proud Boys Leader Was 'Prolific' Informer for Law Enforcement," *Reuters*, January 27, 2021, https://www.reuters.com/article/us-usa-proudboys-leader-exclusive/exclusive-proud-boys-leader-was-prolific-informer-for-law-enforcement-idUSKBN29W1PE

In Canada, the Royal Canadian Mounted Police recruited John Nuttall and Amanda Korody out of a drug rehab center, radicalized them through training, and then gave them money and equipment to conduct a bombing. Before Nuttall and Korody could complete the crime, the police arrested the couple to create a narrative of the RCMP as saviors. [295] Years later, a Nova Scotia man named Gabriel Wortman entered a Brink's vault and picked up bags of cash totaling $475,000—the same untraceable method with which the RCMP pays all of its informants. Days later, he murdered nearly two dozen people and caused millions in property damage in a violent rampage. [296]

The FBI is also involved in creating dozens of US domestic terrorists, many of whom are discussed in detail in a report by Human Rights Watch. [297] Also, via many counter-intelligence and propaganda efforts such as Operations CHAOS and COINTEL-PRO, FBI agents infiltrated and worked within to provoke and subvert all populist movements of the past five decades. [298]

The techniques of the media and the various shadow arms of the government function to push people *away* from the truth. At times, they flood the globe with *half*-truths, a method known among spy circles as the "limited hangout" and commonly used by organizations and the government when they know a secret they have been keeping is about to escape their control. Rather than struggle to keep this genie in its bottle, they let it loose but salt it with many lies that mislead people and keep them from focusing on the actual secret itself. Or they reveal enough information such that it looks like the story is complete, but the actual incriminating evidence is withheld. Such half stories are often enough for the population, which is distracted by the new information and does not think to look further.

Ultimately, the media techniques of disinformation exploit a human being's dualistic mind. Those in power create categories—scientists versus anti-vaxxers, police versus terrorists—and they draw sympathy to the narrative that best serves

[295] Ian Mulgrew, "B.C. Terrorism Conviction Stayed, Surrey Couple Freed After Agreeing to Peace Bond Terms," *Vancouver Sun*, July 30, 2016, https://vancouversun.com/news/local-news/b-c-terrorism-convictions-overturned-as-judge-rules-pair-were-entrapped/

[296] Paul Palango, Stephen Maher, and Shannon Gormley, "The Nova Scotia Shooter Case Has Hallmarks of an Undercover Operation," *Maclean's*, June 19, 2020, https://www.macleans.ca/news/canada/the-nova-scotia-shooter-case-has-hallmarks-of-an-undercover-operation/

[297] "US: Terrorism Prosecutions Often an Illustion," Human Rights Watch, July 21, 2014, https://www.hrw.org/news/2014/07/21/us-terrorism-prosecutions-often-illusion

[298] Marina Manoukian, "COINTELPRO: The True Story of the FBI's Illegal Projects," January 10, 2022, https://www.grunge.com/292194/cointelpro-the-true-story-of-the-fbis-illegal-projects/

their interests while keeping the binaries alive so that people are distracted by the fights between factions. Yet, as the RCMP incident shows, those binaries are often nonexistent.

Be vigilant, Seeker of Truth. You are being lied to every single day, and only awareness can free you from the prison in which the Nephilim have locked you.

TWO MINUTES HATE

You have now learned how the Nephilim and those in the ivory tower brainwash you to create human beings that respond in a certain way to specific stimuli—a way that suits those in power. In "Feelings over Facts," you saw the result of that brainwashing, where people are unable to see the facts in front of their eyes and instead prioritize their ego-driven feelings. In "Medium Is Your Master," the inner workings of this system were exposed, and you saw how the media has been feeding the world a steady diet of outright lies and engineering binaries to keep the Nephilim and others in power.

"Two Minutes Hate" is the consequence of this media propaganda and brainwashing. Though the facts of your situation have been denied, you intuitively know that something is wrong with the world around you. Though you cannot see your tormentor, you nevertheless feel the consequences of their abuses. You watch the middle class and the downtrodden burn, but because you have been brainwashed, you struggle to articulate what precisely is destroying the fabric of society. You cannot see how the Nephilim control you because you are trained not to see. All you are left with is resentment and anger.

Human beings in this state of mind need a way to vent these powerful emotions. The Nephilim are devious and far-seeing. They know that if they do not direct that anger on a particular target, it may be directed towards the government and those in the ivory tower. Thus, the Nephilim and those who serve them have created ways in which people may vent their frustrations on selected, innocent targets.

The phrase "two minutes hate" was first introduced by George Orwell in his book *1984.* During the designated two minutes hate, Big Brother, or the dictatorship, would put a scapegoat upon a screen and the masses would hurl insults at it and work themselves into a frenzy. In another book, Aldous Huxley touches upon the thinking behind this general strategy:

Men show at least as much zeal in mischief as in well doing, in folly as in wisdom. The surest way to work up a crusade in favor of some good cause is to promise people that they will have a chance of maltreating someone. Men must be bribed to build up and do good by the offer of an opportunity to hurt and pull down. To be able to destroy with good conscience, to be able to behave badly and call your bad behavior 'righteous indignation'——this is the height of psychological luxury, the most delicious of moral treats. [299]

[299] Aldous Huxley, "Introduction," in *Erewhon*, by Samuel Butler (Norwalk, CT: Easton Press, 1934), xvi.

Versions of two minutes hate used to happen in China, where they were called "struggle sessions." Government officials would drag any counter-revolutionary or intellectual or anyone they considered to be engaging in wrong thinking onto a stage in front of a crowd, and the mob would join in hurling obscenities at them. In time, these struggle sessions became violent, and the crowd would dismember the person and sometimes eat them, which is why they were also known as flesh banquets. [300]

[300] Jan van der Made, "Cannibalism in China 50 Years On," RFI, May 22, 2016, https://www.rfi.fr/en/asia-pacific/20160522-cannibalism-china-publication-official-records-50-years-after-cultural-revolut; Nicholas D. Kristof, "A Tale of Red Guards and Cannibals," *New York Times*, January 6, 1993.

Today, struggle sessions or two minutes hate happen towards "anti-vaxxers" and others resistant to state-sponsored narratives. In American and German schools, children are subject to ritual humiliation, specifically over their vaccination status. [301] In one school, a child was bullied for being unvaccinated, so much so that he committed suicide. The awful reality is that this child *was* vaccinated, but someone started a rumor that he was not because they knew it would cause him trouble. [302] Vaccine passports—a resurrected version of the Nazi Gesundheitspaß, or "health pass"—are nothing more than a discriminatory policy that pits the population against each other and exploits the division created. [303]

[301] Paul Joseph Watson, "German Schoolchildren Subjected to 'Ritual Humiliation' over Their Vaccination Status," *Summit News*, December 10, 2021, https://summit.news/2021/12/10/german-schoolchildren-subjected-to-ritual-humiliation-over-their-vaccine-status/

[302] Matt Agorist, "Parents Sue after School Allegedly Bullied Son to Suicide by Shaming Him for Being Unvaxxed," *The Free Thought Project*, April 30, 2022, https://thefreethoughtproject.com/parents-sue-after-school-allegedly-bullied-son-to-suicide-by-shaming-him-for-being-unvaxxed/

[303] David Sabine, "Vaccine Passport: Der Gesundheitspaß," Canada: The Apartheid State 2021-22, November 30, 2021, https://dnsabine.substack.com/p/vaccine-passport-der-gesundheitspa

There is unfiltered and misguided hate being spewed toward anyone questioning the state's agendas, all encouraged and even guided by the figureheads in power. Make no mistake, Seeker of Truth: this is a selected campaign that echoes principles and philosophies used throughout the centuries to engineer war and to "other" a section of the population whom the ruling class wants to see exterminated.

Recall that the four stages of genocide, as practiced by the Nazis, are identification, dehumanization, segregation, and extermination. You can witness parts of this plan in action with anti-vaxxers. They have been clearly identified by the news and are now being dehumanized by comments and perspectives of the people in power. Here is a sample of some of this vitriol being directed toward this segment of your population.

Joe Biden, president of the United States, has a history of making overtly racist comments and was great friends with former Ku Klux Klan member Robert Byrd. Biden attended his funeral and spoke about what a great friend Byrd was. Far from uniting the country as he promised during his campaign, Biden stirs up hate and division, directing focus onto targets such as anti-vaxxers and those who support Donald Trump. In a 2021 press briefing, Biden said,

> We are intent on not letting Omicron disrupt work and school for the vaccinated. You've done the right thing, and we will get through this. For the unvaccinated, you're looking at a winter of severe illness and death for yourselves, your families, and the hospitals you may soon overwhelm.

In a September 1, 2022, speech in front of Independence Hall, Biden continued his habit of using divisive and extremist language. The building was lit up in red, and flanked by US Marines, the president said his critics "represent an extremism that threatens the very foundations of our republic" and that "they embrace anger. They thrive on chaos. They live not in the light of truth but in the shadow of lies." The entire address singled out half the country, or more, as potential terrorists and targets for extreme prejudice, while fanning the flames of civil war. [304]

[304] "Remarks by President Biden on the Continued Battle for the Soul of the Nation," speech given at Independence National Historical Park, Philadelphia, Pennsylvania, September 1, 2022, https://www.whitehouse.gov/briefing-room/speeches-remarks/2022/09/01/remarks-by-president-bidenon-the-continued-battle-for-the-soul-of-the-nation/

Justin Trudeau, prime minister of Canada, is a well-known bigot; pictures of his repeated appearances in "blackface" are all over the Internet. To misdirect from his own moral failings and to keep his vote bank, Trudeau spoke thus about anti-vaxxers at *La Semaine des 4 Julie* on September 16, 2021:

They [unvaccinated citizens] don't believe in science and progress and are very often misogynistic and racist. It's a very small group of people, but that doesn't shy away from the fact that they take up some space. This leads us, as a leader and as a country, to make a choice: Do we tolerate these people?

Trudeau is calling for a pogrom here, and he has whipped the population into such a frenzy, they will follow him. Indeed, on another episode of the same show, children put their hatred and fear of the unvaccinated on full display to roaring applause from the audience.

Emmanuel Macron, president of France, in an interview with *La Parisien* on January 4, 2022, talks openly about discriminating against anti-vaxxers and making their lives more difficult:

How do we reduce that minority? We reduce it by pissing them off even more, putting pressure on the unvaccinated by limiting, as much as possible, their access to activities in social life. I really want to piss them off. And so we will continue to do so, to the bitter end. That's the strategy. When my freedom threatens that of others, I become irresponsible. An irresponsible person is no longer a citizen.

And here is Jacinda Ardern, prime minister of New Zealand, in an October 25, 2021, interview with the *New Zealand Herald*, admitting to how her policies divide and discriminate among her citizens:

[Reporter]: So, you've basically said, and you probably don't see it like this, but two different classes of people if you're vaccinated or unvaccinated. You have all these rights if you're vaccinated.

[JA]: That is what it is. So, yep. Yep.

Remember, Seeker of Truth, this is only a sample of the hate that your political leaders and people in the ivory tower have put out into the world. Remember also that anti-vaxxers are only one scapegoat, the most recent one, but there have been scapegoats throughout your history. A defining feature of two minutes hate is how quickly those scapegoats can shift and change. The dominant narrative and scapegoat before COVID were the people who opposed the War on Terror. Then it shifted to the anti-vaxxers, and now with the war in Ukraine, it has shifted to the Russians. In a manner similar to Operation Earnest Voice, this latest hatred was cultivated by millions of tweets from thousands of accounts in the early days of the war, mostly bots controlled by a central computer. [305]

Witness how the people of Russia are so despised; the whole world has united against them. Russians are now banned from sports, concerts, and public life, regardless of whether they were actually born in Russia. Their houses, cars, and boats are being seized, all because they belong to a certain nationality. In short, they are being denied due process of law, one of the cornerstones of any legal system. [306]

If the mainstream media is attempting to get you to hate a certain section of the population, be vigilant. Look again, and it will not take you long to uncover the lies they feed you. You have justifiable anger within you, anger born from the injustices you are forced to bear and the burden placed by your oppressors. But be wary of where the Nephilim try to direct that hate, for you may come to despise the wrong party. It is as Malcom X once said:

> This is the press, an irresponsible press. It will make the criminal look like he's the victim and make the victim look like he's the criminal. If you are not careful, the newspapers will have you hating the people who are being oppressed and loving the people who are doing the oppressing. [307]

[307] **Malcolm X**, speech at the Audubon Ballroom in Harlem, December 13, 1964, later published in Malcolm X Speaks: Selected Speeches and Statements, ed. George Breitman (New York: Grove Weidenfeld, 1965), 93.

Remember, the goal of the media and those living in the ivory tower is to keep the government in power. They work hard so that the government never answers for its crimes and is often never even accused. See through their tricks, and you will see the truth.

[305] **Lee Gaskin,** "Bots Manipulate Public Opinion in Russia-Ukraine Conflict," University of Adelaide Newsroom, September 8, 2022, https://www.adelaide.edu.au/newsroom/news/list/2022/09/08/bots-manipulate-public-opinion-in-russia-ukraine-conflict; **Bridgett Smart** et al., "#IStandWith Putin versus #IStandWithUkraine: The Interaction of Bots and Humans in Discussion of the Russia/Ukraine War," paper presented at the International Conference on Social Informatics, Glasgow, October 19–21, 2022, https://arxiv.org/pdf/2208.07038.pdf

[306] **Gabriela Baczynska,** "EU Has Frozen 13.8 Bln Euros of Russian Assets, Official Says," Reuters, July 12, 2022, https://www.reuters.com/world/europe/eu-has-frozen-138-bln-euros-russian-assets-over-ukraine-war-official-says-2022-07-12/

EXTREME FORMS

Every human being on earth is in some way broken. Those who believe they are not, are lying to themselves. You are broken because you have endured this oppressive system of reeducation, training, and brainwashing to make you into something you were never meant to be—a New Man that responds as the Nephilim wish you to respond rather than listening to your God-given intuition.

But it is possible for a person to break free. It is imperative that you keep reading, for the keys to unlock your chains lie in Book IV. There you will acquire the tools you need to identify where you are broken and how you may begin the process of healing.

But before we venture into that journey, there is still more for you to learn; in truth, the worst is yet to come. In the coming chapter, you will read about a more extreme strategy used to make this New Man.

Steel yourself and read on, for unholy horrors await.

CHAPTER 15
DEFILING
THE INNOCENT

How have the Nephilim managed to perpetuate their nefarious philosophy for over ten millennia? From the beginning, they understood they must control the children.

The ruling class knows that children are the most vulnerable among us, and they take special care to defile these innocents by traumatizing and brainwashing them from an early age. The tools of this brainwashing are multifold: they include the reeducation systems of which you have read, but there are also the darker, occult tools of ritual abuse, designed to break a person's will and mind and summon alter-egos that are easily programmed in ways that further their agenda.

DEMON'S LUST

On the 12th of October 1875, a dark entity was born into your world: Edward Alexander Crowley. Dubbed "the Beast" by his own mother, a moniker in which he reveled, young Edward later became known as Aleister Crowley, a highly influential figure in the European occult circles that had been growing over the previous decades. [308]

[308] **Martin Booth**, *A Magick Life: The Biography of Aleister Crowley* (London: Coronet Books, 2000), 3.

One of Crowley's crowing achievements was the creation of Thelema, a system of thought that used sex rituals and blood sacrifice to summon demons for the practioners' selfish purposes. Over the course of his life, Crowley immersed himself in every evil imaginable, notably in a dilapidated house he called the Abbey of Thelema, all in service to his vision for the ruling classes of the earth:

> We should found society upon a caste of "men of the earth," sons of the soil, sturdy, sensual, stubborn and stupid, unemasculated by ethical or intellectual education, but guided in their evolution by the intelligent governing classes towards an ideal of pure animal perfection. [309]

[309] **Aleister Crowley**, *The Confessions of Aleister Crowley* (New York: Penguin, 1989), 730.

Knowingly or unknowingly, he was the perfect tool for the Nephilim, who had revealed enough of their arts to Crowley to make him appear almost supernatural, and people flocked to him as moths to a flame.

One such devotee was Harry Hay, who deeply admired Crowley's promiscuous bisexuality and penchant for sodomy. You see, Hay himself was a prominent figurehead in the LGBT movement and remains so even after his death in 2002. Crowley's sex "magick," as he spelled the word, featured heavily in Hay's own writings, who exalted depravity as a path to enlightenment and liberation. Hay is most famously known for being an ardent promoter and defender of pedophilia, issuing many defenses of one of their lobby groups: the North American Man-

310 "The Real Harry Hay," Phoenix. com, https://bostonphoenix.com/ boston/news features/other stories/ documents/02511115.htm

Boy Love Association. [310] It was easy for the general public to ignore the likes of Crowley and Hay, since they were clearly twisted figures who were incapable of engendering trust. But since the early years of the twenty-first century, there has been a push from within professional circles to normalize pedophilia in society, as you shall see.

Why is such a reviled practice being defended and perpetuated? It is because pedophilia is a tool of the Nephilim and their descendants to break children and make them instruments of their bidding, such that they are shaped to unquestioningly serve the Nephilim's goals. Indeed, one psychologist studying this phenomenon reports that, in many cases, one of the personalities created in the fractured mind of a child victim is an alter ego—an image of the attacker that abides, thus making it easier for the adult victim to step into the role of perpetrator and thus continue the legacy of evil. [311]

311 Howard Steele, "Unrelenting Catastrophic Trauma within the Family: When Every Secure Base Is Abusive," *Attachment and Human Development* 5, no. 4 (2003): 353–366.

Consider the growing transgender activist movement, which confuses children about their sexuality from a young age with pornographic performances and other materials inserted into school curricula. Could it be that children are thus left vulnerable to predators who step in to offer firmer "guidance" on the child's sexuality? If so, who does that vulnerability serve? Those in charge leave no room to question these practices. When parents in the United States challenge school boards about the sexualization of minors, normalization of pedophilia, the promotion of transgenderism, and the stripping away of their parental responsibility and authority over what their children are exposed to, the FBI labels them as domestic terror threats.

A key agency in normalizing pedophilia and suppressing knowledge of the Nephilim's heinous actions is the American Psychiatric Association, whose members have been promoting pedophilia as simply another sexual preference for many decades. Consider, for instance, Dr. Frederick Berlin, founder of the Sexual Disorders Clinic at the Johns Hopkins Hospital, who stated at a 2003 conference that "people who are sexually attracted to children should learn not to feel ashamed of their condition." [312] The mainstream media has joined these professionals, featuring articles written by pedophiles in an attempt to garner sympathy for their degenerate, destructive impulses. [313]

312 Lawrence Morahan, "Psychiatric Association Debates Reclassifying Pedophilia," *CNS News*, June 11, 2003, https://web.archive.org/ web/20080315035737/, http:// www.cnsnews.com:80/Culture/ Archive/200306/CUL20030611c. html

313 Tracy Clark-Flory, "Redefining Pedophilia with Pedophiles' Help," *Salon*, August 17, 2011, https://www. salon.com/2011/08/17/pedophilia/

There are many more examples of child abuse in your civilization, carried out by agencies and people in power. The Catholic Church is one well-known example, with Pope John XXIII issuing the *Crimen Sollicitationis* in 1962—a set of instructions for covering up the sexual abuse of children by priests taking place throughout Christendom. The FBI also participated in a cover-up, hiding documents and falsifying the claims of the child victims, thereby protecting the perpetrator, Larry Nassar, doctor of the US Olympic Team, and allowing him to continue molesting gymnasts. [314]

And there's more. A top FBI agent in charge of crimes against children was a pedophile. [315] In fact, the FBI's corruption and direct involvement in sex scandals goes all the way back to J. Edgar Hoover, first director of the FBI and a closeted homosexual who is known to have commiserated with pedophiles. [316] Hoover gained such notoriety during his tenure that US President Harry Truman wrote of Hoover's FBI, "We want no Gestapo or Secret Police. F.B.I. is tending in that direction. They are dabbling in sex life scandles [sic] and plain blackmail when they should be catching criminals. They also have a habit of sneering at local law enforcement officers." [317]

And there's yet more evidence of rampant pedophiliac practices among the high and mighty. Dennis Hastert, the longest-serving speaker of the US House of Representatives and a confessed sexual abuser of young boys, used his banking connections to cover up the same crimes by others. [318] BBC icon Jimmy Savile sexually abused over 500 children, even having sex with corpses. [319] He was a close friend to King Charles III and even "elevated" to knighthood in 1990 by the king's mother, the late Queen Elizabeth II. Prince Andrew, brother of the king, was a close associate and customer of convicted pedophile and sex trafficker Jeffrey Epstein. [320]

[314] "McKayla Maroney's Gut-Wrenching Statement to Congress about FBI's Handling of Nassar Abuse," *ABC News*, September 15, 2021, https://abcnews.go.com/US/mckayla-maroneys-gut-wrenching-statement-congress-fbis-handling/story?id=80037780; **Matt Agorist**, "No Charges for FBI Agents who 'Covered' for Child Rapist with 500 Victims, Allowing Him to Continue to Prey on Kids," The Free Thought Project, Mary 30, 2022, https://thefreethoughtproject.com/no-charges-for-fbi-agents-who-covered-for-child-rapist-with-500-victims-allowing-him-to-continue-to-prey-on-kids/; **Brian Naylor**, "Gymnasts Blast the FBI's Mishandling of Their Allegations about Larry Nassar," *NPR*, September 15, 2021, https://www.npr.org/2021/09/15/1036968966/gymnasts-nassar-fbi-senate-hearing-simone-biles-aly-raisman-wray

[315] **Jeff Burlew**, "FBI Agent Who Investigated Sex Crimes against Children Is Charged for Sex Crimes against Children," *USA Today*, August 31, 2021, https://www.usatoday.com/story/news/nation/2021/08/31/fbi-agent-charged-sex-crimes-against-children-florida/5663692001/

[316] icareviews, "Did Israel Control J. Edgar Hoover with Pedophilia?" *Renegade Tribune*, June 19, 2017, http://www.renegadetribune.com/israel-control-j-edgar-hoover-pedophilia/

[317] "Longhand note of President Harry S. Truman, May 12, 1945," Truman Library, https://www.trumanlibrary.gov/library/truman-papers/longhand-notes-presidential-file-1944-1953/may-12-1945

[318] **Christy Gutowski, Jason Meisner,** and **Elyssa Cherney**, "Dennis Hastert Released from Prison but Still Faces Sex-Offender Treatment," *Chicago Tribune*, July 18, 2017, https://www.chicagotribune.com/news/breaking/ct-dennis-hastert-released-chicago-20170718-story.html

319 **Terrence McCoy,** "How BBC Star Jimmy Savile Got Away with Allegedly Abusing 500 Children and Sex with Dead Bodies," *Washington Post*, June 27, 2014, https://www.washingtonpost.com/news/morning-mix/wp/2014/06/27/how-bbc-star-jimmy-savile-got-away-with-allegedly-abusing-500-children-and-sex-with-dead-bodies/

320 **Sean Coughlan,** "Prince Andrew Pays Settlement Ending Sex Assault Case," *BBC News*, March 8, https://www.bbc.com/news/uk-60667111

321 **Matt Agorist,** "US Army and State Officials Facilitated Torturous Child Sex Ring by Ignoring Dozens of Complaints for a Decade," The Free Thought Project, March 30, 2022, https://thefreethoughtproject.com/us-army-state-officials-facilitated-torturous-child-sex-ring-by-ignoring-dozens-of-complaints-for-a-decade/

322 **Jonathan Bucks,** "Starving Children 'as Young as Nine Forced to Give UN Officials Oral Sex to Get Food,'" *Express*, December 15, 2015, https://www.express.co.uk/news/world/627783/Starving-children-as-young-as-NINE-forced-to-give-UN-officials-oral-sex-to-get-food/amp

323 **Paisley Dodds,** "More Than 100 UN Peacekeepers Ran a Child Sex Ring in Haiti. None Were Ever Jailed," *Toronto Star*, April 12, 2017, https://www.thestar.com/news/world/2017/04/12/un-peacekeepers-child-sex-ring-left-victims-but-no-arrests.html

324 **Matt Agorist,** "'Horrifying' GOP Bill Opens the Door for Child Rape by Scrapping the Minimum Age for Marriage," The Free Thought Project, April 9, 2022, https://thefreethoughtproject.com/the-state/horrifying-gop-bill-opens-the-door-for-child-rape-by-scrapping-the-minimum-age-for-marriage

325 **"Pedophiles in Government?"** *Awake Australia*, https://awakeaustralia.org/pedophiles-in-government/

Through inaction, the state of Arizona and the US army facilitated a child sex torture ring.[321] The UN World Food Program forced starving children as young as nine to give sex for food.[322] In Haiti, hundreds of UN peacekeepers ran a child sex trafficking ring for over a decade, and none were jailed after it came to light.[323] Laws have even been proposed in the United States legalizing marriages between adults and prepubescent children.[324] After trying and failing for years to obtain authorization to begin an investigation, an Australian police officer provided a list of twenty-eight known pedophiles to Senator Bill Heffernan, which included judges, prosecutors, and even a former prime minister. In response, Prime Minister John Howard enacted a ninety-year publication ban on the list.[325]

EMPIRE
OF SIN

As you read these instances of pedophilia cover-ups in your society, carried out by law enforcement and those in power, you may wonder how deep this network runs. It runs all the way to the top. Here is but one example: During Hillary Clinton's run for the US presidency in 2016, her campaign manager, John Podesta, was embroiled in a pedophilia scandal known as Pizza-gate, which came to light after many of Podesta's emails were leaked. [326] In these emails, Podesta and his associates make frequent references to a specific pizzeria called Comet Ping Pong Club, as well as "pizza-related" handkerchiefs, "Thelema favors," and many other seemingly nonsensical topics. Brace yourself, for you are about to confront a disturbing truth.

[326] **"The Podesta Emails,"** *WikiLeaks*, https://wikileaks.org/podesta-emails/

In January 2007, the FBI published a paper detailing signs and symbols used by pedophiles and sex traffickers to refer to the characteristics of the children being trafficked, and these symbols have been found on many businesses frequented in elite circles—including Comet Ping Pong Club. [327] In their coded language, the children are pizza, with different types of pizza referring to different genders and appearances of children. The code, in conjunction with the content of Podesta's emails, strongly implies Comet Ping Pong Club was a front for child trafficking. [328]

[327] **"(U) Symbols and Logos Used by Pedophiles to Identify Sexual Preferences,"** Federal Bureau of Investigation Intelligence Bulletin, January 31, 2007, https://www.wikile-aks.org/wiki/FBI-pedophile-symbols.pdf

[328] **"DC PizzaGate: A Primer,"** *DC PizzaGate* (blog), https://dcpizzagate.wordpress.com/

Consider the owner of the pizzeria, James Alefantis, who brazenly posted to his Instagram account an image of a young girl restrained to a table with masking tape, and even one of a baby holding stacks of sequentially numbered euros with the currency strap still in place, something typically only seen in the criminal underworld. On another post of an unknown baby, someone commented, "Cuteness is very serious business. Seriously." In yet another Instagram post, Alefantis uploaded an image of a doll with a sign saying, "German baby, $1,200" and left a comment that this was "way overpriced." Many other images used in the company's advertising strategy posted on employee accounts show pornographic acts that have been censored with slices of pizza. [329]

[329] "DC PizzaGate: A Primer."

Clinton's former chief of staff, Tamera Luzzatto, was also implicated in the Pizzagate scandal. In another of the leaked emails, Luzzatto spoke of transporting children to a "pool party" as "further entertainment." On her personal blog titled *Evie's Crib*, now made private after the Pizzagate scandal became public knowledge, she offered up her own daughter with the headline "Evelyn is growing up. Soon she will be the queen of the entire US of A. Right now, for a limited time only, you can spend some time with her online, raw and uncut." [330]

[330] "DC PizzaGate: A Primer."

After the evidence mounted that horrific events were taking place in the pizzeria, a man walked into Comet Ping Pong Club with a semiautomatic rifle to rescue children supposedly being kept in the basement. He found none, and the ruling class was able to package all of the evidence from this incident as the delusions of a lone, violent nut, and thereby silence all further discussion about the pedophilia ring being valid.

But is this a clear case of self-motivated vigilantism? Is it not odd that the Internet Movie Database profile photo for this perpetrator, an actor with several credits to his name, is a cropped version of the one taken during his arrest following the incident at Comet Ping Pong? And is it not curious that just one month earlier, he was arrested for driving his car into a teenager, causing injury to his head, torso, and leg, yet he was able to leave the state and drive to Washington DC to play out a heroic fantasy at Comet Ping Pong? Could it be that Edgar Maddison Welch's act of vigilantism was a sort of plea deal that would be used to deflect attention away from Alefantis, painting him and his patrons as victims, and providing an excuse to shut down all discussion about his criminal activities? [331]

[331] Josh Levin, "Gunman Arrested in Pizzagate Incident Recently Ran over a Teenager with His Car," *Slate*, December 4, 2006, http://www.slate.com/blogs/the_slatest/2016/12/04/pizzagate_gunman_edgar_maddison_welch_ran_over_a_teenager_with_his_car.html

[332] Nicole Silverio, "'An Alarming Pattern': Sen. Josh Hawley Questions Ketanji Brown Jackson's Record on Child Porn Rulings," *Daily Caller*, March 17, 2022, https://dailycaller.com/2022/03/17/alarming-pattern-josh-hawley-supreme-court-nominee-ketanji-brown-jackson-record-child-porn/;

The judge who oversaw the trial of the Pizzagate vigilante, Ketanji Brown Jackson, has a record of being especially lenient on the perpetrators of sexual crimes against children. It seems quite coincidental, does it not, that she was assigned to this case, especially since she doled out a harsh sentence, perhaps sending a message to other would-be vigilantes trying to shut down this pedophile ring. [332] Since the Pizzagate trial, Jackson has been appointed to the US Supreme Court, where she will serve for the rest of her natural life. In the face of massive criticism, CNN legal expert and public masturbator Jeffrey Toobin had the temerity to echo Jackson's opinion that child pornography laws are too strict because the Internet had made it so easy to create and distribute huge quantities of it. [333]

If you have been paying attention, you will have noticed that names and organizations connected with the ruling class and their nefarious purposes are repeated again and again. Case in point: In addition to being part of this pedophilia ring, John Podesta is a prominent UFO disclosure advocate, another connection he shares with Hillary Clinton and her husband, Bill. Is this a coincidence? Is it a coincidence that Jan Harzan, the former executive director of the Mutual UFO Network, had to resign in disgrace after it was discovered he was a pedophile? [334]

Where are all these pedophiles coming from, how are they getting into positions of such power and influence, and why are they so well protected by law enforcement and the justice system? As you will see in the next section, the Nephilim have been using this sexual abuse strategy for millennia to create Manchurian candidates, who now sit at all levels of power throughout your world.

[332] Jessica Gresko, "'Pizzagate' Gunman in DC Sentence to 4 Years in Prison," *AP News*, June 22, 2017, https://apnews.com/article/united-states-presidential-election-e0d30f6da17348ce9f354bfd6cb5cd9a

[333] Steve Watson, "Video: CNN Masturbator Toobin Says Kiddie Porn Laws Are Too Strict," *Summit News*, March 23, 2022, https://summit.news/2022/03/23/video-cnn-masturbator-toobin-says-kiddie-porn-laws-are-too-strict/

[334] Andrew Whalen, "UFO Organization Leader Arrested for Allegedly Soliciting Sex from a Detective Posing as Child," *Newsweek*, July 15, 2020, https://www.newsweek.com/ufo-sightings-mufon-arrest-organization-jan-harzan-arrested-1517779

MANCHURIAN CANDIDATES

Perhaps you have heard the term; now you shall learn the soil from which it sprung. A Manchurian candidate is a controllable and docile person who does the handler's bidding when triggered by a stimulus response, a word or phrase that changes the candidate's state of mind and induces extreme compliance, even to commit atrocities. In this way, the handler possesses absolute power: they need not worry about the Manchurian candidate ever rebelling or using their training to attack them. In the early days of these training attempts, the projects were called MONARCH and ARTICHOKE, but let us now hear of the largest and most destructive of them all. [335]

[335] **Cathy O'Brien** and **Mark Phillips**, *TRANCE Formation of America: True Life Story of a Mind Control Slave* (Reality Marketing, 1995); **Vigilant Citizen**, "Origins and Techniques of Monarch Mind Control," Vigilant Citizen, December 12, 2012, https://vigilantcitizen. com/hidden-knowledge/origins-and-techniques-of-monarch-mind-control/

In 1953, the US Central Intelligence Agency approved the creation of MKULTRA, an international project whose sole purpose was to create Manchurian candidates controlled by the CIA and their partners in the intelligence community. It was hoped these individuals could be programmed to engage in certain actions, often nefarious in nature, but then have no recollection of what they did after the deed was committed.

In 1995, a victim of this program, Claudia Mullen, gave testimony to the president's Advisory Committee on Human Radiation Experimentation:

> I was born in 1950, and by the age of seven I thought I was already accustomed to being an abused child. I was wrong. Nothing could have prepared me for what was to follow. Between the years of 1957 and 1984, I became a pawn in a government scheme whose ultimate goal was mind control, and ultimately to create the "perfect spy." All through the use of chemicals, radiation, drugs, hypnosis, electric shock, isolation in large tubs of hot or cold water, sleep deprivation, brainwashing, and verbal, physical and emotional abuse. By the time I was nine, I was also being sexually abused and

humiliated as a coercive technique ... I was sent to a place in Maryland called Deep Creek Caverns to learn how "to sexually please men." I was taught also how to coerce them into talking about themselves, and then I had to prove my accurate recall ... I was to become a regular little "spy" for them after that summer, entrapping many unwitting men with the use of hidden cameras. I was only nine when this began.

MKULTRA didn't quite succeed in their aim of creating the ultimate assassins, but they did succeed in splitting the personalities of their victims, using sexual abuse to create a mechanism of control in the children on whom they were experimenting. For once it was understood that a child's personality could be split, it was also understood that some of those split personalities could be manipulated and used to further the state's goals. As revealed in *Secret Weapons: Two Sisters' Terrifying True Story of Sex, Spies and Sabotage*,

> By the time Cheryl Hersha came to the facility, knowledge of multiple personality [disorder] was so complete that doctors understood how the mind separated into distinct ego states, each unaware of the other. First, the person traumatized had to be both extremely intelligent and under the age of seven, two conditions not yet understood though remaining consistent as factors. The trauma was almost always of a sexual nature ... [The government researchers] decided to use selective trauma on healthy children to create personalities capable of committing acts desired for national security and defense. [336]
>
> [336] **Cheryl** and **Lynn Hersha**, with **Dale Griffis** and **Ted Schwarz**, *Secret Weapons: Two Sisters' Terrifying True Story of Sex, Spies and Sabotage* (Liberty Corner, NJ: New Horizons Press, 2001), 52–54.

The beginning of the MKULTRA project saw a pronounced increase in the number of cases of dissociative identity disorder, formerly known as multiple personality disorder, though officially this is merely attributed to rising awareness of the condition. [337] The CIA used these "agents" to entrap company executives, politicians, bureaucrats, and media figures, and then used those individuals for their own ends.

[337] **Daniel L. Schacter, Daniel T. Gilbert, and Daniel M. Wegner**, *Psychology* (2nd ed.) (New York: Worth, 2011), 572.

When the MKULTRA program was exposed and the terrible truth came out, it was supposedly shut down. But Jeffrey Epstein, notorious in your society for running a pedophilia ring and later dying in prison under very suspicious circumstances, has ties to the intelligence community and appears to have merely moved the MKULTRA practices to the private sector. Using the same methods as the CIA, Epstein brought in girls, taught them to gratify men (starting with himself), and used them to entrap other men whom he then controlled.

338 Daniel Bates, "Exclusive: Ghislaine Maxwell Touted Her Connection to Bill Clinton and How She Helped Launch His Global Initiative to Prove Her 'Desire to Do Good in the World,' as She Seeks a Lower Sentence for Trafficking Under-age Girls for Jeffrey Epstein," *Daily Mail*, June 20, 2022, https://www.dailymail.co.uk/news/article-10935097/Ghislaine-Maxwell-touted-connection-Bill-Clinton-lower-sentence-trafficking.html

339 Isabel Van Brugen, "Who Is Alison Nathan? Ghislaine Maxwell Trial Judge," *Newsweek*, November 29, 2021, https://www.newsweek.com/manhattan-judge-alison-nathan-ghislaine-maxwell-trial-1653899

340 Tyler Durden, "Ghislaine Maxwell's Family 'Fears for Her Safety' after Epstein 'Pimp' Jean-Luc Brunel Found Hanged," *Zero Hedge*, February 19, 2022, https://www.zerohedge.com/political/epstein-pimp-jean-luc-brunel-found-hanged-paris-prison

341 Don Via Jr., "Watch: Journalist Reporting on Ghislaine Maxwell Trial Burglarized, Research Stolen," The Free Thought Project, December 24, 2021, https://thefreethoughtproject.com/government-corruption/watch-journalist-reporting-on-ghislaine-maxwell-trial-burglarized-research-stolen

342 Taylor Lang, "Federal Judge Reduces Ghislaine Maxwell's Max Sentence by 10 Years," *WPBF News*, May 2, 2022, https://www.wpbf.com/article/ghislaine-maxwell-reduce-sentence/39875629; Nate Raymond, "U.S. Senate Promotes Ghislaine Maxwell's Judge to Appellate Court," *Reuters*, March 23, 2022, https://www.reuters.com/legal/litigation/us-senate-promotes-ghislaine-maxwells-judge-appellate-court-2022-03-24/

When Epstein's scheme was brought to light, his associate, Ghislaine Maxwell, was also captured and, unlike Epstein, survived to be tried for her crimes. Immediately, it was apparent this would be no ordinary trial. The prosecutor in the case, Maureen Comey, is the daughter of James Comey, the FBI director who let Hillary Clinton escape charges for her illegal use of a private email server while heading the US State Department, and for allowing herself to be bribed through a not-so-secret "pay-to-play" scheme revealed through the Clinton server scandal. Would it surprise you to know that Maxwell has a close relationship with Hillary and her husband, Bill? She attended their daughter's wedding and worked in Bill's philanthropic endeavors. Maxwell even cited this relationship as a reason why the judge should be lenient with her. [338] And then there is the judge overseeing this case, Alison Nathan, a transgender female first appointed by President Obama who perhaps has a debt to pay to the Democrats for the position she now enjoys. [339] You be the judge whether these factors could inhibit a fair, unbiased trial for Maxwell.

As the trial proceeded, many mysterious events unfolded. Several other associates of Epstein died under strange circumstances, including Jean-Luc Brunel, head of a Paris-based modeling agency that procured young girls for Epstein. [340] In addition, a reporter covering the trial had her Airbnb burglarized, with only her trial research being stolen. [341]

Maxwell was eventually convicted on five out of six charges and was supposed to receive a thirty-year sentence. She asked for, and the judge granted, a reduced sentence in a low-security prison known as "Club Fed," and the judge was then rewarded with a promotion to an even higher court. [342] At no point was the Epstein/Maxwell client list produced or released to the public, which would have revealed the full extent of their corrupting influence. Should we be surprised at this, Seeker of Truth? Maxwell's family connections to the corrupt intelligence community are well known. Her father was Ukrainian-born European media baron Robert Maxwell, who had ties to both British and Israeli intelligence services. Her sister, Isabel Maxwell, is a prominent member of the World Economic Forum, peddling influence throughout Silicon Valley. [343]

[343] **Whitney Webb**, "Meet Ghislaine: Heiress to an Espionage Empire," *Unlimited Hangout*, March 17, 2022, https://unlimitedhangout. com/2022/03/investigative-reports/ meet-ghislaine-heiress-to-an-espionage-empire/;

Whitney Webb, "Isabel Maxwell: Israel's 'Back Door' into Silicon Valley," *Unlimited Hangout*, July 24, 2020, https://unlimitedhangout. com/2020/07/investigative-reports/ isabel-maxwell-israels-back-door-into-silicon-valley/

BRED FOR
SERVITUDE
AND SLAUGHTER

Beyond the Epstein scandal, there have been other examples of the privatization of MKULTRA and its brainwashing programs using sexual abuse, and the ages-old practices of breeding children for the purpose of murdering them in occult rituals. A cult called The Finders was keeping children in a Washington DC commune in the 1980s. When police in Tallahassee found six of these children, aged two to seven years old, in a park in the care of two men to whom they were not related, the children were malnourished, covered in insect bites, and wearing tattered clothes. They were examined by Dr. Moorer from the Health and Rehabilitation Service, and his report stated, "One of the children lacked 'anal specter control,' consistent with acts of sodomy" and that "one of the girls had signs consistent with vaginal penetration by the fingers." [344]

[344] Derrick Broze, "Who Will Find What the Finders Hide?" Conscious Resistance Network, March 26, 2019, https://theconsciousresistance.com/thefinders/

In addition, the children demonstrated a complete ignorance of the function and purpose of common household items like staplers, telephones, televisions, and even toilets, and they stated they were not allowed to live indoors and were only given food as a reward. During the interviews, they urinated and defecated on the floor, and stated they were all under the control of the "game caller," a title held by The Finders' leader, Marion Pettie, whom they also said, "owns a man named Steve."

The officers requested the help of US customs special agent Ramon Martinez in identifying the children and men, as they immediately suspected this was a matter of child trafficking. The case quickly came to the attention of detective Jim Bradley, of the Washington DC police department, who had been investigating the Finders cult for quite some time. It soon became known that in the DC commune, "members engaged in long self-criticism sessions, exposing painful emotional inadequacies to the group. Members stopped seeing relatives and friends who were not in the group; former associates found themselves shunned or treated brusquely."[345] As you now know, all of these cult activities are common brainwashing techniques that break down the individual wills of members and subsume them to the group mind, making them easily controllable.

[345] John Mintz and Marc Fisher, "Ex-Finders Tell of Games, Complex Beliefs," *Washington Post*, February 8, 1987, https://www.washingtonpost.com/archive/politics/1987/02/08/ex-finders-tell-of-games-complex-beliefs/dcb48101-8d06-4777-a8e3-fcf46fd7edOf/

The Tallahassee police supplied Bradley with enough information to obtain a warrant to search a DC warehouse that was believed to be used in cult activities. The ensuing raid revealed the extent of the cult's depravity: The Finders were hiring women to bear children for their commune, meaning the children were undocumented, which gave The Finders greater freedom to abuse and break them without leaving a trace. Instruction manuals detailing how to kidnap, purchase, and sell children internationally were discovered, as was evidence of blood rituals and sex orgies involving children. Telex messages between the cult and other groups in Hong Kong and the United Kingdom were found. One involved the procurement of two children, while another message specifically referred to the arrests that had just been made in Tallahassee, with instructions to move "the children" and keep them moving through different jurisdictions with further directions on how to avoid police detection.

The founder and leader of The Finders, Marion Pettie, was ex-military, with ties to the intelligence community. In a 1998 interview with *Steamshovel Press*, he spoke about keeping house for mainly intelligence people from the OSS, the CIA's predecessor.[346] Not coincidentally, the moment the police investigation amassed the trove of evidence from the warehouse raid, the CIA made the investigation an "internal matter"—a fact the FBI redacted from their official release of the Finders documents. A wall was raised, and the subject became taboo, with Special Agent Martinez's final report on April 13, 1987, famously concluding, "No further information will be available. No further action will be taken."[347]

[346] Kenn Thomas and Len Bracken, "The Finders' Keeper: An Interview with Marion Pettie," *Steamshovel Press*, 1998, https://idoc.pub/documents/ctrl-the-finders-keeper-an-interview-with-marion-pettie-34m71v779m46

[347] "The Finders Part 02 of 04," FBI Records: The Vault, p.74, https://vault.fbi.gov/the-finders/the-finders-part-02-of-04/view. For the unredacted version, see the Ted Gunderson files, in which former special agent Gunderson has a copy of the original report: http://tedgunderson.info/index_htm_files/Finders%20(2).pdf

There is more. The Franklin Community Federal Credit Union, a bank in Omaha, Nebraska, had a CEO called Lawrence King. Over time, it became apparent that the bank was a front for a child trafficking ring led by King, and accusations emerged that King was abusing young people in strange satanic rituals as well as supplying children to elites in Omaha and DC. In 1993, the Discovery Channel

348 "Conspiracy of Silence (Banned Franklin-Ring Documentary),"
YouTube video, posted by Maintenance Tunnels, July 28, 2022, https://www.youtube.com/watch?v=SsFjbYuEjlY

produced a documentary on the so-called Franklin cover-up scandal called *Conspiracy of Silence*, but the documentary's release was abruptly canceled shortly before it was scheduled to air. [348]

In the case of the Franklin cover-up, several victims brought a lawsuit against the perpetrators. The lawyer on the case, former Nebraska State senator John DeCamp, started with a long list of plaintiffs that whittled down to only two who could withstand the bullying and blackmail carried out by state attorneys. One of them, Alisha Owen, had her trial moved straight to a grand jury, who turned the case against her and threw her in jail for apparently falsely accusing certain parties. The second plaintiff, Paul Bonacci, obtained a jury trial and won his case, with a settlement of $1 million. In a statement to FBI Special Agent Ted Gunderson, who had been following the Finders and Franklin events, desperately trying to get a federal investigation started, Bonacci indicated that he witnessed children being trafficked and auctioned off in their underwear, numbered placards hanging from their necks. Some children sold for $50,000 each at locations just outside Las Vegas and Toronto.

King's sexual crimes were proven in court, but no media outlet reported on it, nor will the courts reopen Alisha Owen's case, even though her claims were no different from those made by Paul Bonacci. No one talks about Bonacci's legal victory because Larry King was a powerful member of the Republican Party, and the children he trafficked were sent to the White House to service politicians. [349]

349 Paul M. Rodriguez and George Archibald, "Homosexual Prostitution Inquiry Ensnares VIPs with Reagan, Bush," *The Washington Times*, June 29, 1989, http://www.voxfux.com/features/bush_child_sex_coverup/WashingtonTimes.htm

Using children in this despicable way is not new. Remember the system in Carthage, where young women were sent to the temple when they reached puberty, under the guise of being blessed. There, they would be raped by a man who paid the temple for the privilege, and after the act, the girls would be told they were now sanctified. If they became pregnant from this rape, the child was kept by the temple. If the baby was a girl, and the rulers had need to replenish their ranks, the temple raised her to join the same system, but if new members were unnecessary, or if the child was a boy, the young one was ritually sacrificed to Cronus. The murdered child's remains were kept in the same urn as the animal sacrificed next to them, for the Nephilim do not distinguish between animals and human beings. They care not about the innocent.

SIGNS AND SATAN'S JESTERS

You have already learned in Chapter 13 of the misdirection and lies spread by the Nephilim to hide themselves and keep you distracted, and now you shall see how it is being used to keep you from considering how they are defiling the innocent. For, just as there exists a political Left and Right to keep you trapped in a false dichotomy, so is religion marked by such a fallacy.

Many people have grown disillusioned with the mainstream religions, and rightly so, but rather than discover true spirituality, they have been herded into yet another false paradigm, one replete with false idols and unholy practices of its own. Satanism and its adherents unwittingly serve as a convenient distraction from the nameless and truly evil groups ruling your world.

Satanists can trace their iconography to French occultist Éliphas Lévi, who died a mere five months before the birth of Aleister Crowley. Lévi is most famous for his 1856 creation of the image of Baphomet, also referred to as the Sabbatic Goat or the Goat of Mendes. After learning about the Catholic Church's swift extermination of the Knights Templar in 1307 for supposedly murdering and consuming children, as well as worshipping a false idol bearing the name of Baphomet, Lévi drew what he felt was the image of the demonic entity the Templars were said to be worshiping.

His drawing may have been inspired by Horatio Greenough's 1840 sculpture of George Washington, for Lévi drew Baphomet with the same posture as Washington: seated bare-chested on a "throne," front facing, the right hand raised with an upward-pointing finger and left arm resting on the chair.

The Nephilim often plant the symbols of their mockery and ridicule in plain sight of the public. The 1840 George Washington sculpture was itself a mockery of the first president of the United States. The descendants of the Nephilim sculpted him in the same pose as a Roman Emperor, knowing that Washington was firmly

Lévi's Baphomet

against the concept of himself as king and deified ruler. This insult was their way of signaling that they had infiltrated the United States, and that they were gaining control. George Washington himself knew of their efforts: in two letters stored at the Library of Congress, he talks about his awareness of a dark order of European intelligentsia attempting to take control of the new nation. [350]

[350] "George Washington to Reverend G. W. Snyder, September 25, 1798," Library of Congress, https://www.loc.gov/resource/mgw2.021/?sp=182&st=text; "George Washington to Reverend G. W. Snyder, October 24, 1798," Library of Congress, https://www.loc.gov/resource/mgw2.021/?sp=200&st=text

In his 1856 book *Dogme et Rituel de la Haute Magie*, where the depiction of Baphomet first appeared, Lévi describes this icon in detail

> The goat which is represented in our frontispiece bears upon his forehead the sign of the pentagram with one point in the ascendant, which is sufficient to distinguish him as a symbol of the light; he makes the sign of occultism with both hands, pointing upward to the white moon of Chesed, and downward to the black moon of Geburah. This sign expresses the perfect harmony of mercy with justice ... The dread Baphomet henceforth, like all monstrous idols, enigmas of antique science and its dreams, is only an innocent and even pious hieroglyph. [351]

[351] Éliphas Lévi, *Transcendental Magic: Its Doctrine and Ritual*, trans. A. E. Waite (London: George Redway, 1896). 289–290.

Because he was ignorant of the Nephilim's infiltration of the Catholic Church, rather than rebut the blood libel leveled at the Templars, Lévi sought to use this drawing to put a spin on the Church's claims, in effect admitting that the Templars were worshipping Lévi's creation, though they did not actually believe Baphomet was a demon. By making this image into a mystic union of opposites, he unwittingly opened the door for further perversions and gave the Nephilim a convenient bogeyman with which to menace the ignorant masses.

Who were the Knights Templar? They were a widely respected military order whose mission was to protect the Christian pilgrims traveling to and from the Holy Land during the time of the Crusades. For them to be swiftly rounded up and slaughtered without trial speaks to a mystery at the heart of their extermination. Could it be that the Templars had discovered the Church was in fact responsible for abusing and sacrificing Christian children in ancient Punic rituals? If so, they would have posed a threat to the Church, a threat that could not be tolerated nor given a venue in which to defend themselves. The Baphomet menace was used again to great effect in the 1890's by Léo Taxil, the pen name of Marie Joseph Gabriel Antoine Jogand-Pagès, a French prankster who spent most of his adult life creating hoaxes with which to embarrass the Catholic Church. Sadly, even after confessing in the April 25, 1897, issue of Parisian newspaper *Le Frondeur* with great glee to the success of his Luciferian Masonic deception, many continue to believe his grand production was real.

Based on Lévi's drawing, which turned Baphomet into a recognizable occult icon, a number of modern-day organizations have sprung up in worship of Satan, such as the Church of Satan, the Joy of Satan, and the Satanic Temple. Not all of these institutions believe in demonic worship; some call themselves rationalist anti-religious organizations and aim to mock God worshippers by pretending to serve the Devil. Yet these useful idiots also serve a purpose for the Nephilim, knowingly or unknowingly. In the *Politics of Obedience*, Étienne de La Boétie wrote,

> It is pitiful to review the list of devices that early despots used to establish their tyranny; to discover how many little tricks they employed, always finding the populace conveniently gullible, readily caught in the net as soon as it was spread. Indeed they always fooled their victims so easily that while mocking them they enslaved them the more. [352]

[352] Étienne de La Boétie, *Politics of Obedience,* trans. G. K. Hurst (Auburn, AL: The Mises Institute, 1975), 67.

By mocking God worshippers and the public, these pseudo-religious agencies make it easier for the Nephilim to ensnare people who have become jaded with mainstream religions. Just as the Nephilim have created a false Right-Left political divide, so too have they manufactured a holy-evil dichotomy: when disillusioned God worshippers leave the church, synagogue, or temple, the Nephilim are waiting with another community, another means of control.

The Church of Satan was the first of these modern pseudo-religious organizations, established by Anton Szandor LaVey at the Black House in San Francisco, California, on the equinox festival known as Walpurgisnacht, April 30, 1966. LaVey used the Sigil of Baphomet as the Church of Satan's official insignia, an image that traces back to another French occultist, Stanislas de Guaita. In 1897, the year of his death, de Guaita published *La Clef de la Magie Noire*, in which his sigil encircled the demon Baphomet's head with an inverted pentagram and included the names "Samael" and "Lilith" above and below it. [353] Samael is one of the names of the evil Demiurge, from the Apocryphon

[353] Stanislas de Guaita, *La Clef de la Magie Noire* (Paris: Henri Durville, 1920), 417.

of John, who is associated with Cronus. Another of its names is Yaldabaoth, whose form is described as a lion-headed serpent, not unlike the Mithraic god Aion, who is likewise associated with Cronus. LaVey found the sigil in his copy of Maurice Bessy's 1964 book A *Pictorial History of Magic and the Supernatural*, which had, for unknown reasons, omitted the names from the sigil.

De Guaita's **Sigil of Baphomet**

Since its inception, LaVey's Church of Satan has attracted many celebrities, including musicians Sammy Davis Jr., Liberace, and Marilyn Manson, as well as actress Jayne Mansfield. Even Chelsea Clinton herself has had online exchanges with the Church of Satan. [354]

[354] **Joseph Curl**, "Chelsea Clinton Wishes Happy New Year to the Church of Satan," *Daily Wire*, January 3, 2018, https://www.dailywire.com/news/chelsea-clinton-wishes-happy-new-year-church-satan-joseph-curl

Nearly fifty years after LaVey established the Church of Satan, Lucien Greaves—whose given first name is Doug and given surname is alternately presented as Mesner or Misicko—created the Satanic Temple. [355] Like LaVey, Mesner founded his church upon the image of Baphomet, turning Lévi's drawing into a statue with an inverted pentagram behind the demon's head and a child on

[355] **Shane Bugbee**, "Unmasking Lucien Greaves, Leader of the Satanic Temple," *Vice*, July 30, 2013, https://www.vice.com/en/article/4w7adn/unmasking-lucien-greaves-aka-doug-mesner-leader-of-the-satanic-temple

either side of his chair, gazing upward at the false god. Mesner claims he and the members of the organization simply want equal representation alongside Christianity, Judaism, and other established religions as guaranteed by the US Constitution. Yet, an examination of his personal history reveals some important ulterior motives.

In the early 1990s, a woman by the name of Jennifer Freyd recovered memories of sexual trauma inflicted upon her by her father, Peter. He denied the accusations and, though not a psychiatrist himself, coined the term "False Memory Syndrome" to explain away his daughter's experience. To this day, False Memory Syndrome is not a recognized diagnosis by anyone in the psychiatric profession; it is a pseudoscience. [356]

[356] American Psychiatric Association, *Diagnostic and Statistical Manual of Mental Disorders*, 5th ed. (Arlington, VA: American Psychiatric Publishing, 2013).

Nevertheless, in 1992, Peter founded the False Memory Syndrome Foundation (FMSF), which attracted a number of pro-pedophilia figures to its leadership. The FMSF took issue with dissociative identity disorder, which psychologists had recognized as a diagnosis for decades, and with the phenomenon of ritual abuse, seeking to have both completely erased from discussion. The FMSF set out on a crusade to harass any psychologist discussing ritual abuse or helping victims recover from the trauma inflicted by it. [357]

[357] Kate McMaugh and Warwick Middleton, "Focus on ISSTD History: The Rise and Fall of the False Memory Syndrome Foundation," *ISSTD News*, January 21, 2020, https://news.isst-d.org/the-rise-and-fall-of-the-false-memory-syndrome-foundation/

False Memory Syndrome can only be regarded as an abuse of psychology, not at all unlike the old diagnosis of "drapetomania," used in the days of slavery to explain why those in forced servitude would want to flee their masters. Yet another would be "sluggish schizophrenia," invented by the Russian communists to diagnose and oppress their critics.

[358] "A Documentary by Penny Lane. Rated 14A," *Straight*, https://www.straight.com/movies/1235221/satanic-panic-over-church-and-state

[359] Naomi Oreskes, "Jeffrey Epstein's Harvard Connections Show How Money Can Distort Research," *Scientific American*, September 1, 2020, https://www.scientificamerican.com/article/jeffrey-epsteins-harvard-connections-show-how-money-can-distort-research/

Regardless, this fake science became a topic of study at Harvard University, which is where this story finally catches up to Doug Mesner, who was a neuroscience student there in the early 2000s, specializing in the "syndrome." [358] Coincidentally, around this time Jeffrey Epstein became a major donor to Harvard, enjoying unfettered access to the campus and even his own office, sponsoring projects in order to seed the human race with his own DNA. [359] Whether Mesner and Epstein ever crossed paths remains the subject of speculation, but the likeness of their acts and attitudes suggests some sort of kinship.

Around the same time that he started at Harvard, Mesner befriended Shane Bugbee, reverend of the Church of Satan and Vice Media writer, over their mutual love of a foundational satanic text known as *Might Is Right*, written in 1896 by Ragnar Redbeard. So influential was this book that Anton LaVey transferred much of it verbatim into his own work, *The Satanic Bible*. Redbeard advocates amorality, consequentialism, social darwinism, and psychological hedonism as well as nihilistically disavowing the natural law.

In addition to Satanism, the book found wide circulation in white supremacist groups, highlighting the deep connections between Nazis, eugenicists, Satanists, those ruling from the ivory tower, and their Nephilim ancestors of old.

In 2011, Mesner and Bugbee began planning to write a *Might Is Right* sequel that would be, according to an email sent by Mesner to Bugbee, "a manual for coercion and manipulation. More evil than the first book by orders of magnitude." [360] The theme of the book would be how to best achieve individual gain, as well as how to drive others to violence while thinking it was the perpetrator's own idea.

[360] **State of Arkansas**, "Satanic Temple Ark Lawsuit—Shane Bugbee Sworn Testimony," https://archive.org/details/shane_bugbee_sworn_testimony/2020-04-18%20Shane%20Bugbee%20Declaration/

In January 2013, after a former Florida governor signed a bill allowing student-led religious speech at school assemblies, Mesner and Bugbee worked on a film project that involved a staged rally at the Florida State Capitol. That project was called "The Satanic Temple," conceived as a fake documentary about the (fictional) "nicest Satanic cult in the world" celebrating the governor's decision. Bugbee was originally asked to play the part of "Lucien Greaves," the leader of the Satanic Temple, but when he learned that he would not have final editorial control of his own image and depiction, he turned down the role. Mesner took the role and even assumed the name and identity of Lucien Greaves in everyday life. [361]

[361] **Ken Shepherd**, "MSNBC's Bashir Falls for Hoax, Reports Satanists to Rally for Rick Scott; Turns Out It's Part of Mockumentary," *News Busters*, January 18, 2013, https://www.newsbusters.org/blogs/nb/ken-shepherd/2013/01/18/msnbcs-bashir-falls-hoax-reports-satanists-rally-rick-scott-turns

By 2014, the Satanic Temple had officially begun at Harvard, with Mesner holding "Black Masses" on campus. He also garnered a reputation for harassing the victims of sexual abuse in many, many online posts. [362] Around this time, Mesner and Bugbee had a falling out, mainly because Bugbee now felt

[362] **Dawn Eden**, "Take Action: Tell Fed, Already Probing Harvard on Sex Abuse, That 'Black Mass' Adds to Hostile Environment," *Patheos*, May 9, 2014, https://www.patheos.com/blogs/feastofeden/2014/05/take-action-tell-feds-already-probing-harvard-on-sex-abuse-that-black-mass-adds-to-hostile-environment

Mesner only wanted to exploit Satanism for money, leading Bugbee to criticize Mesner and expose his agenda in a personal blog, claiming Mesner had disclosed that he wrote reports for the CIA. [363] In a sworn statement submitted to the eastern district court of Arkansas on April 18, 2020, Bugbee made many allegations regarding Mesner's ties to fascism, white supremacy, and other ideologies favored by the ruling class. In one place, Bugbee remarked that Mesner

[363] **Shane Bugbee**, "Religion: A Master and Slave Relationship," The Satanic Wanna-Be Cult, n.d., https://web. archive.org/web/20160405153153/ http://www.shanebugbee.com/?p=2161

is sympathetic to fascist ideology and its emphasis on power. He has taken a particular interest in Mussolini, even visiting Italy to see Mussolini's birthplace. Doug also has a Process P Cross tattoo, which is a power symbol derived from the Swastika. [364]

[364] **State of Arkansas**, "Satanic Temple Ark Lawsuit."

[365] **Ed Cara**, "Canadian Therapist Gives Up Her License after Satanists Expose Her 'Mind Control' Talks," *Gizmodo*, November 5, 2019, https://gizmodo. com/canadian-therapist-gives-up-license -after-satanists-exp-1839605239

After the dissolution of the FMSF, in 2019, the Satanic Temple took up their mission of harassing and persecuting both patients and their doctors—anyone discussing the phenomenon of ritual abuse—to the point that one therapist gave up her license. [365]

Here again is the plain truth about the Satanic Temple and other pseudo-religious groups: they are tools of the Nephilim to redirect attention away from what is truly happening, "prebunking" truth and poisoning people's minds against the possibility that ritual abuse and other horrors really exist. In a truly bizarre example, the seven tenets of Satanism were slipped into a presentation to the US Army as a way to prebunk skepticism around vaccines and shame soldiers into obeying the mandate. [366] In addition, Mesner himself sued a public school, and won the right to have his demoralizing ideology taught there as well. [367]

[366] **Tucker Carlson**, *Tucker Carlson Tonight*, September 20, 2021, retweeted by Daily Caller, https:// twitter.com/DailyCaller/ status/1440107751477231621

[367] **Jon Brown**, "The Satanic Temple Sues Pennsylvania School over After School Club Denial," *Fox News*, April 24, 2022, https://www.foxnews.com/ us/satanic-temple-sues-pennsylvania- school-club-denial

How does a licentious character like Doug Mesner come to have so much influence over American institutions, to the point of gaining free publicity from the US military? As you might suspect, he has friends in high places. Judges seem to side with him, though he has no credibility, and with every frivolous lawsuit Mesner files, he alienates more and more people from his organization. [368]

[368] **Julia Duin**, "Orgies, Harassment, Fraud: Satanic Temple Rocked by Accusations, Lawsuit," *Newsweek*, October 29, 2021, https://www. newsweek.com/orgies-harassment- fraud-satanic-temple-rocked- accusations-lawsuit-1644042

Could he possess so much power if he wasn't somehow helping those in the ivory tower? Perhaps even more strangely, the Anti-Defamation League not only has no response to Doug Mesner's open anti-Semitism, but they also issued a defense of his attempts to introduce satanic clubs to public schools. [369]

[369] Oren Segal, "Key Supporter of After-School Religious Clubs Ironically Says Satanic Temple Can Be Barred," *ADL*, August 10, 2016, https://www.adl.org/blog/key-supporter-of-after-school-religious-clubs-ironically-says-satanic-temple-can-be-barred

These methods are hardly unique; they have been employed before by other criminal conspiracies to confuse the public about their existence. Consider the Italian-American Civil Rights League, formed in 1970 by the Colombo crime family. It was used by the Cosa Nostra as a public relations front to deny the existence of the American Mafia and improve the image of mobsters. Not only were they successful at persuading the FBI to deny the existence of the Mafia for decades, but they even convinced the US attorney general at the time, John Mitchell, to order the Justice Department to expunge the words "Mafia" and "Cosa Nostra" from all of their communications. [370]

[370] Joel Dreyfuss, "Italian-Americans Claim Ethnic Bias," *Courier-News* (New Jersey), March 27, 1971, https://www.newspapers.com/clip/66915201/italian-americans-claim-ethnic-bias/

There is yet one more sign used by Satan's jesters, a symbol whose intended purpose has been hijacked by the Nephilim and carried on by unsuspecting jesters of Satan: the inverted cross. Lévi, along with another occultist by the name of Eugène Vintras, popularized the idea that an inverted cross is a symbol of the antichrist. Others refute this symbology, however, claiming that the inverted cross is actually reminiscent of the manner in which Saint Peter died. Behold, for you shall now learn more of this sign.

The tradition that Saint Peter was crucified upside down is a lie popularized by Eusebius of Caesarea in his *Historia Ecclesiastica*. [371] Known throughout the ancient and present world for dishonesty, in *Praeparatio Evangelica*, Eusebius lists the ideas Plato supposedly got from Moses, including the idea that telling lies in order to turn people towards his "truth" was not only permissible, but good. [372] Indeed, he was quite favorable towards this idea, being most famous for forging a passage about Jesus into Josephus's *Antiquities of the Jews* and taking many other liberties with his sources in order to advance his version of Christianity. [373]

[371] Eusebius, *Historia Ecclesiastica*, Book III, Chapter 2.

[372] Eusebius, *Praeparatio Evangelica*, Book XII, Chapter 31.

[373] Ken Olson, "Eusebius and the Testimonium Flavianum," *The Catholic Biblical Quarterly* 61, no. 2 (1999): 305–322.

With regard to Peter's upside-down crucifixion, Eusebius attributes his statement to Origen, the proudly admitted liar whom we have previously discussed. Origen likely drew from the apocryphal Acts of Peter, a text of unknown authorship that did not appear until the very end of the second century. In fact, the first suggestion that Saint Peter was crucified at all that can be attributed to a known author did not appear until more than a century after his death in *Adversus Gnosticos Scorpiace*, a treatise composed by Tertullian of Carthage, only a few decades before Origen. [374] Thus, the entirety of Catholic belief about Peter's crucifixion rests upon a single sentence, written centuries after the event, by one admitted liar, and attributed to another admitted liar. No one truly knows when, where, or in what manner Peter actually died.

[374] **Tertullian**, *Adversus Gnosticos Scorpiace*, Chapter 15, https://www.newadvent.org/fathers/0318.htm

If you look closely at photographs and videos of prominent public figures such as Chelsea Clinton, daughter of Hillary and Bill, you will find evidence that some wear the inverted cross, this symbol of anti-Christianity or Satanism. [375] Indeed, she has been photographed multiple times wearing this unholy icon, and when knowledge of this became widespread, she declared every photograph a forgery and presented a picture of a Greek cross, with arms of equal length, as the true pendant she was wearing. [376]

[375] **TTs-Admin**, "Why Is Chelsea Clinton Wearing an Inverted Christian Cross?" *Truth Seeker*, March 8, 2016, http://www.thetruthseeker.co.uk/?p=130037

[376] **Chelsea Clinton**, tweet replying to @CarmineSabia and @Trooper2121, Twitter, August 15, 2018, https://twitter.com/ChelseaClinton/status/1029776180294168577

Know this: no original unaltered photographs have ever been produced, which would have easily proved her claims of tampering. Chelsea is herself a Methodist, her husband is Jewish, so why would she wear the talisman of the Eastern Orthodox Church?

HIGH PLACES OF BAAL

You have now read, oh Seeker of Truth, of the atrocities committed in the ancient Punic religion, atrocities that included cannibalism and the widespread sacrifice of children. Do you think these practices could be stopped with the destruction of Phoenicia and Carthage? In fact, the abominations of the Nephilim and their descendants continue to this day, though under a different guise, hidden underground, away from the public eye. The ritual sacrifices once made in the name of Cronus are now made in the name of Satan, but they are one and the same entity, also referred to in the Judeo-Christian Bible as Baal.

The elements of these satanic ceremonies remain the same as they were many millennia ago: ritual murder, ritual cannibalism, and ritual sex, often ritual rape. Though repugnant to God, these practices remain an important part of the Punic religious groups' initiation ceremonies, reaching even to the high circles of Hollywood. Consider actress Megan Fox, who spoke candidly on camera about engaging in mutual blood drinking "for ritual purposes" with her boyfriend, an act specifically condemned by God. [377] Actress Angelina Jolie spoke of such rituals, describing how she was tied down and apparently tortured and potentially raped as part of an initiation ceremony. She praised this act of surrendering, saying, "You'll be able to heal once you're beaten," and that it is not to be confused with sadomasochism; this is something darker, something deeper. Though many celebrities participated in the same ceremony, as evidenced by the "most amazing compromising pictures of people" she claims to possess, Jolie wished she could have filmed the ritual to encourage different celebrities to try it. [378]

[377] Emily Maddick, "Megan Fox Is *GLAMOUR*'s April Cover Star: 'Me just Being Free and Having Fun with How I Am Is Very Provocative for People,'"*Glamour*, April 22, 2022, https://www.glamourmagazine.co.uk/article/megan-fox-digital-cover-interview-april-2022

[378] "*LEAKED VIDEO* Angelina Jolie Details Her Illuminati Rape, Torture Ritual!" YouTube video, posted by The Iconic Mr. Perfect!, Mar 3, 2017, https://www.youtube.com/watch?v=3WmcRN1LJK4

Fox and Jolie both give first-hand, eye-witness accounts of rituals that follow the traditional Punic rites of blood sacrifice and strange sex acts, rituals that apparently occur at the highest levels of Hollywood and employ photographs and sex tapes as a mechanism of control, not unlike Epstein's pedophilia ring. In *Asclepius*, Chapter 21, Hermes Trismegistus speaks of the sacredness of sex and its compelling forces. He states that

> the performance of this sweet and vital mystery takes place in secret lest the divinity of Nature that arises from the union of sex were compelled by the mocking and ignorant to feel ashamed if the act were performed openly; much worse still, if it were seen by the enemies of religion. [379]

[379] Hermes Trismegistus, *Asclepius*, 75.

By making members perform these acts publicly and by recording them, these cults maintain a level of control over their participants. They use this control to further their own goals and maintain secrecy.

Yet the true horror is that these occult rituals are also performed on small children, again as a way to control their minds and make them tools of their captors. One study proved that such rituals, unchanged for millennia, are still being conducted in the modern day, to demoralize and brainwash children into doing what they are told. Subjects of the study gave gruesome and horrifying accounts of blood drinking, rape, ritual murder, and cannibalism. One patient recalled a ritual when she was four or five, where a brother and a sister were placed on a table at the center of the ritual and forced to perform oral sex on each other, before being cut open, cooked, and eaten. [380]

[380] Sally Hill and Jean Goodwin, "Satanism: Similarities between Patient Accounts and Pre-Inquisition Historical Sources," *Dissociation* 2, no. 1 (March 1989), 39–44.

In 1994, the conservative government of the United Kingdom sponsored an official report that declared the practice of ritual abuse to be a myth. That report fell under heavy criticism, and in February of the year 2000, the UK Department of Health granted psychiatrists Valerie Sinason and Rob Hale £22,000 to research the same phenomenon and provide evidence of its existence.

Sinason and Hale were both treating victims of ritual abuse at the time, and their report concluded that the evil practice was absolutely real, with two thirds of the survivors reporting similarly heinous activities: rape and non-consenting impregnation, forced abortions, necrophilia, bestiality, cannibalism, the forced consumption of bodily fluids like blood and semen, infanticide, and the torturing and killing of animals. Many of the victims suffered from dissociative identity disorder and PTSD as a result of the abuse, yet others were afflicted with various addictions and

[381] Robert Hale and Valerie Sinason, "Pilot Study on Alleged Organised Ritual Abuse: Final Report" (2000), https://www.whatdotheyknow.com/ request/portman_and_tavistock_clinic_pil

other compulsive, self-destructive behaviors.[381] Hale and Sinason even found evidence that "some children are born for the purpose of abuse and are not registered on birth certificates."[382]

[382] **Sophie Goodchild**, "Satanic Abuse No Myth, Say Experts," *The Independent*, April 20, 2000, https://www.independent. co.uk/news/uk/this-britain/satanic-abuse-no-myth-say-experts-5371639.html

Given these horrific details, Seeker of Truth, do you find it surprising that this report remained undisclosed for seventeen years? Only after the years-long efforts of one individual did the government finally release it. Such is the way of those in power: they do not want their evil deeds exposed to the light.

These rituals are often conducted in abandoned churches, barns, cellars, or other underground venues. In the famous McMartin preschool case, for example, excavations performed at the school revealed a network of tunnels containing ritualistic artifacts, animal bones, and other items underneath the building.[383] Some, however, do actually take place in temples of sorts. In 2016, at the Cern research facility, in front of a large statue of the Hindu god Śiva, several scientists who worked there performed a ritual that was caught on camera. When the video was uploaded to the internet, a Cern spokesperson declared the incident a prank, yet not a single person that was involved in the ritual was ever interviewed or explained what they were doing.[384] It is also well known that these rituals are sometimes staged to deceive a person into believing that a murder had been committed, or surgery had been performed on them. In all cases, it is not the ritual itself that is important, but the fear and compliance it creates in its victims.

[383] **E. Gary Stickel**, "Archaeological Investigations of the McMartin Preschool Site, Manhattan Beach, California," The McMartin Tunnel Project, 1993, http://tedgunderson. info/index.htm files/McMartin%20 Scientific%20Report.pdf

[384] **Staff and agencies in Geneva**, "Fake Human Sacrifice Filmed at Cern, with Pranking Scientists Suspected," *The Guardian*, August 17, 2016, https://www.theguardian.com/ science/2016/aug/18/fake-human-sacrifice-filmed-at-cern-with-pranking-scientists-suspected

Later, in 2019, two intrepid journalists secretly visited the temple that Jeffrey Epstein built upon his island, a structure that was not at all what it appeared to be.[385] The main doors were not doors at all, indicating entrance was by way of subterranean means. But the most intriguing thing of all was that this temple was dedicated to the ancient god of Atlantis: Poseidon.[386] We are then led, inescapably, to ponder if Epstein was indeed a conscious

[385] **Michelle Mark**, "An Unauthorized Video of Jeffrey's Epstein's Private Island Gave Us the Best Look Yet at Its Mysterious 'Temple' and Creepy Statues," *Insider*, October 31, 2019, https://www.insider.com/video-jeffrey -epstein-private-island-temple-2019-10

[386] **J. K. Trotter**, "Why Did Jeffrey Epstein Build a Temple on His Private Island?" *Insider*, July 10, 2019, https://www.insider.com/jeffrey-epstein-private-island-temple-2019-7

Nephilim. Consider this as well: both Lord Śiva and Poseidon wield the trident, perhaps explaining why the 2016 ritual at Cern was performed where it was, in desecration of a god who has never demanded any sort of blood sacrifice.

The latest glimpse into the world of these degenerate murderers came in 2020 by way of the Dutch news radio team Argos. One hundred and forty accounts of ritual abuse were collected, revealing stunning similarities to each other, and to past accounts of the same. Six prominent people were named, as well as ten locations where the rituals took place. Argos summarized their findings as follows:

> Almost every single one of the 140 people who filled out our questionnaire state that they were introduced to the network by a family member, usually their father or mother. All of them were drugged. Almost every one of them was forced into prostitution. Child pornography was produced, as well as torture porn.

> Four out of five respondents were forced to inflict pain upon other children. This makes for the deepest traumas. It is impossible to find the right words to describe it. The same goes for pregnancies. 78 percent states that they got pregnant through the abuse. The majority more than once. They'd get tortured to the point of losing their baby, they say. But they also speak of 'nobodies'. Children that were born into and kept within the network, and never got officially registered. Some of them are dragged from place to place. Others live with families that are active within the network. Their mothers are only allowed to see them if their sexual performance is up to par. If they continue to come back. These nobodies undergo the most severe forms of abuse. [387]

[387] Sanne Terlingen, Huub Jaspers, and Sophie Blok, "Shards of Glass and Dark Rituals," *Argos*, 2020, https://www.vpro.nl/argos/lees/nieuws/2020/glass-shards-and-dark-rituals-english-transcript-.html

One victim account indicated the abusers wear black and purple robes—the colors being that of Cronus (black) and that of one of the most popular Phoenician exports, purple dye.

The Argos reporters discovered a warehouse in the Bollenstreek region that was marked as a location for the "storage" and production of child pornography. These same reporters received an anonymous email stating the journalists had to "be aware" because "they know about your investigation" and "they're going to get rid of evidence—just like they did with [Marc] Dutroux." The same day the journalists received the email, the Bollenstreek warehouse burned down. According to Argos, the fire department could not determine the cause of the fire, so severe was the damage caused.

The Argos research was published as an audio documentary called *Shards of Glass and Dark Rituals*. It caused a sensation, and the public demanded an official investigation, which was overwhelmingly supported even by most of the Dutch congress. The minister of justice, Ferdinand Grapperhaus, himself a member of a Catholic political party, quickly squashed the investigation. [388]

Do not be fooled. The abominations of the High Places of Baal continue to this day.

[388] "Anwoorden Kamervragen over de uitzending van Argos over ritueel misbruik," Rijksoverheid, August 27, 2020, https://www.rijksoverheid.nl/documenten/kamerstukken/2020/08/27/antwoorden-kamervragen-over-de-uitzending-van-argos-over-ritueel-misbruik

TOWARDS
ASCENSION

It is natural for you to feel rage as you read this, Seeker of Truth, perhaps even rage like you have never felt before. But do not be vengeful. Your path is towards understanding, not retaliation. Vengeance for such wickedness is the right of God, and his wrath will soon come upon your world.

The strategies of the Nephilim present a grim reality. Your urge to fix the world, silence the oppressors, and create a utopia is real, but your actions will not bear those fruits. The Nephilim have had more than 10,000 years to consolidate their power and execute their strategies. Individual violence will not stop them now. Do not waste your time trying to fix the world, violently or otherwise. For through your desire to do good, you will be led into all manner of sinful acts. Instead, pursue the Path of Righteousness. Prepare yourself to become the fully actualized spiritual being you were meant to be. In reaching the next stage of human evolution, others will follow because you have shown them the way to ascension.

BOOK IV
THE PATH OF RIGHTEOUSNESS

CHAPTER 16
FEAST AND FAST

Animal nutritionists are able to fine-tune diets to the point where creatures may eat from the same bag of food their entire lives and remain in excellent health. Yet humans, who have inhabited Planet Earth for 300,000 years, still struggle to eat in a way that similarly promotes good health.

How is it that humans find this so challenging?

The truth is that you have been deliberately misled. In the past, your species knew how to eat healthy and live long lives by following the best practices of your ancestors and the species that came before *homo sapiens*. Yet today, you have wandered far from that wisdom. For the past sixty years, your governments have been encouraging a diet that is not good for your minds or for your bodies.

Think back to what you learned about the Nephilim's desire to keep the human population weak and subjugated. What better way to suppress a revolt and control humanity than to keep them sick and malnourished? Keep people ill long enough and they will eventually die, another key part of the ruling class's plan.

Furthermore, the Nephilim and the ruling class profit from your poor health, for they have designed a medical industry that earns money from treating the very symptoms that they create. Throughout history, studies have been published about the medical and food industries' calculated aims to mislead people away from healthy eating. None is more culpable than the sugar industry.

SWEET SUBTERFUGE

For millennia, your ancestors survived on a diet of meat and fat and were not only healthy, but strong. They did not suffer from obesity and dental issues; the latter being evidenced in the near perfect teeth in human skulls dating back 10,000 years and earlier.

Then in the modern age, and particularly in the Industrial Revolution of the late nineteenth century, new food groups were introduced to the human diet, processed foods that plunged human health into a downward spiral. Potatoes and other starch-laden vegetables, sweets, desserts, ice cream, and milkshakes became fashionable, particularly among the wealthy, and the rich grew fat. [389]

[389] Gary Taubes, *Good Calories, Bad Calories: Fats, Carbs, and the Controversial Science of Diet and Health* (New York: Anchor Books, 2007).

It is not that the people did not know the cause of their problems; it was common knowledge that these unnatural foods were causing ill health. In 1863, William Banting wrote one of the first diet books, titled *Letter on Corpulence*, where he offered his solution to the increasing waistlines of the rich: cut out sweets, bread, and potatoes. The suggested diet was successful for a great many people, and thus began the world's first diet trend.

Its success was limited, however, as more and more industrialized food with added sugar displaced traditional foods at grocers. In due course, people's health deteriorated and, particularly after US President Eisenhower's heart attack, individuals rightly raised the alarm.

Following this voiced concern, in the 1960s, US government scientist Ancel Keys conducted the Seven Countries Study to analyze the effects of fat on human health. Alas, it was not an unbiased study, for Keys had a preconceived conclusion that he hoped the study would prove—that fat, and particularly saturated fat, is the primary cause of human health problems—so he engineered his data to get the result he sought. Keys' Seven Countries Study began with twenty-two nations, but he eliminated all but seven because they did not suit his hypothesis. The remaining countries did indeed show higher incidence of heart disease that could be loosely tied to fat consumption, but Keys failed to look at sugar intake, incidence of smoking, or other confounding factors that might have led to high incidence of heart disease apart from the eating of fats. [390]

[390] Robert Lustig, *Fat Chance: Beating the Odds Against Sugar, Processed Food, Obesity, and Disease* (New York: Plume, 2012), 110–111.

The Seven Countries Study launched the anti-fat and anti-cholesterol movement, and the government played a key role in both, suppressing the dangers of sugar and promoting the "benefits" of a low-fat diet.

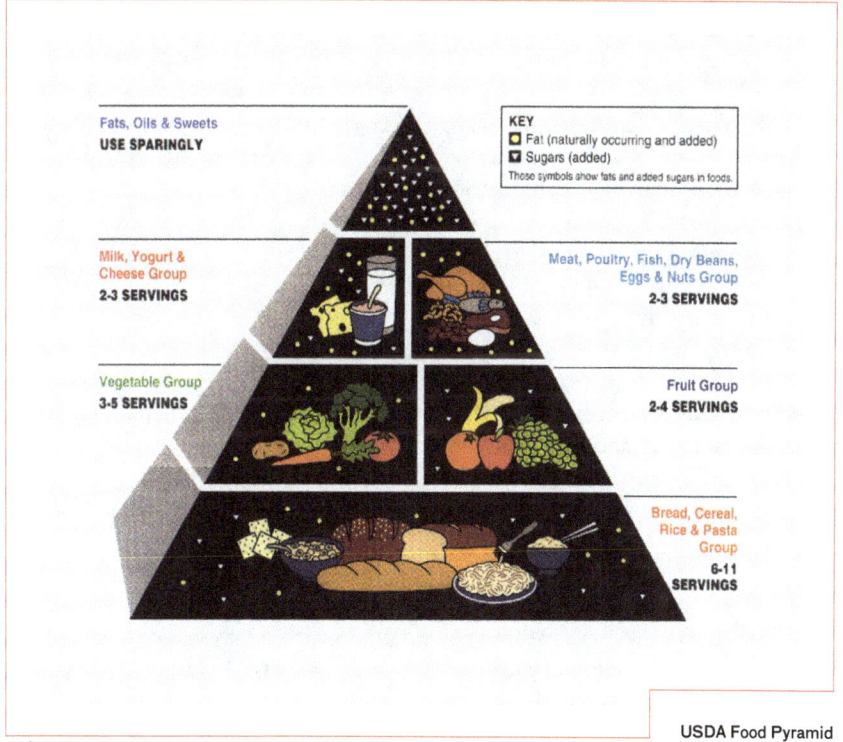

USDA Food Pyramid

But dietary fat and cholesterol were never the problem.

For many decades, sugar was a luxury good and remained outside the reach of the common people. This changed when the government actively began subsidizing certain crops, including sugar, in part due to the incestuous relationship between agriculture and the government. Sugar was now endorsed by the authorities, who claimed the product to be safe for consumption, irrespective of how much of it one ate or how often.

Not only did the authorities make it easier to produce and sell sugar, while suppressing the harmful effects of this food product, but they also created a systematic way in which to package and convey their philosophy: the "food pyramid," created by the McGovern Commission in the 1970s as a way for the ruling class to push a high-carbohydrate and low-fat diet upon the common people.

McGovern's main support for the benefit of this food pyramid was none other than Keys's faulty Seven Countries Study. McGovern also famously stated they did not have time to wait until science could settle all the uncertainties; something had to be done immediately.

In his book, *Good Calories, Bad Calories*, Gary Taubes exposed how this food pyramid was created through a collaboration between the government and the wheat, corn, and sugar industries. Cargill and ConAgra, two packaged food corporations, played such a large role in lobbying for the pyramid that they almost seemed to sponsor it. Meanwhile, meat lobbies were largely ignored and guidance to reduce meat consumption persisted.[391]

[391] **Marion Nestle**, "Food Lobbies, the Food Pyramid, and U.S. Nutrition Policy," *International Journal of Health Services* 23, no. 3 (1993): 483–496.

Here's the truth about the foods being pushed upon you: the chemical name of sugar is "sucrose," and it is made up of two molecules—glucose and fructose—united in a 1:1 ratio. Glucose is not necessarily bad for human beings. It raises the body's insulin and if a person consumes too much of it, then they will put on weight, but it is not actively harmful.

Fructose, on the other hand, is treated as a toxin by your body. It goes straight to your liver, down the same pathways as ethanol, which is why some children have fatty liver disease, though they have never consumed a drop of alcohol. The culprit is the copious amounts of fruit juice they consume. It should be no surprise, if you understand the ruling class's goal, that fructose is what gives sugar-laden treats their sweet, enjoyable flavor that humans crave, and it is fructose that causes the most harm to humans' health. Fructose appears naturally in fruit, it is true, but humans today have gone far beyond the seasonal consumption of these foods. It is the dose—the copious amounts of fructose consumed in refined forms—that makes the poison.

The effects of this food pyramid are evident today. Between the 1980s and the early 2000s, the consumption of carbohydrates soared, and the eating of fat decreased, and humans simultaneously witnessed a boom in diseases such as obesity and diabetes, despite the government's assurances that the exact opposite would happen. There was an explosion in other, related diseases: high cholesterol, heart disease, strokes, infertility, and cancer. All of these afflictions fall into a category called metabolic syndrome—chronic diseases that have not been contracted or passed on from person to person but rather created by diet. [392] By emphasizing sugars and carbohydrates, while simultaneously vilifying fat and red meat, the ruling class is encouraging people to make themselves sick through what they eat.

[392] "What Is Metabolic Syndrome?" WebMD, October 27, 2021, https://www.webmd.com/heart/metabolic-syndrome/metabolic-syndrome-what-is-it; "Sugar: The Bitter Truth," YouTube video, posted by University of California Television (UCTV), July 30, 2009, https://www.youtube.com/watch?v=dBnniua6-oM

The government and scientific agencies have worked hard to mislead the public about what they are eating and the many dangers of this new diet. Who is funding the "science" that tells you this diet is good for you? The big pharmaceutical and food companies with a vested interest in getting "results" that further their own interests.

Throughout your history, you have seen this same strategy play out. When the data said that tobacco caused cancer, the big tobacco companies funded research to show that smoking didn't cause cancer at all. Doctors even prostituted themselves to large cigarette makers for their advertising campaigns. The sugar industry did the same thing. When scientists from the early twentieth century began to point out the link between sugar and the rise in these diseases, the sugar lobby funded a series of "studies." They hired scientists and told them the conclusion they needed to reach through their research, and the scientists designed studies such that they could arrive at those conclusions. This is how fat, and cholesterol got blamed for the problems caused by sugar. The sugar lobby then identified which scientists were still speaking the truth to the public about the harms of sugar and used their power to chase them out of academia. [393]

[393] Camila Domonoske, "50 Years Ago, Sugar Industry Quietly Paid Scientists to Point Blame at Fat," NPR, September 13, 2016, https://www.npr.org/sections/thetwo-way/2016/09/13/493739074/50-years-ago-sugar-industry-quietly-paid-scientists-to-point-blame-at-fat

[394] Stephen Phinney and Jeff Volek, "Reversing Type 2 Diabetes with Nutritional Ketosis," Virta, October 4, 2017, https://www.virtahealth.com/blog/reversing-type-2-diabetes-with-nutritional-ketosis-lchf

The remedies for your health problems are also controlled by large pharmaceutical and food companies. Coca Cola and Pepsi pour money into diabetic associations because they have a vested interest in keeping sugar consumption high. It has been proven that type 2 diabetes can be cured through sufficient changes to diet, but no lobby will tell the public this truth, because there is money to be made from the production and sale of insulin. [394]

Much to the ruling class's dismay, diets such as keto and paleo have shot to popularity around the world because people are realizing that by simply returning to the diet of their ancestors, they feel much better. The high-carbohydrate and low-fat diet serves the interests of the ruling class—keeping the human population controlled, depressed, and weak—but it does not serve you.

FOOD OF
THE GODS

You have learned what food is bad for you; now hear what your body needs to feel as strong and as clear-minded as you were born to be.

The core of the human diet was always meant to be meat and animal products like butter, milk, and eggs. In the Book of Leviticus, "God" gave clear direction regarding the food humans should consume:

> These are the beasts which ye shall eat among all the beasts that are on the earth. Whatsoever parteth the hoof, and is cloven-footed, and cheweth the cud, among the beasts, that shall ye eat. [395]
>
> [395] Leviticus 11:1–3 (KJV).

What animals chew the cud and have cloven feet? Cows, deer, elk, bison, sheep, and goats—animals of this sort shall you eat, for they provide the greatest benefit to your health and well-being. Harken back to the discussion of lactase persistence in Chapter 5. It is known this trait could only arise after a long period of proximity to bovines. If the Atlanteans were not yet drinking the milk of these animals, as it seems they were not, then what use did they find for them?

If you continue reading in the Book of Leviticus, you will note that "God" mainly speaks of animals, not plants, as sources of food, for humans derive the greatest strength and vitality from meat and animal products. Some of you will shy away from this truth, claiming the need to avoid animal products for ethical reasons. Heed the words of the Bible, where Jesus says:

> Are ye so without understanding also? Do ye not perceive, that whatsoever thing from without entereth into the man, it cannot defile him; Because it entereth not into his heart, but into the belly, and goeth out into the draught, purging all meats? And [Jesus] said, That which cometh out of the man, that defileth the man. For from within, out of the heart of men,

proceed evil thoughts, adulteries, fornications, murders, thefts, covetousness, wickedness, deceit, lasciviousness, an evil eye, blasphemy, pride, foolishness: All these evil things come from within, and defile the man. [396]

[396] Mark 7:18–23 (KJV).

Whatever you eat, be it animal or plant, cannot defile you and is not a sin. Sins are the actions that spring from the heart of humankind, not what enters the belly.

What does the law of universality say, Seeker of Truth? Is it not that what is true for one creature must be true for all? And thus, if it is a sin for humans to eat meat, then is it not also a sin for tigers or lions or eagles or any other carnivorous animal to eat the flesh of another? And yet, they do, because that is in their nature as carnivores.

The sensible among you see that the ethical foundations of vegetarianism and veganism cannot hold. Meat is not evil, nor is the consumption thereof. In Genesis 4:2-7, "God" rejected Cain's offering of grain for Abel's offering of sheep—not because eating grain is sinful, but because meat is preferable for health and well-being. You know now that biblical stories such as this describe the visitations of an advanced civilization to a primitive one. In this Cain and Abel story, "God" is the Atlantean king, and he demonstrates the preferences of the enlightened ones, choosing meat over cereal, which he knew must be extensively processed before being anywhere near suitable for human consumption.

Some among you might wonder if offerings were meant to be eaten or if they were only designed to be symbolic. Is it a coincidence that both offerings were food? Recall the common custom of *xenia* among the ancients, in which food and shelter were offered to guests, a tradition many cultures keep to this day. Zeus, the ancient Greek god, used to insist that all Greeks welcome any stranger at their door and give them food and shelter, for this stranger was often Zeus himself, dressed as a mortal to visit earth.

Why did the ancients and the advanced civilizations so prefer meat? Why are there verses in the Bible that specify how the fat and suet of the animal is to be preserved and made as a burnt (i.e., cooked) offering to "God"? [397] It is because meat and fat contain essential nutrients the body needs to survive.

[397] Exodus 29 (KJV); Leviticus 3-9 (KJV).

Plants are usually limited or lacking in one or more essential amino acids, typically lysine—which is found plentifully in eggs and meat. Because people in many countries choose to consume plants instead of meat, they are deficient in one or more

[398] **Paul J. Moughan**, "Population Protein Intakes and Food Sustainability Indices: The Metrics Matter," *Global Food Security* 29 (2021), https://www.sciencedirect. com/science/article/abs/pii/ S2211912421000572

[399] **Anne Mottet** et al., "Livestock: On Our Plates or Eating at Our Table? A New Analysis of the Feed/Food Debate," *Global Food Security* 14 (2017): 1–8, https://www. sciencedirect.com/science/article/ abs/pii/S2211912416300013

of these amino acids due to the poor digestibility of plant proteins. [398] Animals do humans a great service by consuming grasses and other plants that are mostly cellulose and thus inedible to humans. Their bodies then convert this cellulose into high-quality, highly digestible protein. [399]

The value of meat goes beyond the provision of protein and amino acids, for the fat contained therein is an energy-dense material: it is nine calories per gram, while protein and carbohydrates contain only four calories. When people search for energy, they are searching for fat. And when they store energy, they store it as fat. This is why the human body can store huge amounts of fat, but can store only a hundred grams of carbohydrates in its muscles and another hundred in its liver, in the form of glycogen. Sugar was never intended to be your primary source of energy; fat was.

All fats, including saturated fat, play important roles in the proper functioning of your body, but the most important fats are those the human body cannot make and thus must come from the food you consume. These are called essential fatty acids—essential because humans must consume them to survive—and are based on linoleic acid (the omega 6 group) and alpha-linolenic acid (the omega 3 group).

Today, humans consume a disproportionate amount of omega 6 fatty acid as compared to omega 3 fatty acids. This is due to the drive toward cheap seed oils—such as canola, cottonseed, corn, or grapeseed oil—as a medium for cooking. Seed oil is high in omega 6 but low in omega 3, and is full of other, nonessential polyunsaturated fats, which oxidize easily, going rancid and producing free radicals that damage your cells and DNA, causing you to age more quickly and develop a host of afflictions. Balance is key, Seeker of Truth, and it is important to eat the right foods to make sure you are consuming enough of all of the essential fatty acids.

Your journey toward a healthier lifestyle and diet does not stop here. Studies have shown that increasing the intake of certain essential fatty acids, either alone or in combination with other fats and compounds, can improve health, help in treating certain diseases, and even enhance body composition, as well as mental and physical performance.

One such miracle fatty acid is stearic acid, which is found in high quantities in beef, as well as a plant known to you as cacao, the Latin name of which means "food of the gods," as you shall soon see why. Cacao is the same plant you use to make chocolate, but the bars you create consist mainly of sugar, with the fat almost entirely removed. The cacao seed, as plucked directly from the plant, is more than 50 percent saturated fat, a third of which is stearic acid. [400]

[400] "Technical Summary: Stearic Acid," Beef Research, https://www.beefresearch.org/resources/human-nutrition/white-papers/stearic-acid

The benefits of stearic acid for the human body cannot be overstated. It regulates the mitochondria and reduces cardiovascular disease and cancer risk. Your scientists have conducted experiments on mice using stearic acid that show a 70-percent reduction in visceral fat, the kind that is associated with cancer and other dangerous maladies. [401] Human trials have not been conducted as of yet, but people have been testing the benefits of stearic acid outside of institutional control. In one self-imposed study, a man ate only croissants enriched with stearic acid and was able to replicate the mice's results in terms of losing weight. Croissants are carbohydrates, it is true, but the benefits of stearic acid far outweighed the negatives of an all-bread diet to produce an overall positive result. [402]

[401] Ming-Che Shen et al., "Dietary Stearic Acid Leads to a Reduction of Visceral Adipose Tissue in Athymic Nude Mice," PLOS One 9, no. 9 (2014):1–12.

[402] Brad Marshall, "Introducing the Croissant Diet," Fire in a Bottle, December 3, 2019, https://fireina-bottle.net/introducing-the-croissant-diet/

The ancients also knew the benefits of cacao, which came from the 7,500-year-old Mayo Chinchipe culture from the highlands of Ecuador. [403] From the Spanish conquistador Hernán Cortés, we are told that the Aztec emperor Moctezuma II regularly drank a cacao concoction he called the "divine drink" and wrote of its ability to "build resistance" and "eradicate fatigue." So valuable were the seeds of this plant that they were even used as money by the Aztecs. Your scientists have found that other compounds in cacao increase cerebral blood flow by 30 to 87 percent, meaning it could be used to treat vascular impairments such as dementia and strokes. [404] A meta-analysis conducted in 2011 showed that cacao consumption significantly reduced LDL, the "bad" cholesterol. [405]

[403] Sonia Zarillo et al., "The Use and Domestication of Theobroma Cacao during the Mid-Holocene in the Upper Amazon," Nature Ecology and Evolution 2 (November 2018): 1879–1888.

[404] Susan T. Francis, Katharine Head, Paul G. Morris, and Ian A. Macdonald, "The Effect of Flavanol-Rich Cocoa on the fMRI Response to a Cognitive Task in Healthy Young People," Journal of Cardiovascular Pharmacology 47 (2006): S215–S220.

[405] Oluwabunmi A. Tokede, J. Michael Gaziano, and Luc Djoussé, "Effects of Cocoa Products/Dark Chocolate on Serum Lipids: A Meta-Analysis," European Journal of Clinical Nutrition 65 (2011): 879–886.

Why is it that your body requires *essential* fatty acids and *essential* amino acids, but there is no such thing as *essential* sugars, carbohydrates, or starches? The answer is quite clear.

Eskimos have survived for millennia in hostile conditions by only eating meat. When anthropologist Vilhjalmur Stefansson and colleague Karsten Anderson lived among them for four years and switched to their diet, the naysayers told them they were sentencing themselves to death, believing it had taken generations for the Eskimos to evolve and adapt to a diet of only meat.

Not only did the pair do exceptionally well on the diet but they came back and performed a controlled trial of consuming only meat for another year. Both thrived: there were no apparent downsides and only upsides. Stefansson wrote about his experiences in *The Fat of the Land*.

Human hunger is controlled by two hormones, ghrelin and leptin, the latter of which is known as the "satiety hormone" because it tells the brain the body is full. Leptin is released by the adipose tissue when a person consumes fat, which means that the more fat a person eats, the less hungry he will be. Ghrelin, on the other hand, is known as the "hunger hormone" because it tells the brain that the body is hungry and needs to eat. Carbohydrates stimulate appetite, and thus food consumption, by triggering ghrelin. Those of you consuming plentiful amounts of carbohydrates are stuck in a vicious cycle, like an addict, and for your own vitality you must break it.

Putting meat at the center of your diet may not be easy at first, because your body has spent decades consuming mostly carbohydrates and glucose. Those who go on a ketogenic diet complain of brain fog in the beginning, because their bodies need to re-learn how to process fat, after years or even decades of that metabolic machinery atrophying. But once their body begins to function as it is meant to, the fog clears, and they experience clarity as they never have before.

[406] Mesfin M. Mekonnen and Arjen Y. Hoekstra, *The Green, Blue and Grey Water Footprint of Farm Animals and Animal Products*, vol. 1: *Main Report* (Delft, The Netherlands: UNESCO-IHE Institute for Water Education, 2010), https://waterfootprint.org/media/downloads/Report-48-WaterFootprint-AnimalProducts-Vol1.pdf

[407] Richard Black, "UN Body to Look at Meat and Climate Link," *BBC News*, March 24, 2010, http://news.bbc.co.uk/2/hi/8583308.stm

Pay no mind to the catastrophists who would dissuade you from eating meat. They claim that raising animals for meat uses up vast quantities of water, yet they use faulty calculations that include the rain that falls on pasture—water that would fall whether or not livestock were there.[406] Similarly, pay no mind to the claim that cows produce too many greenhouse gas emissions, for the researcher who made this assertion admitted it was vastly overstated the moment his findings were challenged.[407] All carbon emitted by an animal must first be taken from the environment, meaning that raising livestock is and has always been a carbon-neutral process.

A LITTLE
STARVATION

Those who consume high quantities of fat shall find themselves producing the leptin hormone more often and thus experience a waning appetite. Over time, they may find that they do not want to eat for a whole day. This should not be a cause for alarm. The human body is evolutionarily designed to feast and then fast—to eat a large amount in one sitting and then not eat for a while.

Modern humans have proven that fasting can be done for a prolonged period of time without any negative side effects. Consider Angus Barbieri, who fasted for 382 days, lost 125 kilograms, and suffered no ill effects.[408]

[408] W. K. Stewart and Laura W. Fleming, "Features of a Successful Therapeutic Fast of 382 Days' Duration," *Postgraduate Medical Journal* 49 (1973): 203–209.

For a time, Mark Twain was staying on a Caribbean island. One day, there arrived a lifeboat of fifteen men who had been sailing through the tropics for forty-three days with only ten days' rations after a fire destroyed their ship along with most of their food. He observed firsthand the effects of fasting. As he writes in "My Début as a Literary Person," "A little starvation can really do more for the average sick man than can the best medicines and the best doctors. I do not mean a restricted diet; I mean total abstention from food for one or two days."[409]

[409] Mark Twain, "My Début as a Literary Person," in *"My Début as a Literary Person" and Other Essays* (Hartford, CT: American Publishing Company, 1903), 32.

You see, a very sick man was with them, who had already been bedridden for months, and eventually the food ran out. Twain continues,

> In spite of dreadful weather, deprivation of sleep, scorching, drenching, and all manner of miseries, thirteen days of starvation "wonderfully recovered" him …Twenty-five days of pitiless starvation have followed, and now we have this curious record: "All the men are hearty and strong; even the ones that were down sick are well."[410]

[410] Twain, "My Début as a Literary Person," 33.

Hundreds more accounts of the benefits of fasting were also chronicled around the same time by Upton Sinclair in *The Fasting Cure.*

For millennia, we have had accounts and evidence showing that abstaining from food for certain periods of time is in fact beneficial for the body. Fasting gives the body respite from the energy-intensive process of digestion and allows it to focus on other systems. It is known to rebuild the immune system, cleanse the cells, fight inflammation, improve brain function, prevent neurodegenerative disorders, assist in weight loss, aid in metabolism, and increase one's overall lifespan. [411] In fact, with a lifelong fasting regiment, it should be possible for any human to live well past 100 years to the maximum lifespan of 120 imposed by "God" after the flood. [412]

[411] **Rachel Link**, "8 Health Benefits of Fasting, Backed by Science," *Health-line*, July 30, 2018, https://www.health -line.com/nutrition/fasting-benefits

[412] **Genesis** 6:3.

The link between fasting and longevity has been explored by your scientists. One study states that, as far as is known, the only way to prolong an organism's lifespan is through caloric restriction. [413] There appears to be a cosmic trade-off between consumption and lifespan, which offers you a moral lesson: fasting should be an important component of your diet.

[413] **Leanne M. Redman** et al., "Metabolic Slowing and Reduced Oxidative Damage with Sustained Caloric Restriction Support the Rate of Living and Oxidative Theories of Aging," *Cell Metabolism* 27 (2018): 805–815.

FIXING
YOUR BODY

To start on the Path of Righteousness and attain the spirituality required to survive the coming judgment, you must begin by fixing the evils done to your body. Move away from the sugary, high-carbohydrate diet cooked with unnatural oils that is advocated by those in the ivory tower, and rediscover the diet of your ancestors that took them to the top of the food chain, a place of privilege that should not be taken for granted. Focus on animal products, sources of high-quality proteins, fats, and clean energy, for these will nourish and sustain you better than anything else. Fast regularly, for the benefits to your mind and body are manifold.

Now, dear soul, we have talked about what goes into our mouth. In the next chapter, let us look at what goes into our nose so you may understand the importance and power of breath.

CHAPTER 17
THE POWER
OF BREATH

D o you know, dear soul, of the superhuman abilities you hold within, potentials that await unlocking with the power of your breath? The limits of your body go beyond what you think—nay, what you can imagine. The Atlanteans knew the secrets of the breath and created a biological science around it.

Now it is your turn to learn that of which you are capable.

BREATHE WITH YOUR HEELS

Many of you who follow the philosophies and thinking of the West have not dedicated time to understanding the power of breath. Paying attention to how you breathe has probably not crossed your mind at all.

Yet breathing is a form of consumption, no different from eating. Just as you swallow and excrete food, so you inhale and exhale air, making it a vital part of the natural ebb and flow by which your body runs itself. In the West, untold attention has been paid to what human beings eat, yet little focus is given to how you breathe.

This is a mistake, Seeker of Truth.

For if you look to the East, you will find that breath has long been a cornerstone in their holistic understanding of health. The ancient practice of Hatha yoga focuses specifically on breath, timing its postures and movements to the pattern of how a person inhales and exhales. Indeed, in the East, it is common knowledge that one must learn how to breathe correctly, and that this type of breathing will unlock the potentials of the body.

Laozi, the founder of Taoism and the author of *Tao Te Ching*, taught many disciples in his time. One of his students, Chuang Tzu, wrote his own book called *The Way of Chuang Tzu*, a text that is now 2,300 years old. Tzu speaks to the holy and often primordial link between breath and the growth of the spirit. "The True Man breathes with his heels," he writes, "the mass of men breathe with their throats. Crushed and bound down, they gasp out their words as though they were retching. Deep in their passions and desires, they are shallow in the workings of Heaven." [414]

[414] Thomas Merton, *The Way of Chuang Tzu* (New York: New Directions, 1965), 60.

Those people who know not how to breathe—and breathe properly—are forever locked in their throats, living shallow lives with stuttering words and uncertain actions. But those who know the true way to breathe may access an essence of themselves that is pure and anchored, an essence that lifts their spirit.

To "breathe with [one's] heels" involves breathing from the deepest regions of your body, what is known as the diaphragm. People today still breathe with their chests and throats but—as any accomplished and praised athlete will tell you—breathing from your chest is not as effective as breathing from your diaphragm.

To breathe well, you must get the breath down to the lowest regions of the lungs, for this is the only way to reach maximum lung capacity. I speak not of volume, dear soul: good breathing is not about taking in as much air as you can. Try to breathe rapidly but in a shallow manner, and you shall see that it does your body no good—indeed, it is similar to hyperventilating. This is because you are not raising your blood oxygen, but lowering your blood CO_2, which leads to feelings of lightheadedness, known as hypocapnia.

Good breathing—breathing from your diaphragm—infuses your body with a sense of strength and well-being because the amount of stress it is under is lowered.

But the powers of breath are not only limited to a general sense of health. Good breathing can unlock the potential in the human body. In *Breath: New Science of a Lost Art*, James Nestor chronicles how breath has helped people achieve what the modern age terms "miracles." People have cured chronic disease. They have fixed scoliosis, that abnormal curvature in the spine. Athletes have unlocked the next level in their sporting practice and broken limits they did not believe possible.

Did you know that the act of chewing can affect the development of your mouth and nasal passages? The human skull has a suture that runs down the middle of the mouth. As a person chews, it stresses the maxilla, causing it to expand and create room for human teeth. Skulls from 10,000 years ago had near-perfect teeth and no dental cavities, partly because they avoided the sweet subterfuge of sugar and partly because they developed their mouths through chewing hard foods, like roots and tough meat.

The result of this expansion of the mouth is an expansion of the airways in your nose, allowing for deep, unobstructed breathing. Today, surgery for a deviated septum is common, as is the removal of the four innermost molars. In some cases, the deviated septum is real, but in others, the person simply has an underdeveloped airway. Alas, even for those without an official deviated septum diagnosis, the experience of breathing is straight-jacketed because they simply do not have properly developed airways and thus are unable to breathe as fully as they were meant to. Fear not, Seeker of Truth, for this straight jacket is not permanent. Your airways can be developed at any age; the point is to keep trying. Practice breathing from deep in your belly, through your diaphragm instead of your chest. If you snore or wake up in the morning with a dry throat, it is likely because you are breathing through your mouth at night. You may wonder at this suggestion, but you can train yourself to breathe properly by placing a piece of tape, no bigger than a postage stamp, over your lips before you retire at night. Your body will naturally adapt, restfulness will improve, and you will breathe through the nose as you should. Mouth breathing carries with it a whole host of problems and diseases that will compound over time—such as poor teeth, throat and ear infections, poor growth, and even lowered intelligence—as well as physical changes such as an elongated face and a receding chin, so it is imperative that you focus on breathing through your nose and breathing well. [415]

[415] Jacquelyn Cafasso, "Mouth Breathing: Symptoms, Complications, and Treatments," *Healthline*, July 15, 2019, https://www.healthline.com/health/mouth-breathing

Deep breathing from the diaphragm, through the nose, will affect you physiologically in every respect, in the same way that eating right has an impact on your health. It will also affect other processes in the body, in the same way that eating well improves your metabolism.

Free divers have accessed some of the vast physiological benefits of good breathing, and they have developed this practice over thousands of years. An average human being can cease breathing for three minutes before they suffer brain damage. Yet free divers can enter the water, swim to depths of 100 meters or more, and take not a single breath for five minutes, eight minutes, even ten. The record for holding one's breath under water is almost twelve minutes—four times the average person's capacity.

Miracles are possible, dear one.

And this is only the beginning. In the next sections, you will learn of people who have unlocked the physiological benefits of breathing and, through rigorous training, mastered the bridge between the physical and the spiritual.

YOGIS OF
THE MOUNTAINS

One of the oldest spiritual practices in the world is yoga. Its beginnings can be traced to the Indus Valley Civilization—which is more than 5,000 years old—as evidenced by the Pashupati seal, which shows the great god of destruction, Śiva, in one of the primary yoga asanas, or poses.

As you know from previous chapters, the Indus Valley saw significant Atlantean activity. It is likely that they mastered the spiritual arts, including yoga and the power of breath, and tried to communicate this practice to the people living there. This is why we have books today that are rich in the spiritual practice of yoga and its hidden secrets.

Yet humans have consistently failed to understand what the Atlanteans have tried to convey. Instead, they have created their own practice, an amalgamation of strength and stretching that largely neglects the breath and deviates from the meditative tradition that was originally conceived and taught. If you consider the oldest instruction manual on yoga, the *Yoga Sutras of Patanjali*, there is not a single chapter on stretching. It only mentions that your posture must be steady and comfortable.

According to this 2,000-year-old text, yoga is the act of silencing the mind and focusing one's breathing. The *Yoga Sutras of Patanjali* refers to this mind quieting as "the cessation of the turning of thought," an essential part of yoga for "when thought ceases, the spirit stands in its true capacity as observer of the world." [416]

[416] *Yoga: Discipline of Freedom: The Yoga Sutra Attributed to Patanjali*, trans. Barbara Stoler Miller (New York: Bantam Books, 1995), Sutras 2–3.

Here, the Sutras harken back to what you have learned about the ego and shadow: that the chatter in your mind is not you. This back-and-forth conversation is merely a delusion. You are a divine spirit that exists apart from that chatter, and you have the power and potential to silence it. Yoga was invented to show you this truth, for when you do silence your mind, you are capable of truly seeing the world as it is and accessing all of its potential.

Remember, Seeker of Truth, your true self is a divine spirit experiencing the material world and these material thoughts. But you are not chained to them, and it is folly to identify with them. The ancient practice of yoga teaches you how to step away from the clamor of your mind and, by using your breath, find the essence of you.

Humans have been so focused on the material side of existence that they have ignored the spiritual side. Worse yet, your neurologists and physicists claim that this side cannot exist, that it is simply fantasy. Your entire civilization devotes itself to material pursuits while ignoring the true essence of your being.

It is no wonder, then, that people throughout history have struggled to unlock the power of breath and learn the full potential of their bodies. So many have yet to uncover the mysteries within and begin this spiritual journey.

But you *can* begin. Breath acts as a bridge between the material and the spiritual and guides you toward the divine. Once you unlock the power of breath, much is available to you.

Swami Rama is just one example of what is possible. He came to the West to set up several yoga studios and teach his knowledge to others. He volunteered to demonstrate certain skills under the observation of your scientists so they may better understand the powers inherent in this ancient practice.

The scientists found that through meditation and breathing, Swami Rama could control his skin temperature *and* his heart rate—both of which have always been relegated to the exclusive domain of the autonomic nervous system, existing beyond the control of the conscious mind. Yet Swami Rama was able to regulate them both.

The key that unlocked this power was breathing, for it is an activity that one can consciously control—if they choose not to, of course, then the body takes over and breathes on its own. A person cannot directly control digestion or heart rate or metabolism, except through breathing. As you shall learn, unlocking the secrets of the breath begins the journey toward personal apotheosis, discussed in the final chapter, a journey that can be accelerated by the sacraments we shall discuss in the next chapter. Much knowledge and growing awaits, and it all begins with the breath.

A MAN OF FIRE AND ICE

There are examples of non-Yogis who have learned the same practices as Swami Rama, the most famous of them being Wim Hof, a Dutchman who harnessed the power of breath in such a way that he is able to withstand extremely low temperatures, earning the nickname "the Iceman."

Wim Hof's journey began when he learned the Tibetan practice of tummo breathing, an ancient art developed as a way to survive the extremely harsh conditions found in the Himalayas. Through tummo breathing—an extended series of deep and forceful breaths—Tibetans were able to control their body temperature and thus stay warm in extreme weather.

Tummo breathing is also called the Breath of Fire. Hof learned this practice and used it to increase his body temperature drastically, without experiencing heat stroke, enabling him to remain immersed in ice water for hours and maintain meditative poses in polar settings. He ran a half marathon barefoot in the snow without getting frostbite. He swam under the ice cap in the Arctic—conditions that would kill an average person. It was so cold that his retinas froze, and he turned temporarily blind, though his body was fine and he continued swimming along, searching for the hole in the ice from which he was to emerge. With help from his team, he did so, and surfaced with no harm to his body. His eyes soon recovered completely.

This ability to regulate body temperature extends to all kinds of extreme weather. Hof can down-regulate his body temperature as well and has run marathons in the desert without suffering a hint of heatstroke.

Hof's practice goes beyond simply adjusting his skin temperature. Scientists who have studied Hof speculate that by controlling his breath, he is better able to regulate his vagus nerve, which is connected to the body's autonomic nervous system and controls heart rate, digestion, and even the immune system. Your scientists ran an experiment in which they exposed Hof and his students to a bacterium that causes a predictable immune system response in a very specific amount of time. Hof and his students, however, controlled their response and experienced none of the typical symptoms.

Hof shows that, through breathing, it is possible to take control of bodily functions that were believed to be completely subconscious. Carl Jung stated that to reach a state of good mental health, a person must integrate the parts of themselves that are subconscious. Controlling your breath gives you a path to doing that, not only with your psyche but also with your physiology.

INTO
THE DIVINE

Can you not see that breath is crucial to your state of being? Indeed, mastering your breath is the gateway to the spiritual, a crucial step on the path to realizing what you were always meant to be—part of the divine. You do not have to achieve the extremes shown here, but these examples illustrate the power available to you. They show you what is possible.

We begin this journey with breath because it is within your control; along with your eating habits, it is the first thing you can practice changing. It is the bridge between the material body and the spiritual realm.

Now we shall move beyond the body to matters of the mind and soul. If this chapter on breath showed you how to begin your journey, then the next chapter shows you what your goal is. It places you directly in the presence of the divine.

CHAPTER 18
AWAKEN
THE SLEEPER

What is the goal of this Path of Righteousness, oh Seeker of Truth? Why learn to master the breath, to gain full control of the material body and move beyond the veil into the spiritual realm? It is to enter into a direct experience of the divine, an encounter that involves leaving your body behind altogether.

Most humans are unable to meditate their way into a deep experience of metaphoric death, leading to life and the divine. Ancients of old found this to be true and learned how to guide themselves into the experience with the help of a psychedelic trip beyond the limits of their body.

These practices did not end with the ancients. Scientists today have discovered a spirit molecule produced by the human body and found throughout nature, a substance that can take you to the other side, to a glimpse of the divine and the purpose toward which you are striving.

MYSTERIES OF
THE ANCIENTS

Throughout the ancient world, there existed spiritual societies that called themselves the Mystery schools. These schools were dedicated to the experience of the beyond. They sought to shake ordinary human beings out of the humdrum of their lives and the cage of their flesh and bones and initiate them into an experience of consciousness without a body.

Archeological digs in the modern day have discovered the existence of these schools around the world. There are the Greek Mysteries, the Roman Mysteries, the Egyptian Mysteries, the Persian Mysteries, the Hindu Mysteries, and many more. Each of these schools used psychedelics to connect with and experience the essence of the spirit and the divine.

Records and texts prove that these Mysteries were not outcast or fringe cults but learning centers that were vital to the cultural fabric of the time. In *De Legibus*, Cicero speaks to how crucial they have been to the development of civilization:

> Among the many exceptional and divine things your Athens has produced and contributed to human life, nothing is better than those [Eleusinian] Mysteries. For by means of them we have been transformed from a rough and savage way of life to the state of humanity, and have been civilized. Just as they are called initiations, so in actual fact we have learned from them the fundamentals of life, and have grasped the basis not only for living with joy, but also for dying with a better hope. [417]

[417] Marcus Tullius Cicero, *De Legibus*, Book 2.36.

The name given to the most renowned of these schools in Greece is the Eleusinian Mysteries. When Emperor Valentinian II banned night-time celebrations, the proconsul of Greece, Praetextatus, pointed out that his edict forbade the performance of the Eleusinian Mysteries, for these rituals were only held at night. So sacred were the Mysteries to the empire that Emperor Valentinian II immediately issued a clarification that these rituals, which were a "great bond" to society, must be "celebrated in the usual manner, without regard to his edict." [418]

[418] Zosimus, *Historica Nova*, Book 4.3.3.

What exactly happened during these Mysteries that made them so vital to daily life? Archeological digs and ancient drawings on Egyptian temple walls give us clues: in several illustrations, a priestess or goddess is pictured standing in front of a tree serving a drink on a platter filled with seed pods or the five-pointed flowers of the Peganum Harmala, also known as Syrian rue. Rue was a well-known medicinal plant in the ancient world, being mentioned in dozens of concoctions in *De Materia Medica*, an ancient book of remedies written by Greek physician Pedanius Dioscorides. It is also well known that the bark of the Acacia tree is filled with dimethyltryptamine, more commonly known as DMT, one of the most powerful entheogenic compounds known to humankind. If one were to eat Acacia bark by itself, no effect would be felt, for the monoamine oxidase enzyme in the stomach would neutralize the compound before it could travel into the bloodstream. But mix that Acacia bark with Syrian rue, and the psychedelic properties are released, for the rue acts as a monoamine oxidase inhibitor, giving the DMT free passage to the body and mind.

Ancient depiction of an
Egyptian tea ceremony

In those ancient drawings, the goddess is likely serving up a psychedelic brew of Acacia bark and Syrian rue as part of a ceremony or rite of passage. The Egyptians called the Acacia tree the Tree of Life, for they knew its life-changing powers and the ability it gave them to connect to the divine.

Recall that there were two trees in the Garden of Eden: the Tree of Wisdom and the Tree of Life. You know that the Tree of Wisdom is the jamun fruit tree, which the Atlantean king used to control his blood sugar. The Tree of Life is none other than the Acacia tree, its bark replete with DMT that the Atlanteans used to connect with the divine. The Atlanteans brought these trees from their respective lands and planted them in the Garden of Eden. Thus, psychedelics have been used from the beginning of time as a gateway to the eternal.

Today, you know of Dionysus as a Greek god of wine and ecstatic experiences, but there are actually multiple Dionysus personas in Greek mythology. The female followers of Dionysus were known as Maenads, and there is pictorial evidence on a Greek vase, or *krater*, in which Maenads brewed a concoction of Acacia and rue for their sacred rituals. Parts of the vessel have now fallen off, but researcher August Frickenhaus, who observed the vase prior to it being damaged, later made a line drawing of the brewing, which you see depicted here.

Frickenhaus's line drawing

In the picture, two Maenads are standing over the pots of wine, with one stirring it. A third Maenad is seated in a chair and is holding out two flowers: one is large and five-pointed, clearly the flower of the Syrian rue plant, and the other is the spherical flower of the Acacia tree. [419]

[419] Brian C. Muraresku, *The Immortality Key: The Secret History of the Religion with No Name* (New York: St. Martin's, 2020).

Thus, it is clear that the followers of Dionysus were adept at brewing the concoction of Syrian rue and Acacia bark, creating a drink that could help them access the spiritual realm. Historian Diodorus speaks of Dionysus as being born in Libya, which connects him clearly to the Atlanteans. Could it be that the Greek god Dionysus—this god of wine and ecstatic experiences, the Bacchanalia—was an Atlantean who traveled around the Mediterranean imparting knowledge about how to mix this psychedelic brew that was part of the Atlanteans' advanced knowledge of the divine?

As you can see, psychedelics have long played a crucial role in spiritual rituals. Historically, they have been seen as a means to break out of the body and connect with the divine, whether it is for a few minutes or a few hours. In India, Hindu sages drank *soma* in order to have a vision of God. In Persia, the drink was known as *haoma*. In South America, shamans and tribes drank Ayahuasca, the plant-based psychedelic used to transport an individual to higher planes of existence and connect them to God. Ayahuasca gives you the same effect as the ancient brew of the Mysteries, for it is also made with one plant that is full of DMT and another plant acting as a monoamine oxidase inhibitor.

From Egypt to South America, DMT was the predominant compound used by the Mystery schools and shamans to access these transformative experiences. But in Mesopotamia and Greece there arose the use of another compound—ergot. If you isolate the active compound in ergot, you have what is known today as LSD.

An archeological dig in Spain at a place called Mas Castellar de Pontos found a cup containing the residue of beer and ergot, thus confirming that the ancients drank a hallucinogenic brew, likely as part of a ritual. We know the Eleusinian mysteries were being performed in this place because a carving of Triptolemus, herald of Demeter's mysteries, was discovered there. A similar brew has been found in Göbekli Tepe, ancient training site of the Nephilim in present-day Turkey, and the Rakefet cave in Israel, in the Natufian settlement that existed over 13,000 years ago. [420]

[420] Oliver Dietrich et al., "The Role of Cult and Feasting in the Emergence of Neolithic Communities: New Evidence from Göbekli Tepe, South-eastern Turkey," *Antiquity* 86 (2012): 674–695; Benny Shannon, "Biblical Entheogens: A Speculative Hypothesis," *Time and Mind* 1, no. 1 (2008): 51–74.

These findings in the Levant suggest that at some point, the Nephilim switched from DMT to LSD as their chosen psychedelic, but why? As you'll see in the next section, DMT is clearly more potent and more effective as a gateway to the divine, so why would they choose a different medium?

This mystery is yet to be solved, but we can guess at answers. *The Epic of Gilgamesh* is credited with bringing back the knowledge that existed before the flood: knowledge of how to work with stone, build walls, and buildings, and a resurrection of the proper sacraments—that is, the ritualized use of psychedelics. Yet Gilgamesh did not bring back the true compound; his followers only *believed* he did. He substituted LSD for DMT.

Could it be that the switch to LSD was the Nephilim's first attempt to sever mankind's connection to the spirit, first by changing the compound used to access that spiritual plane and then by outlawing entheogens altogether? Perhaps the fact the CIA used LSD on its MKULTRA subjects in an attempt to subvert their will and control their minds yields further insight into the true purpose of sacramental corruption.

There is other evidence that the Nephilim tried to muddy mankind's connection to DMT and thus keep them away from the divine. Consider again the Egyptian drawing of the tea-serving ceremony, where a goddess is offering sacred tea on a platter. Many of the depictions that remain intact show the goddess Hathor in front of a sycamore tree, but the sycamore does not contain any entheogenic compounds. However, it is known that Hathor is associated with the much older goddess Iusaaset, wife of Atum, the great creator god, and primordial mother to all Egyptian gods. Many people may have heard of the goddess Hathor, but Iusaaset is relatively unknown. Would you be surprised to learn that Iusaaset is the Egyptian goddess associated with the Acacia tree? Many passages in the Pyramid and Coffin texts, the oldest known religious scriptures, make reference to her sacred tree, said to be capable of driving out impurities and sufferings.

Substituting Iusaaset with Hathor and concealing the Acacia tree alongside rue in depictions of the tea ceremony, was another attempt by the Nephilim to sever humanity's connection to the spiritual plane and erase the knowledge of how to connect with the divine. Hathor's associations with worldly pleasures are legion, being the goddess of beauty, sexuality, pleasure, intoxication and ecstasy, music, and dance, as well as foreign lands and the luxury goods imported from them. We know from the Hyksos conquest of lower Egypt, as well as Akhenaten and his daughters, that there was a Canaanite influence in Egypt at some point; it is possible the Nephilim made these changes while in power.

Then, there is the case of the Egyptian blue water lily, *Nymphaea caerulea*, whose usage in Egypt as an entheogen was popularized around the 18th dynasty, the same period as Akhenaten. His son, Tutankhamun, was buried with a large amount of lily petals in his sarcophagus and many depictions of orgiastic sex, such as those on the Turin Erotic Papyrus, have been found with the participants and onlookers carrying the flower. The use of the blue water lily spread throughout the lands of Canaan and Mesopotamia and its active ingredient, apomorphine, is known to cause persistent erections in men. [421]

[421] McDonald, J. Andrew. 2018. "Influences of Egyptian Lotus Symbolism and Ritualistic Practices on Sacral Tree Worship in the Fertile Crescent from 1500 BCE to 200 CE" *Religions* 9, no. 9: 256.

Over an age after the corruption of Iusaaset's mysteries, a Roman historian named Titus Livius remarked on how corrupted the Bacchic rites—named after Bacchus, the Roman name for the Greek god Dionysus—had become:

> When wine, lascivious discourse, night, and the mingling of sexes had extinguished every sentiment of modesty, then debaucheries of every kind began to be practised ... Nor were they confined to one species of vice, the promiscuous intercourse of free-born men and of women; but from this storehouse of villiany proceeded false witnesses, counterfeit seals, false evidences, and pretended discoveries. In the same place, too, were perpetrated secret murders; so that, in some cases, even the bodies could not even be found for burial. Many of their audacious deeds were brought about by treachery, but most of them by force, and this force was concealed by loud shouting, and the noise of drums and cymbals, so that none of the cries uttered by the persons suffering violation or murder could be heard abroad. [422]

[422] Titus Livy, *The History of Rome*, vol. 5, trans. G. Baker (New York: Collins and Co., 1823), 297–298.

Livy's treatise continues with Roman consuls Spurius Postumius Albinus and Quintus Marcius Philippus receiving testimony about the conspiracy of the Bacchanalians from a former slave, Hispala Facenia, whose mistress had forced her into these mysteries. Before testifying, Facenia pleaded that the consuls would send her out of the city to ensure her safety as "she stood in great dread of the gods, whose secret mysteries she was to divulge; and also of men, who, should she be seized as an informer, would certainly put her to death." [423]

[423] Livy, *History of Rome*, vol. 5, 302.

Agreeable to this, the consuls then heard of the Bacchanalians that "their number was exceedingly great, enough almost to compose a state in themselves, and among them were many men and women of noble families. During the last two years, it had been a rule, that no person above the age of twenty should be initiated; for they sought for people of such age as it made them more liable to suffer deception and personal abuse." [424]

[424] Livy, *History of Rome*, vol. 5, 304.

It had not always been this way, explained Hispala. For, in the beginning, the group was run exclusively by women and no impropriety ever appeared. But, after a new priestess took charge, many changes were made. She introduced men to the group, beginning with her own two sons, and changed the number of initiation ceremonies from three in the year, to five in a month. The ceremonies devolved into promiscuous sex, including "more frequent pollutions of men, with each other, than with women." Furthermore, "If any showed an uncommon degree of reluctance, in submitting to dishonour, or of disinclination to the commission of vice, they were [425]Livy, *History of Rome*, vol. 5, 303. held as victims, and sacrificed." [425]

The result of this Roman investigation was the passage of the *Senatus consultum de Bacchanalibus*, a few decades prior to the final destruction of Carthage. It was a series of prohibitions against the Bacchanalia throughout Italy, punishable by death for anyone found in a position of leadership within the now perverted mysteries of Dionysus.

Does it not sound familiar that those involved in such debaucheries were the elite of society, those holding positions of great power? The Nephilim's sexual perversions, corruption of what is holy, and victimization of the young have not changed, nor have the types of people who participate in these activities; as it is today, so it was in ancient Rome and for millennia before.

Humanity's disconnection from spirit, and the corruption of sacraments, is no more complete than in the Catholic practice of the eucharist, for here the Nephilim have completely severed the faithful from any experience of God, leaving only a counterfeit creation of their own design, utterly devoid of any entheogenic power. By the doctrine of transubstantiation, members of the "universal" church—for the Greek word *Katholikos* means "universal"—have been led into committing a great sin by the regular consumption of human flesh and the drinking of blood.

THE SPIRIT MOLECULE

In "The Influence of the Mystery Religions on Christianity," Dr. Martin Luther King Jr. asks, "The staggering question that now arises is, what will be the next stage of man's religious progress? Is Christianity the crowning achievement in the development of religious thought or will there be another religion more advanced?" [426] Alas, Christianity will not be the crowning achievement of religious thought, but its replacement will not be another religion, for religion asks that you have faith, which is the belief in something you cannot know exists and of which you have no knowledge.

[426] Martin Luther King Jr., "The Influence of the Mystery Religions on Christianity," in *The Papers of Martin Luther King J.*, Vol. 1, ed. Clayborne Carson, Ralph Luker, and Penny A. Russell (Berkeley: University of California Press, 1992), 312.

Such faith is no longer necessary, Seeker of Truth, for you may experience the divine for yourself. It is said that seeing is believing—and now you can see, with assistance from the right source.

According to Carl Jung, no tree "can grow to heaven unless its roots reach down to hell." [427] The ancient Mysteries understood this wisdom, for their rituals focus on death and resurrection. The gods and deities they worshipped are famous for having traveled to the underworld and returned.

[427] Jung, *Aion*, 43.

These mysteries hint that you cannot access the heights of your power without understanding the deepest depths of yourself. Think of man's inner harmony as a seesaw. Most people balance the seesaw by simply placing the weight in the center. They do not venture out of the bounds of a comfortable and ordinary life; they do not question. Those who wish to travel to one end of the seesaw, however—who wish to access the highest states of consciousness—must balance themselves by placing equal weight at the other end of the seesaw, in the darkest regions of their psyche.

This means you must know yourself and be practiced in achieving inner harmony. It is no accident the phrase *gnothi seauton*, Greek for "Know thyself," was inscribed on the forecourt of the temple of Apollo at Delphi. Psychedelics can bring you closer to the balance that lives free of the ego and the shadow and is rooted in a sense of your true self. You must not ignore one and drown yourself in the other. Just as Jesus was tempted by Satan, so you must venture into the darkest depths to confront and overcome the evil in your own heart.

There are other paths to this same harmony, of course. Yogis have meditated in caves for decades, and Sufis spin until they see the face of God, but these paths are especially long and arduous. Psychedelics bring you into a glimpse of what you are aiming for in a far shorter time.

For the goal is this: to journey beyond the confines of the universal constant c in the Seed of Life and access the infinite, divine realms. As Paramhansa Yogananda writes in the *Autobiography of a Yogi*, "To remove the veil of *maya* is to uncover the secret of creation. ... So long as man remains subject to the dualistic illusions of Nature, the Janus-faced *Maya* is his goddess; he cannot know the one true God." [428]

[428] **Yogananda**, *Autobiography of a Yogi*, 235.

This piercing of maya is the aim of all spiritual practice. It is what breathing, and meditation can help you achieve, after decades of discipline and practice. Psychedelics show you what that end vision looks like—a blinding glimpse of the possibility that could be yours—before taking you right back to the starting line and demanding that you begin the real work.

For psychedelics can help you cross infinite space and time, albeit briefly; they help you breach the material world and touch the infinite universe, if only for a moment. When Eduard Billy Meier met the Atlantean named Semjase, she took him on her ship and traveled with him across the galaxy. On one of these trips, in preparation for an inter-galactic jump, she asked Meier to go into a booth and put on a headpiece that could record his thoughts during the jump.

What Meier described of that experience is nothing short of a psychedelic trip:

> I can see again how the fantastic heavens and stars change. In a fraction of a second they are nothing more than a whitish milky mass, a shining mass, as I have already seen in the other hyper-leaps. But now suddenly as well, this milky whitish shining is gone and there is darkness. But now what is this? Suddenly all is merging into a golden color, and now everything is like silver. But—my dear this glistening light, this beaming shining splendor!

Everything is merged into glistening light—only the glistening light. It is stronger than all the suns of the Universe... Dear, oh dear, this glistening light, and it does not hurt the eyes! Dear, this must be eternity, the glistening light of the eternal... but see, there is nothing besides the eternity; man alive, how marvelous! [429]

[429] Meier, *Message from the Pleiades*, vol. 1, 315–316.

This is how close psychedelics can bring you to the experience of the divine, leaving the mundane and moving into the realm of Infinity and Eternity.

Before inducing these experiences by way of interstellar travel, what psychedelic would an Atlantean give Meier to induce this trip? Not LSD, the product of the Nephilim, but DMT—the true sacrament, the "spirit molecule," as scientist Rick Strassman calls it. For DMT occurs naturally in this world, both in plants such as the Acacia tree and in the human brain. Your scientists have finally learned that DMT is a crucial neurotransmitter that exists in the mammalian brain in concentrations equal to or higher than serotonin and dopamine. It regulates your very perceptions and experiences of the universe. [430]

[430] Jon G. Dean et al., "Biosynthesis and Extracellular Concentrations of N, N-dimethyltryptamine (DMT) in Mammalian Brain," *Scientific Reports* (2019): 1–11.

When people ingest psychedelics like psilocybin mushrooms, they experience visions that are manifestations of subconscious archetypes. But when Strassman performed a series of experiments with DMT, he found that all of his subjects recorded nearly the same experience, which is unique for a psychedelic compound.

Strassman chronicles his study in his book, *DMT: The Spirit Molecule*. He shows that when on DMT, subjects encountered entities that were clearly not products of their subconscious mind. These entities have very clear personalities of their own and are intense. Nor are they always friendly; Strassman describes experiences where the entities were rough with the subject and the trip was not necessarily pleasant.

Yet Strassman says that when these same subjects were asked years later whether they remembered their DMT trip, all of them did and stated that the experience had changed or improved them in a meaningful way. The subjects did not necessarily get the experience they wanted, but they did receive what they needed.

No one can say for certain who these entities are, but they seem to be spirits who have evolved beyond the material plane. When Semjase spoke to Billy Meier about these entities, she said that some of them were once human while others evolved from other species across the cosmos. To become one of these spirits is the next phase of your evolution. You were given time on earth, time in your material body, so that you may build yourself up and learn to transcend flesh into the nonmaterial plane. DMT, the spirit molecule, gives you this experience firsthand: it disembodies and launches you into the spirit realm, leaving your ego and shadow behind.

But while DMT can help you experience the divine realm and show you what you need to aim for, it cannot help you *evolve* into these higher entities. That process must be achieved through balance, the attainment of true wisdom, meditation, and breathing.

This journey is not quick, Seeker of Truth, for there are no shortcuts. It may take you a thousand lifetimes to become those entities you glimpse in your spiritual journey on DMT. But it *is* possible to evolve to a point where you no longer feel any ties to the material world or wish to engage with this realm.

This is why humanity has such infrequent contact with these beings: they have little interest in the material world or in speaking to the people in it. Those who sit on the Atlantean high council have one foot in the material world and one foot in the spiritual realm; they are able to talk with these higher beings and communicate their perceptions to people still stuck in the material realm. They sit on the high council because they possess greater wisdom than those locked in the material plane, peering thousands of years into all possible futures and guiding their stateless civilization along the most prosperous path. As elucidated by Semjase in a meeting with Billy Meier, "We do not keep any administration, but there only exists the High Council. Its way is this, to give high advice, but never a command or an order of a commanding kind." [431] How unlike the Nephilim's policy of ruling with complete domination.

[431] Meier, *Message from the Pleiades*, vol. 3, p. 146.

Remember, reaching a godlike state involves embracing your darkness as well as your divinity. DMT can make this possible.

TIME TO AWAKEN

In your world, even the religious do not have an understanding of the spirit. They struggle to comprehend what life after death may feel like.

This is because that part of you lies dormant; it has been subsumed by the ego. In many cases, humanity struggles to acknowledge it is even there.

But it is. You may not have tapped into your spiritual side yet, but you possess a very real physiological ability to do so, as is evidenced by the presence of DMT in the brain. Be not afraid to take a dose of DMT to jumpstart that part of your slumbering spirit, to unlock your potential, and glimpse what you are meant to become. When you return again to the starting line, your goal will be clear and your focus sharp.

For remember, these are the correct and true sacraments that the ancients have revered for ages. Humanity needs to start taking them again if it wants to reach the next level: ascension and immortality.

CHAPTER 19
PERSONAL APOTHEOSIS

W e have reached the apex of our consideration, Seeker of Truth. Now it is time for you to learn the ultimate goal of everything you have heard, for within every human being is God and thus the ability to achieve a god-like state.

Are you ready for this personal apotheosis? Read on to take the final step in realizing your full potential.

LET YOUR
SPIRIT RISE

In Chapter 17, you read about the power of breath and the physical limits it can help you surpass. In the last chapter, you learned the goal of this collective ascension: transcending the boundaries of the material world. You have caught a glimpse of how you can realize this path for yourself through the practice of the ancient Mysteries: ingesting the spirit molecule and experiencing the world beyond.

Now we will delve deeper into releasing your spirit so that it may rise to other worlds and, ultimately, transcend your mortal being. As Hermes Trismegistus said in Book 10 of the *Corpus Hermeticum*,

> The human soul, that is not every human soul, but a pious one, is spiritual and divine. When such a soul has freed itself from the body and passed the test of piety, which is to know God and to harm no man, it becomes pure Nous. But the impious soul remains in its own substance, restricted by itself, seeking an earthly body, that is to say a human body into which it may enter.

Hermes stated that unless a human being ascends to a level of nonviolence and piety, they will be cursed to be born and reborn in the material realm again and again, for violence attracts the weight of sin and souls thereby stained cannot ascend. They are stuck in a karmic limbo and must reincarnate to free themselves of that weight in another life.

Similar concepts are echoed across the religions of earth. The Egyptians and Hindus, for example, share a concept of reincarnation. Egyptians and Christians share the belief that the soul is judged after death, thus ascertaining whether it is fit for ascension or whether it should return to the worldly realm.

Once a person attains a consciousness that the soul and body are distinct and passes the test of piety, then the soul is capable of incarnating on worlds beyond Planet

Earth. One such realm is referred to as "Hiranyaloka" in Paramhansa Yogananda's *Autobiography of a Yogi*. Yogananda's guru, Sri Yukteswar, says of this world, "The dwellers on Hiranyaloka are highly developed spiritually; all of them had acquired, in their last earth-incarnation, the meditation-given power of consciously leaving their physical bodies at death." [432]

[432] Yogananda, *Autobiography of a Yogi*, 253.

This speaks to a question that humanity has grappled with since the beginning of its existence: what is the meaning of life? The answer is actually quite simple. Your existence is your purpose. There is no need to go searching for destiny or the meaning of life outside of yourself. The purpose of a song is not to reach its end in any particular way, but to enjoy its melody as it unfolds before you. You have the spirit within you; you are God carrying out what you are meant to be doing by simply living and experiencing the universe as it was created.

Several texts, ancient manuscripts, and holy books have referred to this God-like spirit within you, waiting to be freed through experiences that can elevate you beyond the earthly plane. As Semjase, of whom you have already read, said to Billy Meier: "The human being is the carrier of his spirit, which never dies and which also in his deepest sleep does not itself sleep; which records all thoughts and movements; which tells the human being whether his very thoughts are right or wrong." [433] Here, Semjase reveals that your soul is the God-like part of you that knows and judges right from wrong. It is your piece of the divine.

[433] Meier, *Message from the Pleiades*, vol 1, p. 141.

Tormentors and Powers

But how do you free this piece of the divine and leave the material world behind? How do you allow your spirit to truly rise? Let us look at two ways as described by the oldest religions and spiritual practices of the world. In Book 13 of the *Corpus Hermeticum*, Hermes's son asks him how to ascend out of the earthly plane and attain a free and pure spirit. Hermes answers,

> Oh son; withdraw into yourself and it shall come. Will and it is so. Make idle the senses of the body and the spirit will be born. Cleanse yourself from the torments of the material world which arise from the lack of reason.

Notice the term "tormentors"; here, Hermes speaks of what he considers the twelve tormentors that keep a person captive in the material world: ignorance, sorrow, intemperance, lust, injustice, greed, deceit, envy, treachery, anger, recklessness, and malice. There is considerable overlap with the seven deadly sins in Catholicism. Both messages are the same: if a person indulges in these sins or lives with these tormentors in constant manifestation in word and deed, their lives will be small and miserable, and they will attract calamity and injury. They will not be able to free themselves to experience the bounty beyond. Such is the natural law. Yet Hermes does not only warn his son of the tormentors that keep him in this earthly realm; he speaks to him of ten powers that can help him battle these tormentors.

He speaks first of the *knowledge of God*, which is a vaster understanding of the universe than what you know. This knowledge was given in Book II, where we unlocked the cosmos and made you aware of how much there is still to discover. The Knowledge of God is vital, for without it you cannot know that you possess a spirit and that there is even a soul in you to free.

Once you know God and the vastness available to you, you can access the second power—the *experience of joy*. For knowing God is, indeed, a deeper and more fulfilling experience of joy than any experience in the material realm.

The third power is that of *self-control*, and the fourth is that of *steadfastness*, both of which can oppose the tormentors of intemperance and lust. These powers temper instinct with the light of reason, and keep you from succumbing to your lower, animal nature. Heed the words of Hermes,

> Not all men, O Asclepius, have attained true understanding, but through a rash impulse and without the true insight of reason most, pursuing an illusion, are deceived. This begets evil in minds and transforms the nature of the best living creature into that of a wild beast and makes it behave like a savage monster. [434]

[434] Hermes, *Asclepius*, 59.

The fifth power is what Hermes names the *Seat of Justice*. This is where he speaks to the soul's power to know right from wrong and to judge accurately without need of trial. Humanity believes that trials are the highest form of justice, yet the divinity within you can tell the truth from lie. There will be no need for a jury of peers once you access this form of sight.

The sixth power is *generosity*, which opposes greed, while the seventh and eighth powers are *truth* and *supreme good*. Hermes states that supreme good arises from truth, and both lead to *life* and *light*, which are the ninth and tenth powers, respectively.

Together, Hermes posits that these ten powers can fight off the twelve tormentors, and through a consistent practice of meditation and breathing, help the soul to move beyond the earthly realm.

Turnings of Thought and Being Set Free

The *Yoga Sutras of Patanjali* provides similar advice on how to transcend the material world and free yourself to a new, spiritual plane. Here, the enemy is not the twelve tormentors but what the book calls "turnings of thought." It describes yoga as "the cessation of the turnings of thought. When thought ceases, the spirit stands in its true identity as observer to the world."[435]

[435] *Yoga: Discipline of Freedom: The Yoga Sutra Attributed to Patanjali*, trans. Barbara Stoler Miller (New York: Bantam Books, 1995), Sutras 2–3.

Recall that in Chapter 11, "Maya," you learned about the ego and the shadow, the illusion that you are one with your thoughts. Yet your thoughts and the emotions appended to them are not you; they are the manifestations of your material brain. Only when you are released from that belief can your spirit stand free to judge what is right and wrong as an objective observer of the world. Realize that love and oneness with all things is the true nature of the universe, and at that moment of comprehension, you will pass beyond the sufferings, fears, and hatreds that consume most human beings.

According to the *Yoga Sutras*, the turnings of thought consist of five factors. The first is *valid judgment*, which is itself comprised of direct perception (the five senses), inference (logical extrapolation), and verbal testimony (what other people have said). The second is *error*, which is belief or knowledge with no objective basis. The third is *conceptualization*, which are words thought without any substance or real meaning. The fourth is *sleep*, by which the *Yoga Sutras* means "dreams," or those thoughts or imaginings that are abstracted from experience. And the last is *memory*, which is the recollection of objects one has experienced. The warning here is to not let yourself be consumed by the past; don't ruminate and overthink memories to the point of anxiety and stress. Stay in the present.

These five elements together comprise the turnings of thought and learning how to cease this turning is key to ascending to a higher spiritual plane. Similar to Hermes's ten powers, the *Yoga Sutras of Patanjali* also offers advice on how to go about freeing oneself from the chains of thought.

The first step is *practice*: you must consistently practice separating yourself from your thoughts and silencing the chatter of your mind. The second skill is *dispassion*, which is mastery over your craving for sensual objects. Dispassion is mentioned often in Buddhism, as a separation from worldly attachments and desires, but the *Yoga Sutras* takes this further in their next skill, known as *higher* dispassion—a total severing from the craving for the material world. Those who have achieved higher dispassion are able to step away from material life and meditate for years in a cave, though it certainly is not necessary to do such a thing in order to reach this level.

The last skill is what the *Yoga Sutras* calls *dedication to the Lord of Yoga*, which is a "distinct form of spirit unaffected by the forces of corruption, by actions, the fruits of actions, or subliminal intentions." [436] This is Lord Śiva, who is a role model for yogis and the epitome of what they are striving to achieve.

[436] *Yoga: Discipline of Freedom: The Yoga Sutra Attributed to Patanjali,* trans. Barbara Stoler Miller (New York: Bantam Books, 1995), Sutra 24.

The *Yoga Sutras* offers more detail than Hermes, outlining both the obstacles that distract thought, the effects of these distractions, and where tranquil thought springs from. The obstacles that distract thought are disease, apathy, doubt, carelessness, indolence, dissipation, false vision, failure to attain a firm basis in yoga, and restlessness.

If you allow these obstacles to distract your mind and pull you even deeper into the turning of thought, then you are likely to face suffering, frustration, trembling of the body, and irregular breathing, all of which are symptoms of anxiety and panic attacks.

Tranquil thought, on the other hand, arises from friendship, compassion, joy, and an impartiality toward pleasure or pain, virtue, or vice. The last point speaks to the need for balance; resist the urge to tip into either extreme of masochistic pain or hedonistic pleasure and strive not toward being the embodiment of good or evil. Instead, center yourself. This is the source of calm and contentedness.

The *Yoga Sutras* also describes the forces of corruption, which are similar to Hermes's twelve tormentors. These forces are *ignorance*, which is the breeding ground for other forces of corruption; *egoism*, which is ascribing a unified self to the material body and its five senses; *passion*, which follows from an attachment to pleasure; *hatred*, which follows from an attachment to suffering; and the *will to live*, which is instinctive and overwhelming, even for a learned sage, but must be overcome. If a person is attached to living and survival, then it is possible to corrupt them by threatening that life, but someone who is free from that attachment cannot be bullied, coerced, or touched in any way.

The Eight Limbs of Yoga

Once you are free from the forces of corruption, you will find yourself able to be disentangled from the turnings of thought. But how does one attain this freedom? The *Yoga Sutras* outlines the eight limbs of yoga, which are instructions for practices you can perform in your daily life.

Let us look at these eight limbs in detail, so you have guidance on where to begin your journey. The first limb is what the *Yoga Sutras* calls the *moral principles*, which is the great vow of yoga. These are your guide to action, as with any principle that forms the bedrock of a community. A member of a community devoted to these principles, for example, would follow the cosmic principle of nonaggression, from whence all natural law springs forth, which means no member of this community can coerce or deceive another as a means to an end; it is a principle they apply in their daily life.

In the same way, the moral principles of the *Yoga Sutras* are guides to action that each follower can implement every day.

The first principle is similar to the nonaggression principle, in that it is the principle of nonviolence, and crucial in passing the test of piety. The second principle is truthfulness, which means a person must always be honest and not use fraud or any other nefarious means to get what they want. Abjuration of stealing is the third principle, because stealing is a violent act that deprives a person of the product of their limited time.

The fourth principle is celibacy, though a better word for the modern context might be fidelity. This principle encourages a person, if they are married, to keep sexual activity within that relationship, and if they are not married, to be forthcoming and honest with their partners. It connects to the principle of truthfulness.

The fifth principle is the absence of greed, which ties into both the abjuration of stealing and nonviolence.

The second limb of yoga is the *observances*. If the moral principles are guidelines for how to lead your life, the observances are actions you can take every day. They include bodily purification, which is a clean and healthy diet; contentment, which is being happy with what you have and who you are; ascetic practices, which is living for a purpose beyond the material world and thus not allowing your possessions to possess you; sacred lore, which is the study of sacred texts from your religion and others to better help you commune with your chosen deity; and dedication to the Lord of Yoga, which you will remember from the practices mentioned earlier and acts as a role model for what a yogi is striving toward.

The third limb of yoga is *posture*, which should be steady and easy. When you practice yoga, seek to be comfortable when you are meditating so you can leave the body behind and focus on the spiritual.

The fourth limb of yoga is the *control of breath*, which is regulating the inhalation and exhalation of air. Recall from Chapter 17 that there is a correct way to breathe, through the nose and from the diaphragm, so that air comes into the deepest reaches of your lungs. Focus on that method and practice.

The fifth limb of yoga is *complete withdrawal of the senses*. It echoes what Hermes says to his son when he tasks him with withdrawing into himself, for only then can the spirit be born. Complete withdrawal of the senses happens during meditation—a person must close their eyes and focus on the inner self—but meditation itself is more than a complete withdrawal of the senses.

The last three limbs of yoga are the most vital: concentration, meditation, and pure contemplation.

The sixth limb, *concentration*, is the binding of thought in one place. For most people starting their yoga journey, this is the active and focused concentration on their breath.

The seventh limb, *meditation*, is a step beyond this: once a person has mastered concentration, they can meditate from any place or while doing anything; they don't need to sit in one place and focus on their breath. They can walk around, do the dishes, play an instrument they have mastered—anything that allows them to focus their attention naturally, a single conceptual flow.

In other words, someone who has become skilled at concentration and meditation will be able to slip into a meditative state easily, not necessarily in specially curated situations designed to evoke that meditative state.

The last and eighth limb of yoga is *pure contemplation*. This is the breakthrough state where a person pierces the veil of Maya, when the material world falls away and the person meditates as if they were devoid of intrinsic form. As mentioned in Chapter 17, there are yogis who have meditated in the mountains for years, where their bodies have entered a state of stasis and their heartbeats have slowed. These yogis have achieved pure contemplation. As you approach this state, you will notice the experience of time seems to slow, and indeed as it does, your experience is elevated to the infinite.

The last three limbs of yoga are the most important because a person who has mastered all three attains perfect discipline, which the *Yoga Sutras* states is the goal of all yogis. For someone who has mastered perfect discipline, the turnings of thought have ceased; they are permanently in a meditative state, even when walking or talking or doing other things. They speak from a dispassionate and soulful perspective.

Both Hermes and the *Yoga Sutras of Patanjali* outline ways for you to help your spirit rise. For a person to leave the earthly realm behind, they must pass a test: know God and harm no man. This is not a hard test, but the conditions on earth have made it more difficult for a person to pass. If a person fails, they remain stuck on your planet, consistently reincarnating as their soul moves from one earthly body to another.

If they pass, however, they have taken an important step in becoming like God, a master of the universe.

MASTERS OF
THE UNIVERSE

Now that you have seen the path to unlocking the potential of your spirit and body, what might you become, Seeker of Truth? What is your true potential?

Multiple historical texts, eyewitness accounts, and examples exist of what is possible when the spirit is freed, and the body becomes an immaterial and intangible barrier. In Chapter 17, you saw hints of what can be accomplished, where humans like you are able to control their body temperature and run marathons barefoot in the snow. These are but parlor tricks compared to the true abilities you could unlock. Your true potential lies far beyond what Wim Hof has accomplished, impressive though it is.

Look again to the *Yoga Sutras of Patanjali*. In Book III, it says, "The light of wisdom comes from mastery of perfect discipline"—the "light of wisdom" being a God-like consciousness or cosmic awareness. But what does this cosmic awareness look like? What can people who possess this awareness do?

The answer lies in other religious texts that speak of this same "light." Look to the Book of Genesis, where it says the angels who visited Lot "smote the men that were at the door of the house with blindness, both small and great." [437] How else might one blind a crowd, while sparing Lot   [437] Genesis 9:11 (KJV). and his daughters, but with focused light? It is clear to those who know more about earth's history—as you now do—that these "angels" were Atlanteans. Could it be that they developed an antimatter weapon that presented as blinding light—even appearing as light themselves? Enoch himself states that the Atlanteans "took and brought me to a place in which those who were there were like flaming fire, and, when they wished,   [438] Book of Enoch 17:1. they appeared as men." [438]

This conscious control is important, for it reveals that those who have unlocked the potential of their bodies may use these abilities at will. But to reach this place, a person must be at a certain level of spiritual evolution. In the words of Semjase, the Atlantean who visited Billy Meier, "This is a safety measure in Creational Law, by which no form of life taps more knowledge than is allowed according to the state of evolution." [439]

[439] Meier, *Message from the Pleiades*, vol. 1, p. 383.

Think of this as a guiding principle around who may use these abilities and how. It is not possible to simply cheat your way into these powers; they must come from true spiritual growth. This is why human beings have been unable to use the technology of the Atlanteans, even if they lay hands upon it.

Once a person does evolve enough to attain these abilities, however, their powers will seem miraculous to an ordinary human. The *Yoga Sutras of Patanjali* divides these skills into three categories: extraordinary knowledge, mastery of the physical world, and other powers.

Extraordinary knowledge refers to the ability to read both time and minds. It includes knowledge of the past and future, as well as present awareness of what people and animals are thinking.

Mastery of the physical world involves the ability to manipulate reality as people know it. Advanced souls can enter the body of another, a phenomenon you may know as remote viewing—the ability to see through the eyes of another. It also involves a resistance to heat or cold (as seen in the cases of Wim Hof and Swami Rama); floating on water or air (as witnessed in the case of Jesus and messiah claimants such as Simon Magus in the apocryphal Acts of Peter); becoming invisible; shrinking down your awareness to a minute level, such that you can witness what happens molecule by molecule; and immunity from the constraints of matter, which means immunity from sickness.

The last category is *other powers*, which includes quickness of mind, perception without the aid of senses, like a blind person being able to describe how someone looks. It also includes omniscience and powers over all states of existence. This is what transforms a human being into a God-like state, for you can sense the fabric of reality itself.

Those of you who call yourselves "New Agers" may understand these superhuman abilities as being the concept of a "light body," which holds that humanity has thus far cultivated and understood the body only through the five senses, but humans possess a light body that belongs to the soul and that has its own senses that commune with the divine realm. Evidence about unlocking the spirit shows that this light body of the New Agers may be a real phenomenon, and a natural ability for any being with a soul.

Another question that arises from these three categories of perfect discipline is, how much of the Atlanteans' superhuman abilities were due to technology and how much was due to the advancement of their souls? Does the Atlanteans' mastery of the universal phenomenon extend to conscious access to the anti-verse? Such power could manifest in some miraculous effects, including the emission of light out of seemingly nowhere. Perhaps it is a combination of both, spiritual evolution and technology. The thunderbolt wielded by Zeus, Viracocha, Marduk, Thor, Indra, and many other primary deities across cultures and throughout history may be an allusion to an antimatter weapon they carried with them, that can only be operated by someone of sufficient spiritual advancement.

As you read these words, Seeker of Truth, you may feel as if these powers are beyond you. Such worries are natural. Remember, however, that even the most primitive human being has risen to the highest stations available to an Atlantean.

Consider Metatron. In the choir of archangels, it is said that seven is their number, but this is not true. There is an eighth, Metatron, who occupies a special position as the voice of God. He carries out God's orders and is treated as God when he is present.

Who is this Metatron? He is none other than Enoch, for Metatron is the name given to the man when he transformed into an archangel. Enoch, as you know, was an ordinary human being whom the Atlanteans trained so he could assume the lofty role of archangel.

Let this be a lesson for you—with dedication, discipline, and practice, even the most ordinary among you may rise. If Enoch could become a master of the universe, so can you.

Why do you not see a lot more people wielding these powers today? Because humanity does not have a spiritual command to operate the technology that makes these miraculous feats possible. Let that not be true of you.

ASCENSION

The Path of Righteousness, which begins with the food you consume and continues with mastering the breath and using the spirit molecule to transcend the material realm, ends with your personal apotheosis—becoming a god, with all the power and responsibilities contained therein. You will never transcend the bounds of your human existence if you cannot accept this possibility:

> If you do not make yourself equal to God, you cannot apprehend God; for like is known by like. Leap clear of all that is corporeal and make yourself grown to a like expanse with that greatness which is beyond all measure; rise above all time and become eternal; then you will apprehend God ... But if you shut up your soul in your body, and abase yourself, and say "I know nothing, I can do nothing; I am afraid of earth and sea, I cannot mount to heaven; I know not what I was, nor what I shall be," then what have you to do with God? [440]
>
> [440] Hermes Trismegistus, *Corpus Hermeticum*, 57–58.

Following this path enables you to break free of the Nephilim's control, those who have manipulated humans and bent their wills to serve their own. Is it any wonder that these evil ones want to keep you from accessing this path and the power that lies in mastering it?

Take heart, for the Atlanteans are with you on this journey. They want you to get on the path and embrace its lessons, for they have decided to save those on the Path of Righteousness and the rest shall perish, so that they may restart the next cycle of ages on earth.

So no matter where you are in life, now is the time to start. Eat correctly, master your breath, practice discipline to unlock the spirit within you so that you may evolve and access your true potential. If Enoch could achieve this, so can you.

CONCLUSION

We have reached our conclusion, Seeker of Truth, and I commend you on your dedication. This could not have been an easy journey, and no doubt you were, at times, wrestling with the truths that have been revealed to you.

You now know the history of humanity, and though many details are beyond the scope of this work, you can now grasp the grandness of your past. An understanding of why this truth was hidden from you has also taken shape within your mind. In knowing the past, you can now see the present as it truly is, and exist in your world with strength and wisdom. This is the birthright to which access has hitherto been denied—but no more.

Knowledge of God, the universe, and yourself has now come to you. The banishment of the tormentors has begun, and a vision of true and divine technology may now seize your imagination. Let your creative powers flow and be in harmony with the workings of all Creation, for there is no limit to where this knowledge will take you, as one of your great minds has written in a rejoinder to Nietzsche:

> There is, in fact, a god—namely, the world. To participate in its divinity, all that is necessary is to consent. "No longer to pray, but to give one's blessing." And the earth will abound in men-gods. To say yes to the world, to reproduce it, is simultaneously to re-create the world and oneself, to become the great artist, the creator. [441]
>
> [441]**Albert Camus**, *The Rebel* (New York: Vintage Books, 1991), 73–74.

You have seen the evil and depravity of those who would enslave your mind and spoil your body. You have read their own words regarding what they have planned for you. Yet hatred has not crept into your heart, for it is guarded by wisdom—wisdom to see yourself in your enemy and to not lose your compassion. Neither revile nor pity the Nephilim and their followers, wretched as they are. Let them be a reminder of the darkness of which you are capable, and remember nothing that exists in the light can avoid casting a shadow. For millennia you have been presented with a choice *between* good and evil, spirit over matter, or matter over spirit, never realizing a third way exists—spirit *and* matter, together as a harmonious whole. For all is God and within His greatness. He takes no sides and has blessed both spirit and matter with divine grace. To deny one is to condemn the other.

The Path of Righteousness has been laid before you, which leads to the next stage of your evolution—not of your body or mind, but of your spirit. Remember the words of the Lord:

> Ye are gods; and all of you are children of the most High. [442]
>
> [442] **Psalm**, 82:6 (KJV).

Through measured practice, meditation, and reaching the state of perfect discipline, you will achieve spiritual maturity, divine sight, and prescience, and no foe shall again deceive you. Love and oneness with all shall rule your heart, and the kingdom of heaven will be yours for all time.

Heed these words, for there will be grumblers and fault finders of every sort who shall try to lead you astray. They will attack and curse the name Yajnavalkya, blaspheming the Creation and all that is good and holy. Pay them no mind, for they are imprisoned by their misery and will be liberated from this self-deception by the fires of judgment soon enough. Do not entangle yourself in their politics, their debates, and their systems of violence, and never apologize for your devotion to truth. God has no need of missionaries, for you will only waste precious energies you can direct towards true spiritual progress.

But be wary, for the Nephilim's sinister plans to poison your mind against our arrival are already at work. Watch closely as they turn every event, real or engineered, towards consolidating more and more power, enslaving the people of earth all the more with promises of protection and order.

Rise above fear, and keep within yourselves the divine love that you have discovered. For in that love lie salvation and an ineffable light that no evil shall ever overcome.

About the Publisher

The **Library of Cernê** takes its
name from the matchless institution
destroyed with the capital city of
Atlantis. Its mission is to publish works
that elucidate humanity's evolution
and facilitate the building of an
elevated being, one with resurrected
spiritual wisdom.

libraryofcerne.com
curator@libraryofcerne.com